DA

Items should be returned on or before the last date
shown below. Items not already requested by other
borrowers may be renewed in person, in writing or by
telephone. To renew, please quote the number on the
barcode label. To renew online a PIN is required.
This can be requested at your local library.
Renew online @ **www.dublincitypubliclibraries.ie**
Fines charged for overdue items will include postage
incurred in recovery. Damage to or loss of items will
be charged to the borrower.

aying
. .

ltimately, self-belief,
al commitment drive
sights and nuggets of

waterhouseCoopers

as our mentor, critic

**Leabharlanna Poiblí Chathair Bhaile Átha Cliath
Dublin City Public Libraries**

Dublin City
Baile Átha Cliath

and Garden Centre,
dge, County Carlow

Date Due	Date Due	Date Due
16 FEB 13		
23 OCT 2017		

rk ethic and above all
ce, understanding the
atism and work.
Killian, CEO, ARYZTA

on . . .

e-Book

eBook

3/a90/13

D1419982

First published in 2011 by
Management Resource Institute (MRI)
Hospital Road, Wexford, Ireland

Author: Blaise Brosnan
Editor: Michael Freeman
Cover Design: Sinead McKenna, Sine É Design
Production: Daniel Bolger, Liberties Press
Printed in Ireland by: Naas Printing Ltd., Naas, Co. Kildare
ISBN: 978-1-907593-22-2

Enquiries should be addressed to:
Management Resource Institute (MRI)
Hospital Road, Wexford, Ireland
Tel: 00353 (0) 53 914 7774
E: info@mriwex.ie
W: mriwex.ie

Disclaimer

This book offers personal development information and guidance only and is not intended
as direct advice. The author and publisher have no control over the way that the reader
uses the information contained in these pages. The reader has sole responsibility for the
outcomes of any actions he or she takes.

This book is a valuable guide. However, it is recommended that the reader always
employs qualified professional specialist advice.

This book is a work of the imagination.

Jack

*Business Lessons
from Life,
Life Lessons
from Business*

Blaise Brosnan

MANAGEMENT
RESOURCE
INSTITUTE
(WEXFORD)

*To my wife Delia, my daughter Caitriona and
my son Padraig and his wife Anita.*

Contents

Acknowledgements

Jack embodies many people over my lifetime of study and practical experience as an operative and as CEO of dynamic multi-million euro businesses in Ireland and in other countries and currently as management consultant and adviser to thousands of owner/managers and business leaders in Ireland, Europe, Russia and the USA. I have learned from them all, and I am continuing to learn.

The production of *Jack* is the result of the inputs of many people. I would like to record them all, but space does not permit.

For commitment and support throughout the research and writing of *Jack* over the past two years, my thanks to my wife Delia, my daughter Caitriona, and my son Padraig and his wife Anita.

For his wise observations and opinions as the manuscript for *Jack* developed, my thanks to Dr Tom O'Keeffe of Doneraile, County Cork.

For production, layout and design, my thanks to Sean O'Keeffe, managing director of Liberties Press, and Daniel Bolger, managing editor, Liberties Press, Guinness Enterprise Centre, Dublin.

For cover design, my thanks to Sinead McKenna, Sin É Design, Rush, County Dublin.

For promotion, publicity and advice, my thanks to Peter O'Connell, publicist/literary agent, Peter O'Connell Media, Dame Street, Dublin.

For sub-editing, my thanks to Helen Ashdown, sub-editor, Enniscorthy, County Wexford.

For opinions, my thanks to Michael Doyle, broadcaster, South East Radio; Declan Lyons, communications consultant, Dublin and Paddy Whelan, writer, Ballycullane, County Wexford.

For editing, project management, and quality control of typescript from concept to reality as this book, my thanks to Michael Freeman, editor.

Introduction

We are the product of our genetic maps and we are the sum of the positive and negative influences on our journey through life to date. We can do nothing about our genetic maps. However, we can do something about the current influences that are stopping us or slowing us down in our attempts to achieve our potential.

In reality, our current circumstances are the result of how we have worked with what we've got – our resources and the influences of others around us. They are the sum total of how we have reacted to the influences, good and not so good, we have encountered on our life's journey.

Our life's journey has many milestones, many watershed points and many defining moments, such as times of joy and achievement, crises or shocks, and meeting significant people. All cause us to change our attitudes and behaviours. Some events and people in our lives are positive enablers. Others are negative blocks.

As *Jack* travelled his life's journey, he encountered a number of people and events which influenced him in positive ways. Others influenced him in negative ways. He, in turn, influenced many others.

It all begins in the mind. Listed are the views of some of the world's leading philosophers and thinkers.

> Buddha said: The mind is everything. What you think you become.

René Descartes said: I think, therefore I am. (*Cogito Ergo Sum*)

Blaise Pascal said: Imagination decides everything.

Adam Smith said: Man is an animal that makes bargains.

Arne Naess said: Think like a mountain.

William Shakespeare said: There is nothing either good or bad, but thinking makes it so.

Rosa Parks said: Knowing what must be done, does away with fear.

Eckhart Tolle said: When you no longer perceive the world as hostile, there is no more fear.

Edward de Bono said: Many highly intelligent people are poor thinkers. Many people of average intelligence are skilled thinkers. The power of a car is separate from the way the car is driven.

Through the life of *Jack*, I am presenting the influences that made him what he became and, in turn, how his influences helped or hindered others he met along the way.

Jack is the composite life story of many different people that I have met in up to the forty years of business and personal life at college, as a chief executive of major enterprise and as a management trainer, consultant and mediator. He represents the experiences and the emotions and coping mechanisms that most people have.

Whether you are an employee, a manager, a chief executive , an entrepreneur owner/manager, a parent or a student, I earnestly wish you to gain insights, techniques, consolation, empathy, understanding, inspiration, hope and direction from the life of *Jack*.

I believe you'll find something in common with *Jack*. Furthermore, I believe that *Jack* will give you reason to change your present way of travelling along your life's journey.

– Blaise Brosnan

Chapter 1

Mary Anne Cronin's Mission

The man from the Dublin newspaper sat at Kathleen Buckley's kitchen table at her home looking across Dingle Bay. He wanted to know more for his business readers. 'What was it like around here when Jack Cronin was growing up?' he asked.

'We were neighbours and friends,' said Kathleen as she poured another cup of tea for the stranger. Then, in a barely audible voice, she gushed that Jack's parents, Mary Anne and Mick Denny Bill, abstained from sexual intercourse for eight years. Jack was their first child. 'Imagine that – eight years. And over the following seven years, Mary Anne gave birth to three girls and two more boys. I remember them all so well. First of all there was Jack. Then came Sheila, Geraldine and Maura. And then there was Jerome and Mick. But Jack was different.'

It was unlikely that the hand of God was the cause of the childless eight years before Jack arrived. In the protected and protectionist Ireland of 1946 there were no such things as condoms or birth control pills. Kathleen told the journalist that Mary Anne was petite, shy and private, quietly-spoken and 'minded her own business'. Mick Denny Bill was tall, rough and ready, loud, and had poor hygiene. Mary Anne could not easily submit to his amorous advances. But there must have been other reasons.

The Cronins lived in a three-room, thatched farmhouse down a bohreen, or laneway, beside a river in a valley between mountains reaching upwards through the ever-present low clouds. The laneway bent around furze-laden boundaries through a mile of fields. It was built of dry stone. Only the main roads were built with tarmacadam. All the secondary roads and bohreens were built of stone and screenings which became mucky in wet weather and dusty on fine days. Neighbours had to fight for space to pass each other because of the narrowness of the bohreen. Those who were no longer on speaking terms played a silent game of who would pull in first.

The Cronins travelled up and down here on foot and by horse and trap. Status within the community indicated itself by the quality of the horse. Poorer people had a cob pony or a mule to pull their trap or cart. The Cronins were poor, but not that poor – they had a horse.

Mary Anne was one of the McCarthys of The Forge. The McCarthys, who lived about a mile from the Cronins, had a small farm of thirty-six Irish acres, much of it covered in rushes indicating poor drainage. This part of the farm was known as 'the coarse meadow and bottoms'. Like all local farmers, the McCarthys had a couple of dry, high bawn fields which were capable of being cultivated.

They grew tillage crops of oats, potatoes, turnips, mangolds and cabbage in rotation in the bawn fields. The main farm enterprise was twelve dairy cows. The McCarthys milked the cows by hand. They fed some milk to the calves. More was kept for the household and the production of home-produced salted butter. They sent the rest to the co-operative creamery.

They bought maize meal, known as yellow meal, slag fertilizer and bits of hardware from the co-operative on a contra basis. They paid for these out of the milk cheque. The creamery paid the net balance to them at the end of the month. As there was no milk to sell during the winter months because the milk cows were dried off, they put purchases from the creamery on the slate and paid for them from the milk cheques of the following spring.

Mary Anne built her own small farmyard business of producing eggs, chickens and a few turkeys and geese for sale at Christmas. This allowed her to have some petty cash and also the equivalent of a barter to purchase some niceties such as fresh meat, cakes or personal underwear.

The first meeting of Mick Denny Bill Cronin and Mary Anne

McCarthy was not the result of fate. It was a 'made match'. Mickey, the local matchmaker, arranged the meeting. He then brokered a deal between the Cronin family and the McCarthy family. The dowry from Mary Anne could, in turn, be used to 'dowry off' another of Mick Denny Bill's sisters. The more valuable the dowry, the better. Marriage was less about romance and more about finance and the extension, preservation or creation of an aristocracy or dynasty. It was even more about the size of the dowry. Fate, God's will, the laws of nature or romantic notions were mere accidental interventions in the deal.

The valuation process was deliberate. Mary Anne's father and a trusted cousin came to 'walk the land' with the purpose of 'doing the deal'. This was a serious game between both sides. Mick Denny Bill's father, Denny, was clever and dense at the same time. He was cunning. He and a trusted advisor guided Mary Anne's people through the farm. He included a good bawn field belonging to his neighbour, Gerry McCarthy, as if it was part of his farm. Though it might lead to trouble later, this helped to secure a better dowry deal.

The parish priest officiated and thirty people, made up of the Cronin and McCarthy families and their friends, attended the little church in the village for the wedding of Mary Anne and Mick Denny Bill.

Immediately after the wedding, Mary Anne came into Mick Denny Bill's parents' house and shared the kitchen space with his mother. Mary Anne's bedroom was her only bit of privacy. However, a sound made in the bedroom reverberated throughout the entire house – any expressions of physical attraction from the newly-married Mary Anne and Mick Denny Bill were curtailed due to the risk of being overheard by everybody in the house.

The atmosphere between Mick Denny Bill's mother Katie, known to all as Granny, and Mary Anne was tense. On the day before the wedding, Granny was master of her own domain. On the day after the wedding, Mary Anne quietly and firmly took control. No window is large enough for two women to look through.

At all other times, Mary Anne shared the same space as her mother-in-law. The house comprised a kitchen, a parlour, three bedrooms and a loft. The kitchen was the hub of the house. Here the extended family lived, ate, sat around, played cards, gossiped, and made and took decisions.

The focal point of the kitchen was a large open fire, an oven and a crane on which to hang the pots. To the side was a bellows which helped start the fire in the morning. The fuel used was timber and turf. A big wooden kitchen table with a bench lay by the wall. There were some chairs too. At the side was the dresser where they kept tableware and cutlery. Beside the dresser was the settle, which doubled as an emergency bed and a seat.

Hanging from the bare rafters was hairy salted bacon, which was preserved by both the salt and the smoke around the kitchen. There were flagstones on the floor, and the door out to the farmyard was a half-door – really it was two halves. The top half was open and the bottom half was shut much of the time to prevent the farmyard animals drifting into the kitchen. When not shut, the hens and dogs came in and ate the food fallen from the table.

Mary Anne was a good catch for Mick Denny Bill. She was not blessed with good looks, but she brought the McCarthy ethics of resourcefulness, hard work and shrewdness to the marriage. She managed the house and the farmyard with military precision, keeping the kitchen scrupulously clean and her husband, his family and visitors fed on time every day.

Meanwhile, Mary Anne and Granny strove to change their individual behaviour. Deep down they disliked each other, but their thinking and attitude gave different signals from their actions as they controlled the evolving tension in their behaviour with each other. Mick Denny Bill suffered in silence.

Because of the scarcity of money, Mary Anne managed the limited amount that circulated very carefully. She paid mostly by a barter system with the co-operative and the local shop. She nevertheless required cash to pay unexpected bills.

Mary Anne had never heard of the accounting concepts of double-entry bookkeeping or accruals or prepayments – she had her own system. She held small amounts of money in various jugs on the kitchen dresser. She kept some money tucked in her bosom. These monies were the buffer to cover unexpected payments to the priest, vet, doctor, undertaker or solicitor.

Mick Denny Bill Cronin was known to be a good farmer. But he was known better throughout the county as a great judge of animals. His neighbours referred to him for guidance about buying and selling cattle, calves, sheep and pigs. The cattle dealers knew this and, being streetwise, they tried on fair day to complete an early deal with Mick Denny Bill. They paid a better price to him just to get the deal done. They then used this as a reference point for the deals with other farmers. Their motto was, 'If I was able to deal with Mick Denny Bill, then I can deal with you.'

In order to close the gap between the bid price and the price expected by the farmer, the services of the tangler were called. The tangler operated around the edges of deals. The dealers used him to get the farmers to lower their price expectations and engage in negotiations. He brought both sides together and brokered a deal which was sealed not by a written contract, but by a spit on the hand and the clasping of all three hands together.

The farmer drove his sold animals to the railway yard for loading onto rail carriages for transport to their next destination. He then returned to the pub used by that dealer to receive his payment in cash. The fairgreen was surrounded by forty-three houses of which twenty-six were pubs and eating-houses. Here the dealer paid the farmer, but the deal was not concluded until there was another argument over the 'luck penny'. The seller was supposed to give this money back to the buyer, so that he would have luck with his purchases. It was all part of a ritual. Having been paid, the farmer and his neighbours had a big, greasy fry-up. They then drank porter over the next few hours.

Farmers often spent a good part of the money received for their sold livestock here. When a farmer went home to face his wife, there often was little money left. This created great distress as the wife needed this money to pay the shop and the co-operative, and to buy bits and pieces. This distress resulted in a row or in punishment with the ever effective silent treatment and withdrawal of conjugal rights.

Mick Denny Bill fell prey to bad company a few times and arrived home from fairs heavy with porter and light in money. Mary Anne decided when she realised his history that her best strategy was not to fight about it, but to prevent it happening in the future. She went into the fair later in the morning and was there about the expected time of payment for the animals.

Being mindful of what the neighbours would say behind his back, Mick Denny Bill felt embarrassed when Mary Anne intruded on his transactions at the fair. He never understood her. However, it was better than the treatment she could dish out within the confines of the house if he did not agree.

Sometimes Mick Denny Bill brought the farrowing sow into the kitchen for a few days until her litter of bonhams was born and hardy enough to go into the piggery. He brought orphan lambs and other sick animals in too. There were few veterinary services and if even there were services, there was no money to pay the vet. Home medicines were cures. Tim Pat from the mountain had a special bottle from which he cured sick animals. As a man with the knack, people from miles around in the impoverished community treated him with reverence. He treated the sick animal on the kitchen floor. Minutes after he left, Mary Anne cleaned the floor to spotlessness.

Mary Anne showed her strength of resolve and self-confidence. She was not part of the crowd. She stood out from the crowd and gave quiet signals to all, including her husband and children, of her management and leadership. She worked smarter. She believed that operating as before just leads to more of the same.

None of the neighbours who spoke about her considered that Mary Anne might have been managing the course of nature and her own life with a vision, a mission and an agenda they could only guess at. Her mission was known only to Mary Anne herself.

Mary Anne's Philosophies for Jack

- **It's not always the big things that count. It's often the little things.**

- **The people you perceive to have power may have positional power and little personal power.**

- **A plant grows from its roots and is helped or hindered in its growth by its environmental conditions.**

- **If you want a different output in the future, make a different input.**

- **Keep on doing the exact same thing and you can't expect to get a different result.**

- **Every change journey starts with one small step from the point you are at now.**

- **Nobody can persuade another to change.** The gates of change can be opened only from the inside. It is not enough to change your initial behaviour; you must change your thinking and your attitude.

Chapter 2

War-Time and Priest Power

Father Patrick Shanahan, the parish priest, held absolute power over the Cronins and everyone else in the community. He presented himself as the giver of the gift of salvation or the penalty of damnation depending on how his parishioners obeyed the Church's rules. He had the ideal control model built on having Heaven and Hell at polar opposites.

He was supported by other members of the ruling class in the community – the teacher, the doctor, the Garda and the local merchant who knew that fear and dependence kept people under their control. This ruling class knew that they controlled and influenced most people. They had money and knowledge when most were poor and the formal education of most people ended with the Primary Certificate at age twelve or thirteen.

There was power in knowledge, but only the children of the rich few went to secondary school or university. Within the parish structure, the priest, the teacher, the doctor, the Garda and the local merchant had formal education and knowledge. They listened to the radio and bought and read the daily newspapers; they interpreted, edited and communicated the news to the kowtowing and impressionable, the ignorant, the innocent and naive about local politics, the government in Dublin and the war in Europe according to their own values and principles.

The power reached into people's morals and behaviours. Father Patrick Shanahan exercised his power and enforced the rules of the Church as he patrolled the local dance halls, of which he was the chairman and the funds from which went to bolster parish income. He was the master of parish finances and of parish morals.

Mary Anne and Mick Denny Bill, both innocent of much about life and love, exchanged their physical affection for each other for their first time on their wedding night. They were inspired by nature and guidance picked up through the currency of dirty jokes from their friends. The word 'sex' could not be uttered in company.

There were no illustrated books or videos to teach different coupling positions and where to look for the G-Spot. Mothers and sisters advised the young bride to use Vaseline. Only caring and enlightened fathers or brothers advised the young groom to be gentle and caring with the bride, to respect her and allow nature to take its course. Sexual intercourse between a young man and a young woman had the purpose of the procreation of children – it was not for the building of mutual loving relationships.

Few knew about hormones and how they stimulated organs of the human body to act. Priests and parents preached total abstinence from sex as the only safe way to stop having babies.

All of these constraints, in combination with the living of people in close proximity, led to frustrated marriage beds. This, in turn, led to strained relationships between couples and between them and their wider families.

Married couples had large families, mostly because they had no legitimate, effective birth-control mechanisms, or because of ignorance, or because they succumbed to the will of God. They assumed that a number of the weaker children would die at childbirth or soon thereafter. Yet too many people became a problem. An imbalance between population numbers, housing capacity and gainful employment evolved. This manifested itself in unmarried aunts and uncles around the home fighting for the same food and bed spaces. It often prevented the proper transfer of a farm and legal titles to the designated son or daughter.

Like all ecosystems, the rural Irish system came up with an Irish solution to the problem. Sometimes the solution, after much stress and hassle, was to get surplus family members committed to the local mental hospital or asylum. One of Mick Denny Bill's brothers was taken screaming one night to the mental hospital never to be visited or spoken about again. This freed up bed and table space in the house.

The other safety valve was emigration. Emigrants fell into two categories: the people who had access to some money and connections went to America; the less well-equipped people went where the entry barriers were lower – to England . This people-movement was a common sight around the Cronin's home place. Various customs evolved around the process.

The local version of the American Wake was held for those going to America. The neighbours gathered and actively participated in the ritual of celebrating and mourning the last nights at home of the emigrating young man or woman. They assumed and expected that they would never come home again. American Wakes provided an opportunity for all to lend psychological and moral support to each other.

In any cycle of change or bereavement, there are five steps: shock, anger, rejection, acceptance and healing. The American Wake represented acceptance of the reality, both for the departing person and his or her family and neighbours.

Irish emigrants went into the unknown. After that it was a case of sink or swim. They slaved at rough jobs in their adopted country. They often held two jobs so that they could save money, which they sent home to their parents in Ireland to help pay the fare of the next child to take the boat. This money, together with the parcels full of bright-coloured clothes bought in thrift shops in America, brought some relief to the much-stretched home ecosystem, particularly at Christmas.

Disease and poor medical services, combined with poor nutrition and overcrowding, contributed to the higher than normal rate of death. If the child lived, its life expectancy was short.

On the death of a local person, the community sprang into action. A leading woman in the parish manoeuvred herself into an undisputed leadership role for such events. She arrived with candlesticks and candles, a crucifix, Holy water and a white cloth. She arranged to have the body washed and laid out for the wake. Her assistants washed out the house and set the table for the feeding of the masses that drifted in.

The main role of the man was to organise the drink – bottles of whisky and port, and a barrel of porter. The corking of this barrel evolved into a recognised skill where the local pig butcher was considered to be the expert. It could not be done until he arrived and performed this ritual.

The grave diggers had to be kept well-lubricated for their supposedly skilled job. The best grave diggers were recognised for doing a neat job, giving the banks of the grave very clean cuts.

If they were opening an old grave, the general question was, 'Did you find the body of so and so?' If the buried person was a saint and had gone to Heaven, then his or her body would be intact. If the gravediggers found bones only, the poor person had 'gone to the fires of Hell'. This news scared people, facilitating the priest to keep them disciplined within the rules of the Church.

The wake lasted two days and nights, thus giving the grieving family the opportunity to manage the transition period between life and death. It was a social outing for the neighbours as they gathered to show solidarity with the grieving family, while they ate, drank and told stories. The stories were often tales around happenings concerning the dead person. In addition, they participated in the obligatory Saying of the Rosary.

Against this backdrop, the young men and women went out to the hay barn and succumbed to their natural, but 'sinful', hormonal urges. They fumbled and groped, but avoided penetration because of the risk of pregnancy. Pregnancy would be a disaster for the single girl. If she became pregnant, she was likely to be branded a slut and banished from the parish, often to an unmarried mothers' home such as the Magdalene Laundries.

Father Patrick Shanahan often facilitated banishment to the unmarried mothers' home or to the emigration ship. Sometimes he arranged with priests from other dioceses to have the pregnant girl hired by big farmers in their areas so that the scandal was pushed away from his patch. In some situations, if the property rights weren't too complicated, the priest arranged a quickie marriage. The couple then had what was called an 'early child'.

After a funeral, the women of the immediate family mourned for twelve months. The family turned off the radio, or wireless, for the duration of that year. The women were obliged by society to wear a black dress, shawl and stockings. They were expected to stay home, except when necessary to go to the shop, Mass or Confession. The same restrictions did not apply to the men.

The Church blocked women and the poor from the central aisle by a gate so that they had to go to the side aisles. The central area containing the seats of privilege was reserved for the supposed pillars of society – the doctor, vet, teachers, merchants and big farmers. These were the same people who contributed the most money to the 'Oats Collection' for the priest's usage. The priest read out their contributions in public to the attendance at all the Masses after Easter.

Women who gave birth had to be 'churched'. When the crowds had gone home after Mass, the new mother went to the altar rails for a special blessing to cleanse her after giving birth. She was thus churched, or cleansed.

Many women and their respective family supporters lived under the same roof without talking to each other for years. This was a more difficult strategy than to have the parties engaged in open warfare. In open warfare, they released some of the tension at least and it was probably healthier.

'No window is large enough for two women to look out through.' This crowded space led many people to suffer their supposed Purgatory on Earth. The suffering came from the treatment of men by their respective wives in the bedroom.

People had a need and a want to socialise and get out of the confines of their own over-crowded kitchens. Their big release was to walk across the fields to the local Rambling house. Cronin's was one such house. Mary Anne inherited this tradition when she married Mick Denny Bill.

Why some houses naturally became Rambling houses and others didn't deserves scientific, socio-economic study. The personality of the women of the house was the likely determining factor. In the Rambling houses in the area, the wife or mother-in-law had a warm welcoming disposition.

Judge a house not by its physical profile, but by the people who visit it. The Law of Attraction indicates that the people who visit us are a reflection of ourselves.

Neighbours gathered into the Cronin house every night and sat around the fire telling stories and gossiping about what they gleaned from the townland and further afield. If any of the neighbours had been in town, this was an opportunity for new angles on stories. The storytellers embellished them as they retold them to other neighbours later on.

But the focus of these nights was a game of cards. The traditional game played in the Cronins' locality was the game of 45s as many described it. In this game, each player is dealt five cards and the dealer, to indicate Trumps, turns up the top card from the remaining pack. Matches were used instead of money as the currency of exchange. A prize might be a plucked cooked chicken or a sweet cake. However, the winner often didn't get the opportunity to take his prize home because all players, winners and losers, tackled into the chicken or cake and the strong tea made and served in mugs.

A Tilly lamp provided the light, but because of its weakness, it created shadows in the corners and in the loft. Jack and his brothers slept in the loft. They hid in the shadowy background and listened quietly through the floorboards to the gossip going on around the kitchen table below. The bits they missed, they just made up themselves. This was Jack's first lesson in innovation and creativity. Work with what you have and be inventive with the rest.

After the card game, the neighbours scattered and walked or cycled home in the dark. This darkness led to many scary stories with the presence of ghosts and long-dead neighbours operating in the shadows.

Some tricksters enhanced this scare mode by performing shadowy acts on scared neighbours. These acts included the making of strange noises, moans, throwing stones onto the galvanised roofs and the bagging of chimneys. The bags prevented the smoke from their open fires escaping out through the chimney thus filling the kitchen with smoke and forcing the occupants out of the house. It was a cruel trick, and especially cruel for older people.

Local farmers drove their cattle, sheep or horses on foot to the fair which was held monthly in the fairgreen of the local town. These farmers left their farms at about 4 a.m walking their animals along miles of roadway to reach the fair at about 6 a.m. On the roads into town, the buyers known as dealers approached the farmers to talk down the market and offer them ridiculously low prices. This was a conditioning process for the real business later in the morning.

The cattle and sheep were stood at certain spots around the fairgreen, and the game of exchange, which utilises the tactics of bluff and threats, commenced. The dealers were crafty and lived by their wits. They appeared to be in competition, but in reality, they were all together playing games. Having poked the animals and talked down the market, they made a slightly better offer than their ridiculous earlier morning offer. There was generally still a gap between this offer and the price that the farmers expected. The job of the tangler was to broker the deal.

Each family in the townland agreed, on a rotational basis, to have Father Shanahan say The Station Mass in their house. The Station Mass, known locally as The Stations, was a ritual and a tradition dating back to Penal times in the 1600s, when Mass was banned and priests had to say it in secret. Over the years, The Stations became a social meeting event. They also became a stage on which neighbours could make a statement about their personal wealth. All the neighbours were expected to attend. The frequency of hosting The Stations depended on the number of houses in the townland. Mary Anne calculated that her turn for The Stations came around every nine years. Mary Anne knew already that it was their turn next. However, she had to wait until the parish priest read it out from the pulpit at Mass to know what date he had decided to come. In the past, there had been two weeks' notice; Mary Anne was proactive in getting the place ready long before that.

Clearing the weeds around the farmyard and driveway and spreading the dung heap out onto the land were important jobs that had to be done well ahead of the day of The Stations. There were no chemicals. Hard work and sweat kept nature in check. Then the gates had to be painted. The outhouses and the outside of the dwelling house had to be whitewashed.

The whitewashing of the dwelling house was done two days prior to The Stations because of the risk of it being washed off the walls by the rain. The whitewash was a mixture of lime and water which performed two functions: to disinfect the walls and, the main function from Mary Anne's point of view, to make them look clean and bright on The Stations' morning.

Two days before due date, Mary Anne and Mick Denny Bill went into town with a long list of shopping. This was their opportunity to demonstrate to their neighbours that their status within the local community had not slipped. They would show, if possible, that it had actually improved. They bought food calculated by Mary Anne to be necessary, and they bought bottles of sweet sherry and cases of porter. When they arrived home, they packed the food and drink away carefully. Mary Anne made out a work programme of jobs for everyone to do the following day. The work focused on cleaning and cooking. They would borrow tables and chairs from some neighbours. These had to be collected and cleaned on the quiet.

On the morning of the Stations, the fuss around the house was frenetic. The farmyard jobs had to be completed, the farmyard had to be cleaned up and fresh straw spread over the bad patches of the yard and cow shed.

At 7.15 a.m., Mary Anne, Jack and the rest of the family dressed in their Sunday best. They then checked around to ensure that everything was in best condition.

At precisely 7.50 a.m., Mick Denny Bill walked down to the gate to greet Father Shanahan and accompany him up the driveway into the house. The neighbours gathered.

The host didn't have to invite the neighbours to The Stations. They were expected to come. Even if they weren't on speaking terms with the host, they were expected to attend. The host only invited relations and friends who were from outside the townland.

When Father Shanahan entered the house, the people bowed their heads in submission and respect. He went straight to the parlour where there was a blazing fire with two chairs set out. The more comfortable of the two chairs was for him to sit on; the other was for people to kneel down as they went to confess. This open Confession was difficult for people – they did not have the comfort of the darkness of the Confession box to protect their identity. However, they knew that even in the Confession box, Father Shanahan knew who was on the other side of the slide of the grill.

Confessions complete, Father Shanahan put on his vestments for Mass and came back out to the people-packed kitchen. Johnny, the parish clerk, arranged the Mass altar. The Mass altar was the kitchen table balanced on two chairs to give it height for convenience for the priest. The Mass and the Holy Communion progressed as normal. At the end of Mass, Johnny read aloud the list of Stations' money due from each household in the townland. The people lined up; Johnny collected the money. This public declaration of the different rates per household was, in its own way, a differentiating factor and ranked people within the townland based on money.

Mick Denny Bill and some specially invited neighbours went into the parlour to have breakfast with Father Shanahan. This was a privilege for those invited, even though it was generally uncomfortable for those chosen few. Men only were invited. It was uncomfortable for them because they had to mind their manners and be careful of what they said.

Mary Anne had introduced a new addition to the breakfast menu for the occasion. The locals weren't sure what it was or how to tackle it. They adopted a 'wait-and-see' attitude. They observed how Father Shanahan went about eating it, and then they tried to copy him as naturally as possible. They had never seen a grapefruit before. It was bigger and paler than an orange, and when they eventually put segments of the grapefruit into their mouths, they realised that it was bitter. But they followed Father Shanahan's lead and pretended that it was nice and refreshing.

People milled around, smoking, talking and waiting for Father Shanahan to leave so that they could enjoy their meal and a few bottles of porter without restriction. No porter could be served until he was safely gone. After breakfast and a few porters, many of the neighbours went home to do their farmyard jobs while the hosts invited cousins and friends to stay back and continue to eat and drink more.

Because theirs was a Rambling house, Jack's parents decided that they would hold a house dance that night. Gerry O'Connor brought his 'box' – his accordion – to provide the music for the dancing. Many neighbours came back as soon as they had their cows milked and yard jobs done. They had more to eat, drink and discuss about various subjects and their own unique angle on these subjects.

The kitchen floor cleared and Gerry started the music to encourage the first people onto the floor to dance. The Sliabh Luachra set was the main dance form in this region. The men knocked sparks out of the flagstones as they tapped out the music. There were always a few shy, sly types who stayed back in the shadows. They observed everything that was happening or about to happen. They watched who danced with whom and tried to see any signals being exchanged. Jack was delighted with the great attention and praise that the guests gave him. The more porter or sweet sherry they drank, the more praise they gave. Jack loved the excitement of it all.

As the dancing got into full swing, some young men and young women went out the back door. As unobtrusively as possible, they went to the hay barn. Jack followed them from a distance. He observed and listened. Their movements were a mystery to him. Nevertheless, he loved the adventure and said that he would do the same at other Stations when he grew up.

Inside the house, the music and the craic raised the spirits of the locals. They toasted Mary Anne and Mick Denny Bill for having put on a great show, which pleased them and helped solidify their relative position within the local community.

Nobody can please everyone. One of the women said: 'Did you see the get-up of Maggie?' Another said: 'Those buns were a bit sticky.' The most critical ladies were those who refused to have The Stations in their own homes. Instead, they persuaded Father Shanahan to transfer their Stations to the local school. The Stations held in the local school were strong on religion and had none of the social trappings. More importantly, they were less expensive.

People dreaded TB. Whole families were wiped out by this disease. Because it was so infectious, once it came into the house it spread like wildfire. Cramped, over-crowded, badly-ventilated houses facilitated this spread.

When a member of the family died, the family members took their clothes and bedding out to the yard and burned them. By doing so, they thought they were breaking the cycle of infection.

Some families were more susceptible to the disease than others. There was a stigma attached to the families who had TB. Some parents ordered their children not to marry the offspring of infected families. This manifested itself with the comment, 'They have the Weakness'.

Paddy McCarthy and his wife, Mary, owned a farm of forty-five acres. Of this, about twenty acres was good dry, bawn-type land and the rest was wet and rushy. They were dairy farmers with ten cows. They had a two-storey standard designed house with a chimney at each gable end. This design type can still be seen scattered throughout western Ireland. The front door was into the kitchen with the parlour door to the left. The stairs was in the kitchen and led to three rooms upstairs. Out the back from the kitchen was an additional room known as the Scullery.

Mary died from TB in 1955. Paddy had three young children to rear. He was pragmatic and got on with doing what he had to do as best he could. The neighbours, including Jack's mother, were good to him.

Over the next few years, he and the children managed to muddle through on their scarce resources. Mary Anne noticed that Paddy had lost weight. One day he came to Mary Anne and asked her to drive him and the three children into town as he had some important business to do. Mary Anne drove them and waited for them.

Paddy was not the usual heavy drinking man who went over the top when he went to the pub in town. But on this occasion he was. Mary Anne tried to get him out of the pub and get him home. She grew very angry with him and threatened to leave him there to make his own way home. Eventually she got him and the children out of the pub and brought them home.

As he was about to go into his home, Paddy turned to Mary Anne and told her about his business in town that day. He told her that the doctor had diagnosed that he had TB and that he had to go into a Sanatorium. He was in town to purchase lengths of timber to board up the windows and to arrange to send the three children to the Industrial School in the north of the county.

Mary Anne was so shocked and ashamed of her earlier reaction that she burst out crying. They hugged each other in a public demonstration of emotions that was very unusual between neighbours at that time.

Jack still remembers the shallow noise as Paddy hammered the boards into place in front of all the windows, never to be taken away.

Paddy went into the Sanatorium the following week. His children were sent to the Industrial School. Paddy died within the year. Some years later, the children escaped from the unfair and harsh regime of the Industrial School. However, they were already damaged by the bad hand of cards that fate had dealt them over their early lives.

Like many before them, they finished their lives as displaced people. They worked on building sites in London. They never again visited the place where all their hardship started.

Theirs was not an isolated case. Boarded windows were never again opened up in many houses around this western area, where whole families perished.

Jack, a six-year-old boy in the '50s, was unaware of the effects of the traumatic events. He was unaware that, like everybody, he was a product of his genetic map and his environment. The events that happened around him and to many people he knew had a bigger and more lasting influence than he could ever know.

Lessons for Jack from Rural Life

- **Show me your friends and I'll tell you who you are.** Judge a house not by its appearance, but by the people who visit it. The Law of Attraction indicates that the people who visit us are a reflection of ourselves.

- **Good Communication has two important elements – the sender and the receiver.** Mary Anne was an effective communicator; she was a good listener and, when she spoke, she said something profound that conveyed her messages with impact to her audience. Of those who say nothing, few are silent.

- **'There is no art to find the mind's construction in the face'** (from *Macbeth* by William Shakespeare). Nobody really knows another's personal agenda. Mary Anne was a good listener and was concerned for her neighbour, Paddy McCarthy; however, she failed to pick up on Paddy's turmoil as he prepared to board up his home and send his children to Industrial school. Resist giving advice based on your first interpretation.

- **Lukewarm is displeasing to the palate.** Mary Anne and Mick Denny Bill were not going to be lukewarm in the way they planned to hold The Stations in their house. This was an opportunity for them to anchor their place within their neighbourhood. They were determined to grab this opportunity within the lifetime of this opportunity.

- **Resentment is a poison that you take while waiting for your enemy to die.** Mary Anne's neighbours saved money by holding their Stations in the school. However, they had to pay the price in the energy-sapping emotion of resentment.

- **Some stubbornness and arrogance can help achieve your goals.**

- **You will never plough a field by turning the sods over in your mind.**

- **Power is when you change the behaviour of someone who would not change.** Father Shanahan and his colleagues used their positional power to regulate people's moral behaviours.

Chapter 3

Great Expectations

Mick Denny Bill was intelligent. His neighbours said he was lazy but smart. He didn't sweat for the sake of sweating. He was methodical. He did not tear blindly into the work as the other farmers did. He took each task step by step to its completion.

Mary Anne had clarity about what she wanted. She knew what she needed others to do so that she could achieve her mission. She delegated work to Mick Denny Bill and to her children.

Her way to rear children was to discipline them in a regimental way. She drilled into them high standards of good manners, truthfulness, obedience and respect for the elderly. These standards were non-negotiable. She dealt with non-conformity in a severe and consistent manner so that over time, Jack and his brothers and sisters understood clearly the correlation between the breaking of the rules and their associated punishments.

In the '40s, '50s and '60s, corporal punishment was the norm – both in the home and in the schools. It was all about conformance to rigid rules. Any child trying to be innovative and daring was dealt with harshly. In every house, there was a rod which was generally a sally stick. It had a spring in it so that it didn't break easily.

Unlike some other neighbouring mothers, Mary Anne was not for delegating this punishment task to Mick Denny Bill. In other houses, the mothers threatened to get the fathers to administer the punishment when they got home. This usually took the form of the father taking off his leather belt and threatening to use it.

Mary Anne just lashed out with the sally rod, or whatever else she could get her hands on, at the moment of her discovery of the breach of rules. For bigger transgressions, such as telling lies, which hit at her core values, she gathered all of the children to witness the lashing. The lashing lasted until the offending child admitted his or her wrongs.

There was also a lot of love and hugging between Mary Anne and her children. It was a counterpoint to her harsh disciplinary regime. Fathers did not engage in a public demonstration of emotions or love. Mick Denny Bill too kept his emotions and his expression of love to himself.

Since Jack's home was a Rambling house, neighbours visited them frequently, coming and going at will at all times of the day. They spoiled the children by bringing them sweets and playing games with them. This genuine attention made the experience pleasurable and satisfying for the children. Children punched uncles, aunts and neighbours. In turn, uncles, aunts and neighbours punched and tickled the children. The children laughed and laughed and came back for more.

It was a natural, fun-giving response. Mary Anne warned the children to keep away from some men because they 'were not nice'. Mothers knew more than was said. They came up with their own practical tactics to safeguard their young from particular danger. Nature tends to balance its plusses and minuses over time.

Other than the neighbours, the only other people Jack and his siblings met before starting to go to school were their aunts and uncles and other family relations who visited in their pony and carts on special occasions during the year. When Mick Denny Bill's mother was alive, his brothers and sisters and their families descended on their house to visit her every Sunday. Mary Anne catered for them with a smile. They expected it.

At the same time, she resented the ungrateful intrusion on her already over-crowded home. They often ate her out of house and home, resulting in her own children going short on food. Sometimes the visitors brought a pound of tea, a loaf of bread or a sweet cake. Other times they came with 'their hands hanging'; these were the cousins whose arms were too short to reach their deep pockets.

Jack and his siblings got to know their cousins while they played games around the farmyard. Like all children, they were preoccupied with their fun and did not sense their mother's tension in the house. They often suffered through the release of this tension when the visitors departed. They were often blamed for things they did not do and had to accept the accompanying punishment administered by Mary Anne.

They faced a full culture shock when they attended Primary School for the first time.

There were no crèches or pre-school facilities. Their only preparation was the horror stories told by neighbouring children about the terrible things that had happened to other children.

Mary Anne sent Jack to the local Primary School when he was four years old. She took him to the school gate where he joined the other crying children as their mothers left them to face this new ordeal.

Their mothers were supportive, but to Jack and his co-sufferers at that time it felt like abandonment. It was like the trauma that suckler calves go through when they are weaned away from their lactating mothers. Their crying and bawling was deafening and doleful.

The school was built in the early 1900s. There were four teachers, but only two classrooms. Two teachers per classroom tried to teach their respective classes.

The school had no running water, except what came in through the poorly fitting windows or the hole in the roof. The toilets were known as dry toilets. A dry toilet was a plank of wood with a hole drilled out directly over the slush heap. This heap built up over time and every few years had to be physically cleaned out and spread on the nearby fields.

The principal of the school engaged Mick, the handyman, to spread quicklime over the slush heap every few months. The quicklime and the openness of the dry toilet to the weather was the school's contribution to hygiene. The boys' urinal just drained out to the back of the schoolyard and soaked away. A strip of green grass indicated its fertilizer capabilities.

Mrs O'Connor was Jack's teacher. She was a small, wiry woman with tight lips and her hair was tied tightly in a bun at the back of her head. Akin to Dickens' Mrs Thingummy in *Oliver Twist*, she was a junior assistant mistress, or a JAM, teacher – the label for non-qualified teachers.

How to handle newly-weaned children sensitively and with understanding was foreign to her. Her first priority was to establish her authority with a structured disciplinary code from the start. This was difficult since Jack and his new classmates had their own uncomfortable agenda and were not mindful of hers. He and the others were given small blackboards, like current day clipboards, and chalk. As far as Mrs O'Connor was concerned, they now had the tools for the start of their formal education; all she had to do to motivate them to use those tools was to slap them. While it wasn't common practice to slap junior infants, Mrs O'Connor had her own punishment formula and slapped the children whenever she saw fit.

As Jack moved from junior infants to senior infants to first class, he built up more and more hatred for school with its conflicting nonsensical rules and regulations. He had no interest in any of the material that Mrs O'Connor taught. He just wanted to be out of the intrusive, oppressive environment and have the opportunity to do what he wanted. The seeds of negativity towards formal education were being cultivated in his mind. In his view, the only good thing about school was the holidays, even though home was not a bed of roses, especially when his mother lashed out. The difference between home and school was the loving relationship between him and his mother. He was, at best, just about able to survive the school regime.

Nearing his seventh birthday, the big school focus was the preparation for the sacraments of Confession and First Holy Communion. Jack was excited about the prospect that he would get some better clothes. His new teacher, Mrs Murphy, worked with the class for months drilling into their heads some of the basics of The Catechism of the Catholic Church. Father Shanahan came to the school every Thursday asking the First Holy Communion class questions from the Catechism. Jack and his classmates were expected to recite the answers, word for word as written in the Catechism. They were like parrots reciting the pat answers – they had no understanding of what it all meant.

They faced the ultimate threat if they didn't know the answers to Father Shanahan's questions when asked. That threat was that they would not be allowed to have their First Holy Communion. But it was an illusion. Even the illiterate got through.

Preparing for the First Confession was a serious effort. Jack and his mother discussed the list of sins he should confess. But he could not understand the difference between mortal sin and venial sin. The concepts of Full-knowledge and Consent were beyond his understanding. This worried him. Jack was showing the first signs of wanting to work out things in meaningful ways in his own head.

When the day of the First Confession arrived, Mrs Murphy marched the class from the school to the church and assembled and lined up Jack and his classmates in front of the Confession box. It was Saturday morning at 11 a.m. Father Shanahan, in long robes and purple stole, went into his middle section of the Confession box. He put the bottom of the curtain out over the half door to indicate that he was present and ready to purge the young sinners of their sins.

Mrs Murphy placed two children before Jack, lining him up in third position. When each of the two came out of the Confession box, they were blushing.

Jack stood up from his pew, crept into his section of the Confession box and pulled the door closed after him. He placed his knees on the kneeler, joined his hands together and waited in the dark with his heart thumping and his breath on hold. On the other side of the box, Father Shanahan was hearing the confession of a girl who had been in the girls' line up at the door. Jack could hear muffled voices of meek girl and loud male adult priest.

Then it happened. Suddenly he was there. Behind the black mesh grill, the shutter pulled back, and in the shadows, Jack could see the priest. He assumed that Father Shanahan could not see him in the dark. Jack spoke as Mrs Murphy had instructed. 'Bless me, Father, for I have sinned. This is my First Confession, Father.'

He then stopped. There was silence. Jack saw through the grill that Father Shanahan was surprised at the silence; the sound of the rustle of his white robes meant that he was upset. The other children had sung out their rehearsed list of supposed sins. But not Jack.

Father Shanahan turned towards Jack and asked, 'What sins have you to confess?'

Jack said, 'I killed . . . I killed . . .'

'You killed?' said the priest.

'Molly,' said Jack.

'Molly who?' asked the priest.

'Molly, the yellow chicken,' said Jack. 'And I don't want to go into the blazing fires of Hell.'

Jack couldn't think of all the usual venial sins, like being bold, or telling a few lies.

Father Shanahan probed Jack where and how this terrible deed had taken place. But Jack was now speechless.

Father Shanahan's voice rose, scaring those still in the queue outside. Mrs Murphy wondered what was going on.

Father Shanahan said to Jack, 'You have been a bold little boy. For your penance you must say five Hail Marys. And you must tell your mother the truth.'

Jack blurted out that he had only *thought* about doing it and not actually done it.

His thought was the sin.

Sunday was the First Holy Communion day. It was the day after the First Confession. The candidates for First Holy Communion had to fast from food, which meant they had no food from the previous midnight if they wanted to receive Holy Communion on Sunday morning. Jack had no breakfast on that Sunday morning.

Mick Denny Bill put the tackle on the horse and trap. The whole family squeezed onto the trap, and the horse, with family in tow, trotted his way to the church. Mick Denny Bill allowed Jack to hold the horsewhip. This was a big event for Jack. He was wearing his first suit of clothes and shiny shoes, which Mary Anne had bought in Culloty's Shop in town. She had bought them three sizes too big so that they would still fit as his feet grew over the next few years. She pinned the Holy Communion badge on the lapel of his coat. Now he was given the horsewhip and allowed to steer the horse. It was a symbol of power and control, and that he had reached the age of reason. He had reached an important milestone in his life and was being rewarded for it with permission to drive the horse.

Mary Anne was both spiritual and practical. She had gone through the motions with Jack on how to receive the pieces of bread she used to represent the Sacred Host. She kept talking to him about the fact that he would be receiving the body and blood of Jesus in the form of the Sacred Host. She showed him how to tilt back his head, close his eyes, gather some spittle into his mouth and stick out his tongue to receive the Sacred Host. The practical reason why she was suggesting the spittle tactic was to prevent the Host sticking onto the roof of his mouth if his mouth was dry at the receiving point. If that happened, he would be unable to release it without using his finger. But, only a priest could touch the Sacred Host. The dilemma and the paradox stressed Jack.

Jack's First Holy Communion went according to the teacher's plan, and Mary Anne, Mick Denny Bill and family all returned home in the horse and trap to have a special celebration.

Commercialism and efforts to beat the Jones' made Holy Communion and other traditional Church events an excuse for people to parade trappings of wealth, irrespective of whether they had wealth or not.

Jack got a half-crown from Nora, their neighbour, and a ten-shilling red note from Aunt Sheila. Aunts and uncles and some of the benevolent neighbours gave something to the boy or girl on receiving their First Holy Communion. That was tradition. Mary Anne confiscated the money and put it into a savings box. She promised to open a savings account at the Post Office where it would be safe and would grow steadily for Jack.

Back at school after the First Holy Communion, Mrs Murphy focused her class on reading, spelling, sums and especially Irish. To Jack, this meant increased boredom and hardship. The harder he was forced to learn, the more difficult it got for him. But he was afraid of the consequences of getting his lessons wrong. His brain was no longer a dry sponge that would absorb information – it was a wet sponge now loaded with fear.

It was so loaded that he could not absorb Mrs Murphy's lessons. The slapping by his former teacher, Mrs Moynihan, last year had eroded his confidence. Mrs Moynihan called him a dunce and made him stand in the dunce's corner beside the door. But Mrs Moynihan instilled such a deep fear in Jack that she capped his hope for a long time.

Jack's move into fourth class was the best period of his formal schooling.

Mr Ryan, who had taught this class for the previous thirty years, died suddenly. Joan Crowley replaced him. Joan was a newly-trained young teacher and was full of new ideas. From her professional training, she knew the methodology to adopt in encouraging young children to be interested in learning. She did not have to resort to punishment. She was young and vibrant, and Jack and the others were only too willing to please her. She knew how to earn their trust. She gave out praise, recognition and love to which the children responded positively.

Jack had no idea about the first stirrings and the flutter of sex hormones. He could not understand that he was falling in love with Joan Crowley. The new and young teacher with her fresh approach was his first crush.

Meanwhile, Mary Anne and Mick Denny Bill were learning how to become parents. Their only role models were their own parents. Mary Anne was merely repeating the strict regime of her father and mother. Being the eldest child, Jack had no older siblings to confide in.

Mrs Moynihan told Jack that he was a dunce, and the others in the class had accepted this labelling of him without much questioning.

As time went on, mainly through the encouraging influence of his teacher Joan, Jack became more self-aware. He was a survivor. His classmates started to look up to him because he showed a natural flare for sport. He was a good footballer.

Joan taught him the rich philosophy of the Gaelic Athletic Association, or the GAA. She told him that the GAA has facilitated its playing members and administrators to become team members and team leaders. It has had a profound impact on the youth of rural Ireland.

The GAA is a grass-roots organisation. The psychology of its survival and success is competition. Competition, or in other words 'battle', raises the spirit in people. In turn, this spirit fuels one tribe to beat the other tribe.

The planning and preparation for battle on the hurling or football field provides training for a range of participants to hone their skills away from the drudgery of earning a living and putting bread on the table. Local parish rivalry is legendary. Not only do the competing teams tear scalps off each other, but their respective supporters often do so as well. The rivalry grows in intensity if the parish is divided and the competitors both meet in the local championship. Ground yielded to your rival is an act of treason.

Problems often arose where there was intermarriage among people from opposing parishes. This often caused internal family strife as these inter-family battles occurred. Some team mentors took winning so seriously that they tried to influence the genetic pool within their parish patch. Their strategy was to influence who the local lads married. They were encour-aged, if at all possible, to make a match with women from a good GAA-playing gene pool. Daughters from a good football family in a neighbouring parish were earmarked.

At the parish GAA Annual General Meeting, where the members lamented the lack of silverware again for that year, they held a brainstorm exercise to expose the real issues. They then formulated a strategy to rectify the situation so that they could energise their vision of building their club to become the top football club in the county.

In formatting their strategy, they considered many options. One said that sourcing wives from identified neighbouring gene pools was a viable strategy. Jimmy, who looked after the playing pitch, and who was a shrewd judge of football, said to make sure they were 'suitably impregnated' before they came into the parish, because the lads here were no use and would only neutralise the 'potential' of these women.

The games provided a safety valve for people to vent their feelings and frustrations, and thus prevent local explosions from being ignited in other ways. On the positive side, it provided opportunities for the locals to take positions of public pride. This facilitated the growth of excitement, moti-vation and confidence.

At national level, the inter-county league and championship became more interesting, fuelled by the tension and excitement generated by com-mentator Michael O'Hehir. The games were broadcast from Croke Park far away in Dublin through radios powered by wet batteries. Only the priest, doctor, teacher, vet, merchant and bigger farmers had radios. When the county team played in the provincial final or the All-Ireland, the neigh-bours gathered around one of these radios to listen to the broadcast of Michael O'Hehir. Some sat inside the house; most gathered outside and lis-tened to the broadcast through the open window.

Radio was a one-dimensional medium of communication, and the neighbours had to paint their own mental pictures from Michael O'Hehir's commentary on what was happening. But mental picturing was much more exciting than the factual situation of the teams playing their hearts out on the pitch as the tension and excitement took on an intensity way beyond reality.

Individual neighbours added to the tension with their own comments. Someone always established himself as the recognised 'expert pundit' and the rest relied on him for reassurance about what was taking place and the likely outcome. It was fertile ground for the expert. He could see the match without the limitations of actually being at the match.

If the wet battery ran out of juice at a critical point of the match and the commentary broke off, disaster ensued. The owner of the radio was in danger of being physically attacked. The listeners had no mercy even though he was facilitating them. His neighbours and his family expected him to provide the means through which they could listen to the match. If he could not do so, he was useless, a fact that would be repeated in the pub and the wider community.

People react with extreme actions when something very important to them is snatched away without warning. Similar snatchings have triggered wars.

This county identity and group excitement helped create Jack's belief systems and culture. Playing football and, more importantly, being good at it, carried local encouragement, approval and the support of hundreds in the parish. Today's teens rave about boy-bands as they are indoctrinated by peer pressure and by media to become part of the boy-band cult. The fundamentals don't change – only the details and form do.

It is critical for all of us to recognise our strengths as well as our weaknesses. We are all good at something, and we need to crystallise this fact. This will give you a status and a following which will facilitate the building of your *genuine* confidence, not just confidence from the teeth out.

Jack's growing football skills and the encouragement of his teacher, Joan, set him on a path he never thought existed. He never thought he could feel so good. Others looked up to him and wanted to be on his team. He had started a series of little victories which built on each other. His confidence grew day by day.

Jack's other classmates were better at different things. Some were better at reading, writing, singing, painting, and arm wrestling. Some were better looking. Some had bigger muscles. One proclaimed that he had the biggest willie.

Mrs Moynihan had no level of expectation for Jack. 'Jack you are a dunce. Go to the dunce's corner,' she said. Jack declined to her level of expectation of him. Joan Crowley demonstrated a higher level of expectation of him. Jack rose to this expectation.

What Jack Learned from Church and Primary School Influences

- **When a person or a thing of importance to you is snatched away without warning, you are left in a heartless vacuum.** You must quickly fill that vacuum. Reflect on how you would feel if people and things which are dear to you were no longer around. Decide if you are treating these as you would if you were given a second chance. It's too late to cry when the coffin is being lowered into the ground.

- **There is direct link between cause and effect.** A breakdown of law and order is because of lack of respect for legitimate authority, and the fuzzy relationship between deeds and their consequences.

- **For every effect, there is a cause. If you want a different effect or outcome, you must adjust the cause or input.** You are this input. There is no place for you to hide. You are responsible, but you need help from those who have the capacity to help you.

- **The person who breaks silence tends to lose. Ask with a smile and then be silent.**

- *We should not let our fears hold us back from pursuing our hopes.*
  – President John F. Kennedy addressing the world in New Ross, County Wexford, during his visit to Ireland.

- **The eldest child in a family is expected to be the trailblazer for the rest.** The eldest is first to go to school, receive the sacraments and get involved in sports and social events. This is why the youngest of families tend to be the best balanced. By the time they are born, their parents have learned from the mistakes they made with the older children. Where you or your partner fits in your family rotation may be the cause of your mannerisms, reactions and attitudes.

- **Positively influence children to understand the importance of their strong points and you give them the key to their success formulas going forward.** This provides a solid base upon which to build their future. Treat the child as he/she could be. They will surprise you but not themselves.

- **Man grows not by what is given to him, but by what is expected of him.**

Chapter 4

Lessons from Farm Life

Jack's neighbours, his Aunt Sheila, his Uncle Tom, the GAA and the farm were of far greater interest to him than school. They taught him valuable lessons, lessons which were at least as valuable as those taught by the teacher. They were also influencers whose influences ranged from positive to negative. They taught him lessons for life that he could not have gotten anywhere else. In the invisible cumulative curriculum of his home and rural community, Jack, unknown to himself, learned how to interact with people, how to manage projects and how economic, political and social community systems and politics worked. In the transition years from child to teenager, he was exposed to the facts of life.

His neighbours dropped in and out of his home without any questions asked. One neighbour called every day to play a never-ending game of Rings with Jack and his brothers and sisters. The game lasted ten minutes each time. The neighbour then went away to continue his work. He came back to continue the game next day.

Family and neighbours met during the day interacting through a quick chat and a cup of tea. At night, the neighbours gathered to play a game of cards. The open fire was always on, and the black kettle hanging from the crane was always boiling. This encounter with adults was an opportunity for Jack to compete in a stretching but supportive environment.

Mary Anne was a disciplinarian given to expressions of rage when her rules were broken. Whenever Jack got into trouble, the neighbours pleaded for him and often eased the path to reconciliation. By the time they left, they would have consoled her; her rage would have subsided and Jack would be safe again.

His Aunt Sheila was another safety valve. She married into a farm, and she and her husband, Tom, lived close by. Her only child, a daughter, died of pneumonia at three years of age. Aunt Sheila encouraged Jack to come over to her house; she adopted him unofficially as the son she never had. Because the regime was a lot easier at her house and farm, it was a more comfortable space for Jack. He was the undisputed centre of attention there. Aunt Sheila encouraged him to do many tasks. Work on the farm and with the animals came natural to him.

This supportive opportunity opened up his interests and gave him the confidence to tackle jobs. No matter what the outcome of his endeavours, Aunt Sheila said, 'Well done, Jack.' When she spoke with her husband or with her neighbours, she always told them how good Jack was and what he was able to do now. Jack soaked this vote of confidence into his heart, and he began to believe the publicity that Aunt Sheila threw out to the community.

Jack learned that we tend to become expert in what we are interested in and what we want to do. Lessons and concepts that we crave will be more easily digested than those rammed down our throats.

Jack developed another important trait: an understanding of territory. He didn't want any of his brothers or sisters invading his space. Aunt Sheila's house and farm had become his territory, his comfort zone. Like a dog marks out his territory by piddling at strategic points around his domain, Jack marked out his territory and he prepared to defend it by whatever means necessary. He used innovative tactics to hold this space for himself. He told Aunt Sheila not to invite the others. He told his mother not to let others go there because of the bull. He told them the dog might bite them.

Jack's questions about the facts of life were answered by his study of how nature worked on the farm. Aunt Sheila had a prize bull that was severely restricted by its nose ring and heavy chain. The bull was housed in a secure pen within the cow house. During the grazing season, the bull was let to run with the cows in the fields near the house.

Jack watched this love-play from a safe distance. He was fascinated by it and questioned Aunt Sheila and Uncle Tom on the meaning of it. They told him about the working of the reproductive cycle.

Neighbours brought their cows to Tom's bull when they were in heat. Tom guided the bull out of the cow house by the restraining chain, and the public expression of love-play began. In order to facilitate the bull in mounting the neighbour's cow, Tom dug a sixteen-inch deep hole in the yard. He backed the cow into this hole to fix her two back legs. This lowered the height of her back and allowed the bull to mount her more easily. Tom pulled the cow's tail to the side to expose her vulva and allow the bull to penetrate her with his poker to hopefully make her pregnant.

Jack listened intently to the conversation between Tom and his neighbour. The mystery of the bull and the cow love-play solved itself. Jack and his friends at school put the pieces of the jigsaw about sex together. They now knew that their parents' story of finding their baby brothers and sisters under heads of cabbage in the garden wasn't true.

Jack and his friends acquired the knowledge about the facts of life through self-discovery. They had no television, no cinema and no glossy magazines. Each classmate contributed bits to put the whole picture together. As Jack's hormones rose, his desire grew, and his hunger for information and guidance about sex intensified. He now knew that girls were different from boys and that they grew breasts. The mystery became less of a mystery.

The better farmers started to use AI. They learned that artificial insemination for impregnating their higher yielding cows with the semen from better-bred bulls would yield better milk returns. The agricultural advisors now taught farmers about the value of better cattle breeding. The big buzz was to try to change the cow breed from the Shorthorn to the black-and-white Friesian.

Instead of mating his cows with the Shorthorn stock bull, Tom decided to get better breeding into his herd. When his three best cows were in heat, he sent for the AI service. The AI men drove white VW beetle cars, and from miles away the neighbours could hear the purring engines of these cars travelling the little roads around Uncle Tom's and Aunt Sheila's farm.

When the AI man came, Tom held the designated cow by the nose. The AI man rolled up his sleeve, put on a long rubber glove up beyond his elbow, stuck his hand into the cow's rectum and cleared it of its dung. He held the round muscle guarding the cow's uterus with this inserted hand. With his other hand, he inserted a long glass plunger holding the semen and pressed it, ejaculating the semen into the cow's uterus.

Castrating the male bonhams frightened and, at the same time, fascinated Jack. The bonhams were about six to eight weeks old when Tom caught each one, turned him upside down and held him between his legs. Then with a sharp knife, he held the bonham's testicles with one hand, slit the scrotum skin, and nipped out the individual testicles. He rubbed a powder into the wound to stop it festering.

The screeching of the bonham and the blood frightened Jack, but he got used to it and wanted to participate with Tom in the gruesome task. He asked Tom direct questions and came to understand the purpose of the testicles and why he castrated the bonhams. By his determination to find out things, and his insistence on asking why, Jack learned quickly.

Uncle Tom's and Aunt Sheila's farm had what the locals called a servant boy and a servant girl. Larger farms hired servants to do the heavy work on the farm, in the farmyard and in the house. There was no mechanisation available then – everything had to be done by hand. Farmers hired men and girls on a year's basis.

Tom had two different servant boys during Jack's young years. Each had a different approach to work.

Denis, in his early forties, was renowned for his strength. He came in the first week of January and left at Christmas. He lived in one of the spare rooms attached to the house. He was a bachelor and visited his sister's family every Sunday evening. Other than that, he lived in his room. He worked the six days and milked the cows on Sunday morning. He collected £3 from Aunt Sheila each Saturday from his agreed yearly contract of £400. From this, he bought Woodbine cigarettes and had a few pints of porter after Sunday Mass.

While he had great physical strength, he had little method to his work. He broke the handles of implements and even the point of the single-sod horse plough. Tom had a war of words with Denis.

Paddy Daly was hired on a yearly basis and was very neat and tidy, both in his room and in his work methodology. Even though he didn't appear to be as hard a worker as Denis, he was a better performer.

Of the two, Jack preferred Denis. Denis let him try out things and tended to be more comfortable in giving bits of advice and praise. Paddy was more like Jack's mother.

Kitty was the servant girl. She worked closely with Aunt Sheila in both the house and the farmyard. She lived in the other spare room. She kept her distance from both Denis and Paddy.

In both cases, they ate with the family and generally got on well with Aunt Sheila and Tom.

On other farms, servant girls were often exploited and abused by their master. When they got 'into trouble', they were sent to the Magdalene homes for unmarried mothers. It was not much better than slave labour, but it existed because servants had few other options. These girls were caught in a vicious circle.

Because of lack of means, most of them did not marry and lived very frustrating lives. For many, their only alternative when they reached the age of about eighteen to twenty was to take the boat to England, substituting one form of slavery for another.

On the surface, the local farmers had a workable, local, self-sustaining community where everyone looked out for each other. They were, nevertheless, human, with all the accompanying frailties. They had a natural pecking order which evolved over the years, and which tended to be based on wealth or the means of it. The priest, the bigger farmers and the professionals, including the local doctor, teachers, Gardaí and hardware store owners, tended to be near the top of the pecking order.

Farmers had a pecking order within their own group of big, good-sized and small farmers. They were mostly jealous about who had more land. For farmers, there is no desire more intense than the desire to acquire your neighbour's land.

One of the shadowy tactics to acquire more land was to use piseog culture. This was an Irish form of voodoo used to send a curse so that the victim farmer would be motivated to stop farming. Eventually, the land would depreciate so the benevolent predator farmer could buy it at a knockdown price. One signal of this curse was the finding of rotten eggs under haystacks. The eggs would be placed there sneakily by someone eager to take the land. When drawing in his stacks of hay, the victim farmer would find the rotten eggs and, as expected, he feared bad luck to happen over the coming months. The unexplained death of some of his cows would give credence to the curse. In this superstitious community, everyone used every limited resource for survival.

As people became more mobile and better educated, these shadowy tactics evaporated. However, the piseog tactic still shows its ugly face during times of high tension.

Jack's neighbours, and sometimes Jack himself, assumed that he would become a farmer and that he would either inherit the farm from Aunt Sheila or that she would gift it to him in her old age. Expectations play a vital role in everyone's forward journey. When provoked about Jack's future, Tom told the neighbours that the word 'ASSUME' means that an expectation can make an 'ASS of U and ME'. Jack's mother, Mary Anne, had different ideas in her head for Jack. She wasn't yet ready to express them in public.

Mary Anne took all her children to the local church on the last Saturday of every month for Confession. Institutional religion had a major influence on Jack and the general society in the rural countryside. Three priests heard Confessions. Long queues of young and old waited to bare their souls to the priests within the confines of the Confession box.

As Jack and his friends grew smarter and more confident, they learned to avoid Father Moore because he asked probing questions and waited in silence for answers. He tended to give more severe penances, also. The old priest, Father Shanahan, was hard of hearing and appeared to be going through the motions and just clearing numbers. Jack tried to get to him rather than go to the others. Sometimes his smartness didn't work.

At school, Jack and his classmates now prepared to receive the Sacrament of Confirmation. This was a more intense preparation than what took place for the First Confession and the First Holy Communion. The major concern for Mrs McCarthy, his teacher, was to prepare her pupils to answer the Catechism question that the bishop might ask at the altar rails during the administration of the sacrament. However, Jack and his classmates were more concerned with how severely the bishop might slap their faces. Rumours about the slap circulated prior to the big day. In reality, the bishop merely stroked each candidate's face gently as part of the ritual of confirming them.

Mary Anne had bought a suit of clothes and shirt and tie for Jack. The girls in his class were dressed in white dresses and veils. A number of other schools from the other parts of the parish had their Confirmation classes there that day as well.

Aunt Sheila was very excited for Jack. She gave him £5 and lots of sweets. She stood as one of his sponsors.

After the ceremony, Mary Anne had a party in the house. She laid out specially baked sweet cake and fresh beef meat. The neighbours dropped in, in ones and twos. She offered the men bottles of porter and the women glasses of sweet sherry. Jack was allowed to keep his new suit on to show it off.

A photographer took an official photograph of the Confirmation class at the church. It would be displayed on the photographer's shop window in the following week. Aunt Sheila said she would be in town and would have a look and order one for herself and Mary Anne.

The sixth class were being prepared for the Primary Certificate. This was the exit exam from the State's Primary School cycle. Not everyone, however, did this exam. The 'less intelligent' were never promoted beyond fourth class lest their failure in the Primary Certificate would bring disgrace to the teacher and the school. Many of Jack's friends left school as soon as they reached fourteen years of age and went to work for farmers or started working in the local shops or in the trades.

When Jack reached sixth class, there were nineteen pupils including himself. However, only six of the nineteen wanted to go for second-level education. These were the children of the higher social classes within the parish. Jack wanted to go to the Technical school, known locally as The Tech. This was a more attractive option than the Diocesan secondary school for Jack and his immediate friends. They believed that The Tech was less onerous for discipline and exams. Jack's group had heard that the punishments and food in the Diocesan school were horrific. The Tech was a gateway to getting an apprenticeship to the trades, such as carpentry, plastering and metalwork.

The Primary Certificate was an exam in Irish, English and Mathematics. The Mathematics examination was divided into two exam papers. In Part One, known as the Mental Arithmetic examination, the participating pupils were asked to answer twenty questions within a thirty-minute time frame. This required them to work out the answers quickly in their heads. Jack and his friends sweated blood about this challenge. But their parents and the teacher, Mr Ryan, forced them to do it.

They were innovative in trying to cog the exam. They wrote Mathematics formulas on the palms of their hands. Others used large writing in their answer papers and positioned these answer papers high on their desks so that their friends could copy from them. They used other secretive and innovative ways too.

If Jack and his friends had put the same focus into understanding and absorbing the information they were trying to cog, they would have been better off. When Jack and his exam colleagues returned to school the week after the exam, they found that their teacher, Mr Ryan, had no interest in teaching them any further. Mr Ryan left them to their own devices for the remainder of the term. During all of this free time, Jack and his colleagues put into place many of the missing pieces about the facts of life.

Sport was now a big part of Jack's life. His team and supporters regarded him as a good footballer. His favourite position was centre-forward. He was the star of both the school and club Under-14 football teams. The divisional selectors spotted him and selected him to play midfield for the juvenile divisional football team. His team went on to win the county final in August. This elevated his status in the local area. The status associated with his football achievements, together with the praise heaped on him by Aunt Sheila, fed into enhancing his self-worth. A strategic question now had to be faced: 'Where would Jack be next term?'

Philosophies for Jack from Uncle Tom and Aunt Sheila

- **In your life, watch out for milestones and defining moments that can give you reference points and valuable lessons.** In the invisible, cumulative curriculum of his home and rural community, Jack, unknown to himself, learned how to interact with people, how to manage projects and how economic, political and social community systems and politics worked. In the transition years from child to teenager, he was exposed to the facts of life in a natural way.

- **As we grow up we are not isolated from the reality of living.** Jack's neighbours dropped in and out of his home without invitation or formalities. His natural interaction with them taught him many practical lessons which underpinned his capability later in life as he successfully addressed critical issues.

- **If you want to find out about something badly enough, there is always a way of finding it.** It is our lack of inquisitiveness that keeps us dull. Jack was encouraged by Aunt Sheila and his neighbours to be inquisitive.

- **As a manager you can be as hard as you like provided you are perceived to be fair and consistent.** Mary Anne was a disciplinarian given to expressions of rage when her rules were broken. She balanced this by also being a loving and supportive mother.

- **It is important to be good at something and to build from this enhanced base.** To gain an 'edge' in your own area is important for your ego and for your reputation. This edge can be based on anything that the significant people in your area consider to be important.

- **An ounce of method saves a pound of sweat.** There is little relationship between sweat and business success. In business you need to work SMARTER rather than harder.

- **We are all victims of habit and we naturally resist change, even if it's for our advantage.** We all have to work out these resistances in our own heads and enjoy the fruits of the new opportunity.

- **A dream remains a dream if it doesn't have a deadline.**

Chapter 5

Milestones and Meeting Points

Jack, his parents, brothers and sisters, neighbours and members of the community gathered naturally at social meeting points or hotspots at different times of the day and on different days of the week. They came to one social meeting point, the water pump at the crossroads, to fetch their spring water. This they used for cooking and to make tea. The rainwater that fell on the roofs of the house, the hay-barn and the cow house was soft water. This was gathered through long shoots into water barrels and used for washing clothes and for drinking water for the housed animals.

At the water pump at these *ad hoc* meetings, neighbours exchanged much of the local gossip, often in supposed confidence.

The church yard on Sunday mornings after Mass was another social meeting point. A wider network of neighbours congregated here to exchange news and gossip about events in the wider parish and the world. The local shop and the creamery were other meeting points for the members of the community. They contributed more than their basic service. They were social-gathering opportunities as well. Here the social glue of the community set and sealed.

The killing of the fat pig was a ritual and a social meeting point; an event that involved the community and also provided food for the family. The killing of the fat pig was Jack's first introduction to a major co-operative event which had all the elements of a business management process;

from an established culture to managing people, to inputs, to processing, to outputs and their associated economics and profit. Unwittingly, Jack was learning first from witnessing and participating in the University of Life.

The neighbours killed a pig once a year. One of the pigs was held back from the litter when the rest were taken to the fair to be sold. This pig was fattened further, mostly on ground maize called yellow meal. When this pig weighed about sixteen stone, Mick Denny Bill organised the killing. Patsy, a local farmer who had developed the technique and the reputation for killing pigs, was the butcher. Neighbours said that the pigs bled well from his butchering.

When he established that Patsy was available, Mick Denny Bill put the other parameters of the killing project in place. These included procurement of a sturdy table upon which to stretch the live pig for killing. Each of four men would hold one of the pig's legs. This table was mounted on blocks so that the men could work at a comfortable height. Mary Anne lit a huge fire in the kitchen. Mick Denny Bill brought in a milk churn and placed it near the fire. Mary Anne and Mick Denny Bill boiled pots of water over the fire and then emptied them one by one into the milk churn until it was full of boiled water.

Patsy and three other neighbours arrived. Mary Anne had a meal ready for them, and Mick Denny Bill gave each a bottle of porter. Having washed the meal down with the porter, they were ready for the kill.

Mick Denny Bill quickly put a rope halter into the mouth of the pig, secured it and guided it out of the piggery to the slaughter table. Each of the four men took hold of a leg and lifted her screeching, as they laid her on her back, but at a slight tilt. She kicked with all her might as the four restrained her to allow Patsy do his job with precision.

Patsy pre-edged his butcher's knife on a special sharpening stone. He marked out where to inflict the neck wound with care so that he could sever the jugular quickly, clinically and painlessly. As she roared and kicked against the four men, Patsy swiftly cut her neck with a small blade and inserted another knife to cut the jugular. Mary Anne held a container up to the neck to capture the blood; the blood was an important by-product and was to be the main ingredient of the black puddings to be made by Mary

Anne next day. The screeching and the kicking eventually muted. Then followed the most vicious kick, the final kick, which the experienced men expected before she died.

Mick Denny Bill hung the pig head down from an upright ladder so that the gravity flow of the blood helped drain it all away. While the pig's body was still warm, they shaved her. To facilitate this job, the four men transferred her back to the table.

They poured the boiling water constantly over the now dead pig to keep the flesh warm. In a forty-minute process, they shaved the hair and the scale using their sharpened butcher's knives. During this team operation, the four men worked in coordination and in close proximity to each other, all the time telling outrageous stories about the adventures of characters in the locality. Jack picked up salacious gossip that was not intended for his ears.

Having fully shaved the pig, they again hung her from the ladder with her head facing the ground. With his long butcher's knife, Patsy cut off her head and put it face up on the table. The staring dead eyes of the pig frightened Jack.

Patsy then slit the full length of the pig's belly and exposed her internal organs. He took these out and put them on the table for sorting. He left the carcass hanging on the ladder to cool off overnight. He cut the heart, liver, kidneys and bladder out and put them to one side. He cleaned the bladder and gave it to Jack, telling him and his friends to blow it up and use it as a football around the haggard.

Patsy teased the gut out and cleaned it of its contents. Mary Anne used the gut as the casing for the black and white puddings. Patsy cut out the pork steaks and put them on the table.

The custom then was to divide the pork steaks among certain neighbours. They would, in turn, return the compliment when they killed their own pig. There were no fridges at that time, and this fresh meat had to be cooked and consumed within the week.

Mary Anne made ready a big supper which included fried rashers, puddings, eggs and boiled potatoes. The customary drink with the meal was sour milk. Today, this sour milk is refined and sold as yogurt.

During the supper, the men told more outrageous stories which gathered legs as they drank more porter. Patsy encouraged Jack to sip the porter.

It tasted sour. However, his curiosity and the encouragement from the men motivated him to take more sips. As he took a sip, his face curled up as the harsh, sour taste hit his young taste buds. On this day, he had taken part in the killing of a pig and had taken his first alcoholic drink.

At midnight, Patsy got up to go home, and the others followed his lead. There was no payment for this job since it was done on a barter system. Mick Denny Bill would go and hold his neighbours' pigs when they killed their own.

The barter system operated through the *comharing* model. Two neighbouring farmers would lend horses to each other to complete jobs requiring the joint strength of two horses pulling together. These jobs included ploughing and the pulling of the hay-mowing machine.

The flow of cash for everyday activity took root only as the economy started to grow in the late '60s and people became more independent. They moved from a status of mutual interdependence within the local community towards a status of individual independence, as they thought. In reality, no person or family is an island. This becomes obvious to all when trouble strikes.

Jack's father and mother were up early next morning in order to prepare the pig for the preservation stage of the cycle. This job was divided into two. Mary Anne took responsibility for the making of both types of puddings, known locally as the white and the black puddings. In conjunction with the pig's blood collected on the previous day, she made up her own mix of ingredients, mixed them with measured quantities of blood and boiled the lot for a designated period over the open fire. This preserved the puddings.

Mick Denny Bill set to work on the pig's carcass. He first sectioned the carcass into manageable pieces. He rubbed salt into the meat ensuring that all the crevices were salted. He placed each of these salted pieces into the bacon barrel and added more salt between the layers of bacon. He closed the top of the barrel and put a heavy stone on top to keep it down. He then left the bacon for six weeks to cure. During this time, the salt reacted with the meat juices to produce brine, which acted as the preservation agent for the meat. Electricity or fridges had not yet arrived in this part of rural Ireland. The people had their own workable formula for preservation.

After six weeks, Mick Denny Bill opened the bacon barrel and extracted the sections of the meat from the dripping brine. He cut a hole in each piece of meat, pulled a cord though it, and knotted both ends. He hung each piece from the hooks in the kitchen rafters. The impregnated brine helped by the smoke from the kitchen's open fire preserved the meat. Flies or bluebottles that dared to land on it died on impact or flew away from the hostile environment.

This bacon, which was very fat, was the staple diet for the family dinner on most days. Mary Anne boiled the slices of this bacon on its own initially to soften it. When cooked, she divided it up into the various dinner plates. She then added either cabbage or turnips. She tipped the pot of boiled potatoes onto a jute bag placed in the middle of the kitchen table. The only savoury available was yellow mustard. She gave mugs of sour buttermilk to everyone.

All the men-folk were involved in digging, ploughing with horses, mowing hay, cutting corn with scythes in wet areas and cutting the turf. Nutritionists of today would be horrified with their constant intake of fat and salt. But all of these jobs generated gallons of sweat. The men burned off the fat and lost the salt through their sweat.

Beef, or fresh meat as it was then called, was bought only for special occasions and some Sundays. Mary Anne often bought a few pounds of beef from the butcher's shop when she went to town shopping. It would be either beef or mutton.

Mick Denny Bill and his neighbours had to be self-sufficient to acquire the basics of life. This included food, shelter and heat. The heat was generated by a combination of timber logs and turf which burned in the open fire in the kitchen and in the fireplace in the parlour on special occasions such as when the priest visited.

The kitchen fire never died. At bedtime, Mary Anne stacked up the embers and screened them over with the ashes so that they maintained their latent heat without the supply of oxygen to burn them out. First thing in the morning, she stoked out these still hot smouldering embers to give them oxygen.

She put some kindling, which combusted easily, on top of them. They soon started to flame, helped by the extra air blown through by the bellows fan which Mary Anne turned very gently. Like all jobs, there was a knack in doing this. She added a few sods of whitish turf which would combust easily. When the fire was well under way, she added the normal daily amount of timber logs and black turf.

Over the fire was the crane from which all the pots, the kettle and the bastable hung. The fire was the focal point of the house where family and visitors tried to gain a position. It did all the cooking and provided the heat for the kitchen. Jack's parents had their bedroom at the back of the chimneystack which gave this room some airing. The other rooms of the house had no form of heating and were damp in the cold wet winters. Over the open fire, Jack and his siblings could look up the chimney and at night could see the stars in the sky.

One of the parameters of an 'edge' in rural Ireland was a good chimney. If your chimney had a good draught, the outside air sucked the smoke from the open fire out and away from the top of the chimney. This created a good flow of oxygen through the fire and kept it burning at a good pace. If you had a poor chimney, the draught was weak and you had a smoky kitchen. Its intensity depended on the weather and from what point the wind was blowing.

The chimney in Jack's house was good. 'Jesus, Mary Anne, that's a great draught,' said Patsy the night he killed the pig. This was an ego booster for Mary Anne. If someone said that to you today about your chimney, what impact would it have on your ego? Your reaction will give some indication of the repositioning of our priorities within Ireland over the last forty years.

Mick Denny Bill organised a *meitheal* every May to go to the bog and cut the turf. A *meitheal* was a community group of neighbours who came together to work as a team for a specific job. Today, our label for it would be a project team. The project team would have a project leader who would scope out the project and pull together the necessary resources to deliver the measurable outputs within an agreed time-frame. The project leader would use some project management software to produce Gantt charts to keep it all organised, neat and within budget.

Mick Denny Bill was the project leader and manager for the turf-cutting project. He had measurable output targets such as getting the five-sod deep turf bank completed on day one and the two lower turf banks completed by the end of day two.

He organised the men to work in mini-teams of three. One cut the sods with the *shlawn*. One pitched the cut sods onto the bank. And one organised the sods in rotation on the bank so that they would be exposed to the weather to start the drying process. The weathering evaporated the moisture from the sods. When cut, the sods were about 90 per cent water. In order to keep the project interesting, the three men rotated their jobs every thirty minutes. At the thirty-minute changeover, they took a break and smoked their pipe or a fag.

There was a skill in preparing a pipe. Mick Denny Bill cut the plug of tobacco into small pieces with his penknife. He rolled the cut pieces between his palms to break them into powder. He scraped the ashes out of the head of the pipe with the penknife onto the upside down pipe cover. He took apart the stem of the pipe and cleaned the central channel of any dirt or spittle that may have lodged at the end of the previous smoking process. He blew out the lodged dirt. If it was very stubborn and didn't go with the blowing, he used either a pipe cleaner or a strong rush to poke it out. He reassembled the pipe and filled the head with the powdered tobacco. Then he topped it off with the ashes from the upside-down pipe cover and gently pressed the contents down to a more firm composition.

The pipe was now ready. He struck a match and applied the flame to the ashes, meanwhile sucking air into his lungs through the channel at the centre of the pipe stem. This gave the flame the necessary oxygen to start to burn the tobacco.

The ash has a high combustion point and, when heated, would catch fire easily when accompanied with the air being sucked through. When glowing, the ash heated the tobacco underneath. This then passed its combustion point and began to burn. Mick Denny Bill kept pulling this smoke into his mouth and some of it into his lungs.

Lighting a pipe required art and skill, and Jack's father was a natural. Each man had his own procedure and style for lighting and smoking a pipe. You would recognise them by observing their process, even if their faces were shielded.

Those considered naturals had status among their peers and in their community. It enhanced their ego and their confidence level.

Mick Denny Bill brought, among other food items, spring drinking water for the men and himself. He brought this in a recycled sweet can which had a tight fitting cover. This tin can had been half-buried into a water hole in the bog in order to keep the water cool. He passed the water around among the men in order to keep them hydrated.

At 10 a.m., Mick Denny Bill lit a small fire and balanced another can of water on top of it. He brought it to the boil, added tealeaves from the bag and then re-boiled the lot. He put a headless match on top of the tea to keep the smoke out of the brewing tea. A scientific basis for this old technique cannot be found. Nevertheless, the locals making tea in the bog believed that it worked. To them it was gospel.

When the tea was brewed, the men gathered around the fire area and sat down in a circle. Mick Denny Bill served tea in mugs and gave slices of homemade brown bread with lashings of butter and jam.

At lunchtime, Mary Anne arrived with the dinner. It consisted of lumps of bacon, cold cabbage and more home baked-brown bread. She gave each man a bottle of tea enclosed in a woollen sock to keep it warm. There was something about the bog air and the hard physical work which made everyone hungry. The food always tasted better than the same food eaten in the kitchen.

Mrs Murphy, the teacher, allowed Jack take two turf-cutting days off from school to help his mother prepare the dinner and bring it over to the bog. He sat beside the men and absorbed all of their banter and gossip. After dinner, the men stretched out. Some fell asleep in the sun.

Mick Denny Bill was in charge. Although he had no positional power over the men because they were getting no monetary payment, he used a leadership tactic to lead by example rather than order them back to work. He did this by standing up and, directing his attention to the better men, saying, 'Do you think we will finish this turf bank today?' They responded to the challenge and all went back to their production routine again. They took another tea break at 3.30 p.m. and drove on to finish this turf bank by 6 p.m. They assembled at the bog the following morning at 9 a.m. to finish the other two smaller turf banks.

There was no money payment. The only public manifestation of thanks for the work was that Mick Denny Bill, the receiver of the service in this instance, said to the men at the end of the day, 'God save you'. They understood. Mick Denny Bill would help them in their own *meitheals* in the weeks to come.

Jack and his siblings took on the backbreaking job of turning the sods to the weather. When the cut turf had dried somewhat, Jack caught each sod with his bare hands and turned it over without breaking it. He bent down all day at this job, and his back became sore. Why people did not use pitchforks for this backbreaking exercise, nobody could tell. Nobody questioned generations of habit, tradition or ritual.

Mick Denny Bill told Jack to foot the drying turf. Stand five sods on their ends and balance them against each other with the sixth sod placed lying across the top of the five standing sods so as to bind them together. He explained that this structure allows the air and wind to circulate around the sods to enhance the speed of drying. After a few weeks, depending on the weather, the sods would be reasonably dry.

The next task was to stack the turf into stooks. In other words, build around thirty sods in an 'architectural' format so that the drying could continue. All this work was done with bare hands and bent back.

By mid-August, the turf was dry enough to be brought home for the winter fire. In wet weather, these stooks would be redone in order to turn the wetter sides up to the weather elements.

Drawing home the turf was a phased exercise. The first job was the transport of the turf from the turf bank to the bog road. It was usually done with a donkey and cart, with turf creels in place. If the underfoot conditions were very wet, Mick Denny Bill and the lads filled up jute bags with the sods and carried them to the bog road on their backs. This was a tough job, and was hard on their shoulders. The friction from the jute bags burned their shoulder skin.

The horse cart and turf creel transported the turf from the bog road back to the farmyard. Some neighbours clamped the sods neatly away above the top of the creels. Others were careless and they brought smaller loads, often losing sods along the way. The skill of clamping gave status.

Mick Denny Bill built a turf reek in the farmyard. This too required skill. The outside sods were clamped in such a way that they would guide the rain water down the side of the turf reek and keep the turf in the centre of the reek bone dry.

With the turf in the yard and the bacon hanging from the rafters in the kitchen, the critical essentials of life and living for the year ahead were in place.

The *meitheal* gathered again for the Threshing – the separation of the oat seed from its straw. The Threshing was another hot spot, a rural socio-economic event at which there would be women present. That meant the opportunity to have a dance and whatever would follow.

Jack's Early Lessons from his Neighbour about the Realities of Living

- **Nature ensures that symbiotic relationships keep evolving.** In rural Ireland the direct or indirect support of neighbours was critical to their journey through life. There were many gathering points such as the water well, the Church gate, the Rambling house, and the killing of the pig where neighbours naturally met. Here the social glue of the community was set and sealed.

- **The University of Life is a great teacher.** Unwittingly, Jack and his siblings learned naturally from witnessing and participating in local activities.

- **Cash for everyday activity began to flow as the economy grew in the late '60s and people became more independent.** People moved from mutual interdependence within their local community towards, as they thought, a status of individual independence. No person or family is an island. This becomes obvious when trouble strikes.

- **Gain a relevant 'edge', so as to differentiate yourself from the pack and get noticed.** In Mary Anne's day, having a good chimney was an example of having a relevant edge. Life is about contrasts. You would never know how good your chimney was, if it couldn't be compared with your neighbour's chimney.

- **Lighting a pipe was an art and required great skill.** Each man had his own procedure and style for lighting and smoking his pipe. If their faces were shielded, you could recognise them by observing their process. Those considered as 'naturals' had status among their peers and in their community. It enhanced their ego and their level of confidence.

- **The Threshing was a natural gathering point.** Women attended the house dance which followed the day's work and provided the opportunity to socialise. Members of the opposite sex could be intimate here and their hormones allowed relative release.

Chapter 6

From Darkness to Light

Jack and his friends watched the electricians strap on their leather climbing equipment and climb the newly-driven ESB poles. The teeth of their wrap-around stirrups dug into the wood of the poles to give a firm grip as each climbed up into the sky to secure the power line.

Timmy, the local electrician and handyman, came to wire the house and put in the fuse box that would connect to the power line outside and make safe the flow of power to each power point in the house.

Mary Anne and Mick Denny Bill debated the possible positions for the power plugs and how many should be installed. They debated whether to put a light in each room and one in the yard. They debated the crazy idea of putting a light in the cow house. These debates, which often turned into intense arguments, showed the difference in perspectives between men and women. The men were reluctant to have too many power points or lights. The women looked at this opportunity to take some of the drudgery out of their daily grind.

Until then, the open fire in the kitchen, the Tilly lamp and candles dispelled the darkness. Farmers had flash lamps powered by dry batteries for light around the farmyard. The dynamo lamp on the bicycle was a big innovation. The back tyre of the bicycle turned the wheel of the dynamo as the cyclist peddled forward. The dynamo turned this energy into light through the lamp mounted on the handlebars. The Gardaí stepped out on roads at night to check bicycles for lights and brakes.

There were many dark and shadowy corners in rural Ireland in the '50s. Because of such darkness, poets and artists shed light on the strange happenings of the time by creating imaginative stories and recycling the performances of night spirits and ghosts.

When the ESB crew arrived, the neighbours gathered in intense excitement. This was the arrival of rural electrification. It would light up the land and would transform lives forever. First to arrive was the installation crew who erected the poles. The poles reeked of creosote, used to preserve them. The crew delivered them in big trucks to pre-arranged dropping points. From these dropping points, they dragged each pole through the fields using horses hired from the local farmers. This gave local farmers the opportunity to generate some cash flow from an asset they already owned.

The implementation of the rural electrification scheme was a major feat of engineering. Just as importantly, it was also a psychological process. It involved the planting of the idea, then public relations and marketing to promote it. There was a felt need, among early adopters, to get the electricity in as soon as possible. Representatives of the ESB came to explain all the advantages at meetings organised by local leaders with the blessing of the most powerful leader of all then, the parish priest, in the parish hall.

The early adopters in the body of the hall kick-started its acceptance. The Church supported the scheme from the altars.

The leaders who were the early adopters became advocates and influenced the early majority. Over time, those, in turn, influenced the later majority. The laggards refused to take the service.

The ESB executives quickly learned that the real decision-makers in households were not men, but women. The men signed along the dotted line, but the women used their own personal tactics to influence these signatures. As the scheme progressed around the country, the ESB got smarter. They got to know the hot buttons to press with women. They sent female domestic science professionals to information meetings. They put on simple cookery and household demonstrations to show how ESB energy was superior to the energy from the open kitchen fire.

Jack watched the ESB officially switch on the electricity in his locality. It opened up the world outside to the people of the parish. Radios powered by wet batteries and saved for the broadcasting of the matches by Michael O'Hehir were put aside. Radios powered by electricity could now be put on everlastingly for Mass, music, plays, sponsored programmes such as the Kennedys of Castle Ross, Harbour Hotel, Din Joe, Mrs Dale's Diary and even discussion programmes.

As the ESB became less of a threat and more of a necessity, the countryside brightened and the shadowy and dark corners disappeared. Most of the ghosts also disappeared. They obviously did not like the light.

Doctor Moriarty bought the first television that appeared in Jack's townland in the early '60s. The doctor was the trailblazer. Mick Paddy McCarthy, a farmer and a cattle dealer, followed quickly. Jack saw this box in the corner with its hazy snowy screen showing the Telefís Éireann test card. The clarity of this card indicated what the reception was going to be like for the night. There was a strong relationship between the reception quality and the prevailing weather conditions. There were many debates about whether the weather or the skill of tuning was the critical factor. The participants were gaining a technical knowledge that previously they hadn't known existed. They were also now interacting differently.

The locals who had gathered to listen to Michael O'Hehir's match commentary on radio now gathered in Mick Paddy McCarthy's kitchen at night to watch the television. Even the advertisements were a novelty. They liked Mr Ed, the Talking Horse. As the months went by, more early adopters purchased their own televisions. An important social meeting point or hot spot gradually disappeared from the countryside, gradually replacing community with individuality. Neighbours no longer called as often to the house – they were watching the television in their own homes.

Mary Anne nagged Mick Denny Bill for ages to get the running water in. They had drawn water for generations from the well. Like lots of other men, Mick Denny Bill was a creature of habit and resisted change. The deadline of The Stations was the catalyst to replace the water well with pipes which would bring water directly into the house.

Jim, the water diviner, walked slowly around the house and farmyard, holding a sally stick at chest level between both his hands. The sally stick moved and thus identified the location of the water at the top of the yard. This showed the spot where the well driller should sink a borehole. Jim was a god in his own field. The magnetic power transmitting through his body from an intersection of two underground streams far down below ground bent the sally stick held in his hands into the shape of a horseshoe. Jack later went around the yard and the nearby fields holding a sally stick in his hands. The sally stick failed to bend. His father told him that that he wasn't blessed with the gift.

Paddy Joe, the well digger, drove the ram with its pounding thumping mechanism down into the earth below to create a borehole and shatter the rock. On its way down through the earth, the ram mechanism flushed rock debris out of the borehole and a stream of thick muddy liquid flowed down the farmyard. After two days of drilling, the driller had reached 150 feet. Jack watched and listened as Mick Denny Bill and the neighbours debated and agreed with the well digger that this depth was adequate.

Paddy Joe hammered steel pipes to line the top fifty feet of the borehole to prevent it filling up with debris. He fitted an electric pump to the end of a rubber pipe and then lowered it into the well. This was a submersible pump system. He attached another pipe to the tank at the top of the well and brought it underground through a drain dug in the yard as far as the new sink installed in the kitchen. He attached the water pipe to the tap above the sink. Mary Anne now had tap water at her kitchen sink.

He dragged another pipe link to carry water via a drain dug across the yard to the former dry toilet and hooked it up to the new toilet cistern that Mick Denny Bill bought in the hardware store in town. Weeks before, Mick Denny Bill had built a new septic tank in the ground. Then he dug a drain and put down the piping to the toilet bowl to carry the waste between both. Jim Morrissey, the local electrician and plumber, worked on the system for two weeks before it all worked seamlessly.

The water in the kitchen tap was dirty brown at first, and it took at least a week to clear. Although now clear, all the neighbours said that the quality and the taste of the water from the tap was not as good as the water from the hand pump down at the crossroads. The initial stages of change are fraught with doubt.

Mary Anne continued to use the water from this hand pump to make the tea. However, following initial resistance, she succumbed to the convenience of the water in the kitchen tap for cooking and washing. Over time, she lowered her resistance more and used the tap for water for tea and other water requirements in the house.

The Cronins had the option of staying in the past or changing. They decided to change. Within a month, the life, the living standards and part of the culture of Mary Anne, Mick Denny Bill, Jack, and his brothers and sisters were transformed forever.

Influences of Major Change on Jack's Quality of Life

- **Change is difficult for those who perceive their current status to be more comfortable than the unknown.** The first step of a change journey is winning the debate in your own head that the poorer option is to stay as you are.

- **Focus on the early adopters when introducing a new 'offering'.** The implementation of the rural electrification scheme was a major feat of engineering. Just as importantly, it was also a psychological process. It involved the planting of the idea to the early adopters and using them to influence the others to sign up.

- **Don't waste your time with pretenders.** Understand who the real decision makers are and where their 'soft underbelly' is.

- **The hangman's rope concentrates the mind.** The deadline of The Stations was the catalyst to replace the water well with pipes which would bring water directly into the house.

- **The grindstone of life will either grind you down or polish you up.**

- **Clarity about the measurable outputs and the areas of responsibility is the secret to commercial success.** Plan to manage by exception. Inspect what you expect. Give your team the authority as well as the responsibility in order that they can deliver the agreed output results.

- **Lead, follow, or get out of the way.**

Chapter 7

Mary Anne's Management

Jack struggled through the Primary School cycle but went from the extreme of being called a dunce by Mrs Moynihan to later being above average.

Jack's mother was cute and determined. Under a different set of circumstances, on a larger and more transparent stage, she would have been a leading entrepreneur or the general manager or managing director of a large corporate business entity. She had all the ingredients that management seek in the profile of high-achieving business people.

Mary Anne had the critical parameters of this success profile. She stretched beyond realistic vision. She was street-wise. She was capable of securing the necessary resources to make events happen. She had the determination and consistency to do what was necessary to energise the defined vision.

Happiness consists not in having what you want, but in wanting what you have. You may be poor and still happy. However, to be ambitious beyond your means causes unhappiness. Mary Anne was ambitious beyond her current obvious means, which led to her private unhappiness.

Families in Jack's locality had their own business model. They had a bull in the field, a pump in the yard and a priest in the family.

Mary Anne had the vision to see beyond this ring-fenced, comfortable scene. To have a priest in the family would be nice but was not necessary. She understood the strategic importance of the value of formal education for her children. She saw this as their better meal ticket away from the 'more of the same' cycle in which she herself was stuck. Not only did she recognise this, but she was prepared to pay the price to make it happen. She was prepared to operate the economic concept known as opportunity cost.

In simple terms, opportunity cost is the cost of foregoing something in order to get something else. Mary Anne was prepared to forego many of her personal comforts, like buying a new winter coat, in order to build up her war chest of net money from the sale of the farm produce to the co-operative and at the fair. She had no bank account, or overdraft, or term loans or education loan facilities. There were no such facilities for most ordinary people at that time and none especially for poor rural people. Mary Anne operated a closed-loop, cash-in and cash-out system. She held any surplus cash in secret places, keeping it for the education investment in her children.

You can't make a silk purse out of a sow's ear. Building up the funds to pay for their further education was of no use if the children didn't have the capacity to take advantage of the opportunity. To his teachers and others, Jack didn't have this necessary capacity. However, Mary Anne knew better. She could see in him the latent spark that could eventually ignite in a more attractive combustible environment.

Education then and even up to this day, is based on a narrow academic definition which has its limitations as an indicator of future suitable capacity to optimise business opportunities.

Everyone has comfort zones. The academics have theirs based on the self-perpetuating importance of theory. This is where they have come from. They know no better. There is also a cohort of people who understand what will work in practice but who will later have the luxury of reflecting on the possibility of whether it fits in theory or not. Mary Anne never reasoned it out like this. She, like the embers in the early morning hearth, saw the spark. She was determined to give it oxygen.

Jack's father adopted a survival strategy to never interfere in this area. He was passively supportive and inwardly proud, but he was afraid it might all blow up. He didn't want to be embarrassed in front of his conservative neighbours. It was safer to stay in the middle somewhere, even though it always led to more of the same.

Mary Anne was a leader and was prepared to come out from the centre, to walk at the front and take the consequences. More than that, there was a balance within the team of Mary Anne and Mick Denny Bill. Their combined total strength was far greater than the sum of their individual parts.

Lessons Taught by Jack's Mother

- **Jack's mother was smart and determined.** Under a different set of circumstances, she would have been a leading entrepreneur. She had all the ingredients that high-achieving business people possess. She had a stretching vision and she was street-wise. She was capable of securing the necessary resources to make events happen. She had the determination and consistency to do what was necessary to achieve her goal.

- **Happiness consists not in having what you want, but in wanting what you have.** You may be poor and still happy. However, to be ambitious beyond your means causes unhappiness. Mary Anne was ambitious beyond her current obvious means, which led to her private unhappiness. Yet she was prepared to pay this price in order to energise her longer vision.

- **In simple terms, opportunity cost is the cost of foregoing something in order to get something else.** Mary Anne was prepared to forego many of her personal comforts, like buying a new winter coat, in order to build up her war chest of money from the sale of the farm produce and have it available to pay the planned education fees.

- **Self-survival is our strongest natural instinct.** Jack's father adopted a survival strategy to never interfere in Mary Anne's area of responsibility. He was passively supportive and inwardly proud, but he was afraid it might all blow up.

- **To successfully deliver the leader's vision, it is critical to have a balance of skills and personality types within the team.** The team of Mary Anne and Mick Denny Bill had this balance. Their combined total strength was far greater than the sum of their individual parts.

Chapter 8

Leaving Home

Mary Anne drove alone to St Patrick's, the Diocesan College. She made it her business to meet with Father McCarthy, the reverend president. Father McCarthy saw that Mary Anne was a determined woman and didn't ask her many questions. For Mary Anne, this was going to be education for a tangible purpose. It wasn't just education for the sake of education. Education was a potential gateway and meal-ticket for her children, and by implication, for herself in the long term. In her opinion, education for its own sake was a luxury that people at her level could not contemplate.

Mr Ryan, the teacher, told Mary Anne that he had taken Jack's education in the Primary School as far as he could.

Mary Anne and her family were at the base line. Their real need was survival. She said to Mick Denny Bill, 'It's okay for those in the big houses to have notions. They don't have to worry about having enough to eat. They can educate their children to acquire the niceties of life.'

For Mary Anne, education was the means to a tangible end. No more, no less. She paid the deposit to the reverend president from her private war chest. She announced that evening at supper what she had done.

Jack was shocked. He had not known about his mother's plan. He thought he had made progress in influencing her to let him go to The Tech. The Tech was the lesser of two evils. He had used Aunt Sheila to try and influence his mother as well, but to no avail. She wasn't for turning. Mick

Denny Bill was shocked too. He just sat there without comment. When Jack tried to engage with him about this critical issue, he muttered something meaningless, as he knew from bitter experience that it was dangerous to get involved in his wife's area of expertise.

Jack tried to manipulate Mary Anne by saying that she had previously agreed that he could go to The Tech and that he would be at home in the evenings to do some of the farmyard jobs. He told her that it would be cheaper, since he could ride a bicycle to and from The Tech. At St Patrick's he would have to become a boarder because the distance was far too long to cycle.

When the 'rational' tactic failed, he tried the 'crying' tactic and attempted to convey sadness and loneliness. It too failed. Over the following few weeks he tried his last known tactic, the 'silent' tactic. He withdrew into himself and broke off communication with everyone.

During this silent period, he visualised all kinds of disasters for himself. He had heard stories from other lads and from some of the adults about the horrific discipline tactics adopted by the teachers in the Diocesan College. He had heard that the food served there wasn't fit for a dog. His horror magnified to the point where he considered ending it all there and then. He would throw himself into the big water hole in the bog or he would run away. As he reflected on the impending horror, he built up a resolve to energise either of the relief options. Then he flunked it. And then he got more depressed.

The only person who seemed to have any sympathy for him was Aunt Sheila. But she had to be careful. Mary Anne had warned her that it was none of her business; Jack was *her* child, and she would make these decisions without any outside meddling. He told his classmates. They jeered him. Their jeering drove him demented.

It was a lonesome summer. But he went daily to Aunt Sheila's farm and to the local GAA club where he played football and hurling with his friends. He went through the motions with a heavy heart.

There was now one certainty; his mother was not for turning. She was moving on with her plans to complete the deal by September 1st. Certainty is a great tactic, and it gives clarity. Jack now had certainty and clarity. As his initial emotional outburst and silent treatment passed, he moved into the passive acceptance of reality.

When a young horse is harnessed, he screeches, kicks and tries all sorts of escape runs. He gradually realises that resistance will get him nowhere. The more he fights the trainer, the more the trainer resists. Over time, he learns that he is treated better when he reacts in a particular way. Eventually he adopts the instructions of the trainer.

Jack went through the mourning period hankering for the past. He hadn't yet accepted the future reality.

The postman delivered a letter addressed to Mary Anne from the college one morning in late July confirming Jack's place in St Patrick's. In the envelope was a list of the clothing and schoolbook items that all new students were to bring with them on September 1st, the official opening day for the new academic year.

Mary Anne looked at the list, did a quick mental tot of the total cost and fell back against the kitchen sink, shaken. Recovered, she went through the list again, this time eliminating any items she thought she could get away with in order to reduce the total cost. She tried to do this readjustment quietly, but Jack sensed what she was doing. He couldn't be seen not to have everything on that list, and if he was short of any items, the consequences would not be good. He argued and fought with Mary Anne. In his mother's management view, at least, Jack was starting to engage in the process.

She engaged in managing the list. She tried to get as many as possible of the listed items second-hand.

On the list were three pairs of underpants. Jack and his friends just wore trousers. Although the lack was less than hygienic, underpants were for wimps and weaklings.

Another item on the list was three pairs of pyjamas. Jack had none. As a boy going to bed, he just dropped his pants on the floor and slept in his shirt. He sometimes slept in his jumper. Mary Anne got one pair of pyjamas from a neighbour who had got it in a Christmas parcel from America and didn't have any use for it. It was miles too big for Jack, but for Mary Anne it ticked off another box on the school list. Unlike many of the other items, it cost no money, even though it probably had a price in kind.

When Mary Anne arrived home from town with a toothbrush and a tube of toothpaste, she got him to try it out. He didn't see the practical need for a toothbrush, and in any case, he didn't like the peculiar taste of the toothpaste.

As she worked her way through the list and did her monetary tots, it became obvious to her that all these items needed identification names so that they wouldn't be lost in the school laundry and have to be replaced. Replacement would cost more money. The letter from St Patrick's stipulated that each item should carry the student's name. This was to be done by writing Jack's name on special tapes sewn on to the individual items using a water resistant ink. This was more expense and more work for Mary Anne. She went to town specifically for this tape and special ink – the local shops had no reason to stock such items.

She tried to empower Jack by getting him to write a series of his name in block letters on the tapes. She then stitched them onto the individual items. She and Jack worked together like a factory production line to complete the job.

As September 1st approached, the mood in the house was tense. It was exciting in one way yet gave mixed emotions in another. Mick Denny Bill, Mary Anne and Jack's brothers and sisters would pack into the car to travel with him for support on this lonesome journey. Mary Anne gathered the last few items on the list and packed them in the brown suitcase she had used herself during the few days she and Mick Denny Bill were in Dublin for their delayed honeymoon. Just looking at the suitcase and the offspring from that honeymoon made her proud and sad all at the same time. It was a bitter and sweet experience.

The Saying of the Rosary, all of five decades, was a nightly half-hour custom in all the neighbouring houses. All members of the family, each pair of hands joined and pointed towards Heaven, knelt down around the kitchen. In Jack's house, Mary Anne led the Rosary and, having said the first decade, Mick Denny Bill said the second. Jack said the third; his eldest brother and sister said the other two decades.

Mary Anne had a list of other prayers which she tagged on to the end of the five decades. These were the Trimmings of the Rosary. She then prayed special prayers to cover special events for special people. For the month of August her special event was the new life Jack was about to embark on. She prayed that the Virgin Mary and her son Jesus would look after Jack and that he would make the family proud. For Jack, this inclusion of his departure as a special intention reaffirmed in him that this disaster was now definitely going to happen.

The neighbours called in the days before Jack's departure to St Patrick's. They called to say goodbye to Jack and to wish him all the best. One gave him a bag of sweets. Another gave him a few shillings.

Aunt Sheila got lonesome for Jack. She saw that her secret pre-planned career for Jack as a farmer on her farm was now a pipe-dream. She and Tom were sad to see him go. They saw that they had failed to deliver a definite proposition for inheritance of their farm by Jack. It was all nods and winks. Nothing definite. Nothing substantial. Mary Anne knew that. She had seen many similar cases over the years. The attachment of the land to the male bloodline was the culture. It would continue. Unless, of course, a mother like Mary Anne or a son like Jack would break the line.

On the morning of September 1st, Jack delayed the departure from home for as long as possible. Mary Anne had packed the brown suitcase and put it in the car. She got the rest of the family to dress in their Sunday best so that they wouldn't embarrass Jack.

Even Spotty the sheepdog seemed to sense something unpleasant. He looked sad and kept out of the way. As Jack got into the car, he went over to Spotty and they rubbed each other's noses. It would be the last bit of loving contact that Jack would experience for some time.

Mary Anne tried to break the silence in the car a few times on the long journey but with little positive response. She recited the Rosary in order to make Jack's journey into the next phase of his life worthwhile. After three hours' driving, they came within sight of the large gates guarding the sprawling building which was St Patrick's. The large gates underpinned Jack's preconceived view that he would be imprisoned behind these for the foreseeable future. Mick Denny Bill drove into the big yard full of parents and new recruits. The new recruits, easily identified from their uncertain gait, hair cuts and fresh faces, looked lost and reluctant to let go of their mother's protection. Some senior students mingled with the crowd. The priests of the college had organised them to meet up with the lost souls and take them to their dormitory and lockers.

Joe, one of the senior students, came over and introduced himself to Mick Denny Bill and Mary Anne. He told Mary Anne that he would take Jack and show him his place in the dormitory. He told Mary Anne and Mick Denny Bill to go to the office to complete the paperwork and finalise the payment.

Mary Anne and Mick Denny Bill joined the queue to the office. When their turn came, the priest at the hatch opened the ledger and checked Jack's application. He noted that Mary Anne had paid a deposit of £20 and that a balance of £80 was due. She could pay this upfront or could spread it into three instalments of one per term.

Mary Anne tried to negotiate a lower price. She pleaded the difficult year it was in farming and assured him that she would try and pay the full amount the following year. The priest was having none of it. After much arguing with him, she agreed to pay the first instalment of £40. She knew that she would try and do a deal for the remainder at a later date. She took her purse from inside her bosom and counted out the £40. She waited for a receipt.

The priest advised Mary Anne and Mick Denny Bill to go straight home. They were not to wait around to say farewell to Jack. The priest said that this procedure would be easier for everyone. Jack's brothers and sisters were shocked. Mary Anne and Mick Denny Bill were too. But they obeyed the priest. That was the norm.

Though the open fire was still smouldering when they arrived home, the house felt cold and empty. There was an empty place at the table, around the fire and in the bed. Aunt Sheila too felt the emptiness. But it was different. An aunt must remain remote and aloof.

The enquiries about Jack from the neighbours compounded the emptiness and made the unoccupied spaces around the house seem even more poignant. Some neighbours were genuine, some were jealous and others enquired just for gossip.

When your voice and your physical presence are absent, you are missed emotionally and at the same time more appreciated.

Jack's brothers and sisters asked all sorts of direct questions, but neither parent gave truthful answers. Mary Anne was a pragmatic woman on a mission. She nevertheless had a heart full of emotion. Now that Jack was out of view, tears for him came down her face. She sobbed uncontrollably. A mist appeared in Mick Denny Bill's eyes. His tears were silent, private, internalised. The children, now frightened, had never seen their mother sob like this before.

What Jack Learned about Loss and Leaving Home

- **We are constantly being influenced and, in turn, influencing others.** Try and reflect on the implications of this fact in your own life.

- **Influencing outcomes is a game and we need to get better at it if we want to be more successful.** Jack thought he had influenced his mother to agree that he could go to the secondary school rather than The Tech. His influencing tactics such as manipulation weren't effective enough to redirect his mother from her planned journey.

- **An obstacle is something you see when you take your eyes off the goal.** Mary Anne kept her eye on the goal.

- **Where you are positioned in the hierarchy of life influences your perception of the value of formal education.** Mary Anne and her family were at the base line. Their real need was survival. She said to Mick Denny Bill, 'It's okay for those in the big houses to have notions. They don't have to worry about having enough to eat. They can educate their children to acquire the niceties of life.' For Mary Anne, education was no more and no less the means to a tangible end.

- **Certainty gives clarity.** Jack now had certainty and clarity. As his initial emotional outburst and silent treatment passed, he moved into the passive acceptance of reality. When a young horse is harnessed, he screeches, kicks and tries to break away. Over time he understands that it's easier to obey his master.

- **Loss and emptiness manifests itself in many different ways.** After Jack left, there was an empty place at the table, around the fire and in the bed. Enquiries about Jack from the neighbours compounded the emptiness and made the unoccupied spaces around the house seem even more poignant. Some neighbours were genuinely sincere, some were jealous and others enquired just for gossip sake.

Chapter 9

Alone in Secondary School

Tim guided Jack to the dormitory designated for first years. It was a big barn of a room. There, Jack saw four straight rows of single beds. Each bed had a thin mattress, a pillow, two sheets, two blankets and a bedspread. All were neatly folded at the bottom of the bed. A bedside locker divided one bed from the next. At best, the space between beds was four feet.

Jack was amazed to see this vast range of beds, which was some difference from the loft room he occupied with his brothers back home.

Tim brought Jack to bed Number 29 and told him that this was where he would sleep during his first year at the college. Tim instructed him to dress his bed neatly and to put away his clothes in the locker. He told him to put his empty case under the bed and that, when finished, he was to sit at the end of his bed until he heard the bell for assembly, which was to take place in the sports hall at 4 p.m. sharp. Tim then left.

Jack felt sorry for himself. At age thirteen, he had felt that young men of his age could not be seen to cry. However, he was not alone. The other raw first year students too felt sorry for themselves as the senior students guided them to their designated places in the dormitory. They were too shocked and too shy to speak with each other.

Jack had never made a bed before and now struggled to do so. He tried to copy the others. But it was a case of the blind leading the blind. He continued with his struggle, wanting to appear busy while he waited patiently for the bell.

It now dawned on him that his parents were gone. He had lost the chance to make a last desperate plea for freedom, or even to say his tearful farewells. He now knew that he was alone. He felt worse by the minute. In the midst of his heroic but unsuccessful effort at making the bed and putting his clothes into the bedside locker, the college bell rang. Jack and his newfound fellow students marched out into the sports hall for their first assembly.

All the first year students were corralled into the front rows in the sports hall. In the next rows were the second years and so on back through the hall. On the stage stood a priest in a long black cassock. The priest in black called for silence – the response was immediate. He formally welcomed the students back after their summer holidays. Then he made special mention of the new students. He laid out the rules and regulations which were going to put a structure in the way that the college was going to be run for the coming academic year.

The message was clear to Jack: 'Mess with us and you can expect to be appropriately punished, as determined by the relevant priests.'

Father McCarthy, the reverend president of the college, in tone of voice as solemn as his long black cassock, said that everyone should respect the strict code of conduct consistently. It was best and it was fair, he said. He said also that the senior students would be the first line of management of the college and that they had his authority to monitor students and administer some initial punishment.

They also had the responsibility to report on non-compliance with the rules and regulations by the juniors. His signal, which passed over Jack's head, was that this school, like most others, aims to produce conformists rather than rebels. This made it easier for the authorities to regulate the day-to-day running of the school. Support and encouragement for the aspirations and potentials of the individual students was an entirely different matter.

The students' eventual interpretation of this culture was to stay in the middle. It was the relatively safer place to be. If they noticed you and saw that you were out at the edges, the teachers considered you to be non-conforming to the formula. This led to painful consequences for the identified student.

Many otherwise brilliant students were destroyed by the conformance strategies and regimes of schools and colleges. Their innate talents, necessary in the more rounded development of society, were ground down to such an extent that their entire self-worth was drained from them, thus wasting their great potential.

Jack could both see and feel the net tightening and that this was going to be a different regime from home or being the top notch on Uncle Tom's and Aunt Sheila's farm. There he was someone. Here he was just student Number 29.

The reverend president gave a brief outline of the time-table for the rest of the day. He then announced the structured time-table for the days ahead. The students were to be organised and were to march in silence in and out of the church, dining hall, dormitory and their classrooms. They were to walk slowly and on the left-hand side when going along corridors. The teachers and heads of departments would give more detailed instructions over the next few days.

Just as he had started it, he finished the assembly with a prayer. He instructed the students to march slowly and in silence to the refectory for their first meal of the term. The long journey towards becoming institutionalised had begun. Jack's stomach churned. He felt sorry for himself.

Since he was Number 29, Jack was allocated a place at table four. Each table had ten spaces, of which nine were for the new students and the top spot or tenth spot was reserved for the monitor. The monitor was a senior student whose job was to manage the table and its nine junior students. Each monitor had day-to-day responsibility for the nine juniors at his table. The monitor for table four was Tim, who had earlier guided Jack to his bed in the dormitory.

They stood beside their chairs at the table, hands folded, and faced the stage. They remained silent.

Wrinkles, whose real name was Father O'Shea, was the priest in charge of the refectory. As Wrinkles now stood before them and spoke to them, one of the boys whispered to Jack that he was nicknamed Wrinkles because of his reputation of causing boys' skin to wrinkle up after he beat them.

Wrinkles, with raised voice, told them what the drill was and what the punishment would be for failure to comply. The drill was that the students would silently march slowly into the refectory with their eyes looking at the floor. They would stand beside their designated chair and face the stage until Wrinkles said the Grace Before Meals. Only then would they sit down and break silence. The monitor had the responsibility and the authority to divide out the food from the large containers.

A cook in white uniform wheeled in a big trolley carrying massive teapots which had two handles to carry their weight. Each table got one teapot. The kitchen staff had already mixed milk and sugar into the teapot. This was convenient for administration, but hateful if you disliked too much milk or too much sugar.

Two slices of white sliced pan and a small knob of butter, which tasted like margarine, were laid on the table for each student. The cook placed a bowl of watery jam in the centre of the table. Another cook wheeled another trolley into the refectory. She gave one container of greasy potato chips, fried eggs and sausages to each table. This was Tim's first opportunity to demonstrate his height in the college hierarchy and his privileges of power. He first picked what he wanted from the container for himself and divided what was left among the nine juniors.

Jack got one sausage, one fried egg and four chips. They were cold and barely cooked. He just couldn't eat them; he merely picked and tried to shield his picking. Hunger was the least of his worries at that moment. Tim advised the juniors to eat up as this was their last opportunity to eat until breakfast next morning. He told them that they would get less 'picky and choosey' as the weeks went on and as the hunger kicked in. There was a lot of chatter in the senior section of the refectory, but in the junior section there was little talk as awkward new students shed some shy tears as they fumbled with their new situation. Jack's stomach churned, but not from hunger. His problems were deeper than that.

The bell rang and Wrinkles told them to be silent and to stand up beside their chairs and face the stage for the reciting of the Grace After Meals. He told them to take their dishes, scrape away any bits of food, and stack them neatly on the provided trolley. They were then free to go to the play yard and remain there until the bell would ring at 8.30 p.m. They were to then queue up in front of the church.

Jack, like most of the other new students, hung around a corner in the yard avoiding notice. The older students seemed to be having a good time playing ground soccer and basketball. Groups of them were in animated discussion about their experiences over the summer holidays. They gloried in the fact that they had now climbed a further rung of the college ladder. Einstein said that everything is relative. The absolute situation of the older students was not good, but it was relatively better than that of the new lost souls scattered in corners around the college yard.

The bell rang at 8.30 p.m. Jack and the new juniors queued up as instructed and marched quietly into the church. The hierarchy applied here too. The front of the church was reserved for the new juniors.

The reverend president took night benediction and sang hymns. He recited a long list of prayers which a senior told Jack and his colleagues they would get to know verbatim over the next year. He then gave the night's homily, which was built around a particular Church teaching principle. His theme for that first night was that all present should thank God for the opportunity they had been given to attend such a renowned college. They should pray for those lucky enough in life to have had this opportunity. Jack could not see that this was an opportunity. To Jack, it was more like a prison sentence.

The reverend president spoke again about the drill for the remainder of the night and through to Mass time in the morning. He instructed the new juniors to go in silence to the dormitory where Father O'Sullivan would assume responsibility.

Father O'Sullivan called all eighty-six new juniors together and ordered them into a circle around a bed on which the bedclothes were badly organised. He pulled all the bedclothes off the bed, made a ball of them and threw them onto the floor. He shouted with cutting personal remarks at one boy and ordered him to remake his bed properly. As the boy bent down to pick up the sheets and blankets, Father O'Sullivan, shouting, red-faced and foaming at the mouth, gave him a kick up his backside. He said that because it was the first night, he wasn't enforcing his normal regime of punishment. In Jack's opinion, Father O'Sullivan's treatment of this boy was brutal and horrific.

Jack wondered what a full regime of punishment would be like. Over the next thirty minutes, the targeted boy used terrified trial and error to make his bed to Father O'Sullivan's standard. Father O'Sullivan told the rest of the students that this would be the minimum standard he would accept and that he would enforce this standard. No one dared to question him.

A monitor said that Father O'Sullivan hated this menial task every academic year and that he had to release this hatred in some way.

Father O'Sullivan instructed the new juniors to go to the toilet, wash their teeth and get ready for bed. This communal bathroom setup was strange and embarrassing for Jack. He was more used to the shelter of ditches, where he could use a fist full of grass to wipe his bottom. The privacy of the outdoor toilet at home was more comfortable than this very public, open plan toilet. He wasn't going to get into any arguments about this tonight. He would suffer through the whole process in the least conspicuous way possible. He had been used to just dropping his trousers on the floor, leaving on his shirt and jumping into bed with his brothers. His comfort of this was now gone. Now, he had to strip off to the skin and put on his new pyjamas. He slid under the blankets and waited for lights out at 9.30 p.m.

Jack didn't sleep. Sharing the loft room and attic with his brothers didn't prepare him for a room with eighty-six beds. The beds were creaky as the restless new juniors turned and twisted in the dark. He heard soft sobs, even crying, from some beds. Though Jack wanted to go to the toilet, he was afraid of getting up and going out in the dark. He didn't know the drill and held on to his stomach rather than go to the toilet to evacuate his bloated bowel. He couldn't afford to fall asleep.

The morning bell rang at 7 a.m. On the dot, Father O'Sullivan came through the aisles of the dormitory loudly clapping his hands. Get up! Get up! Before lights out the previous night he had given details of the morning procedures:

When the morning bell rings, jump out of your bed immediately on your left-hand side;

Proceed quietly to the washroom and wash your hands and face after first going to the toilet;

Come back to your bed and make it correctly;

Dress yourself as it says in the college dress code;

Make your way in silence to the chapel and be in your designated seat by 7.30 a.m.

As Father O'Sullivan walked through the aisles, one boy was still in bed, half asleep and sobbing. Father O'Sullivan caught the corner of his mattress, toppled him onto the floor and shouted that more would happen in the future if any boys didn't do as they are instructed. Directing his attention to the boy now crouched on the floor, he shouted, 'You are now a big boy, seeing that you are in secondary school. You don't have any Mammy aprons to hide behind. Get up and stop your crying!'

Jack had to queue at the urinal before he could relieve himself. Having relieved himself, he had to queue at the wash hand basin in order to wash his face. There was no hot water, but this didn't bother him. However, it did bother another boy who had facial hair and wanted to shave.

When he got back to the dormitory, he had the task of making his bed. He had not yet perfected this skill. He struggled to learn from the horrific experience of his dormitory colleague of the previous night. As if from nowhere, Father O'Sullivan was there observing. Jack was now nervous and more liable to make mistakes.

Father O'Sullivan shouted at him, 'Have you any bed at home? Did you ever make it?' Too frightened to look up, Jack just spluttered out that his Ma used to do it. 'Well, you have no Ma here!' screamed Father O'Sullivan as he tumbled Jack's mattress onto the floor. He shouted 'Do it right this time!' Jack, his insides about to explode, made his bed in some sort of fashion that was acceptable to Father O'Sullivan. He got dressed as fast as he could and got to the chapel just in time for morning prayers and Mass at 7.30 a.m.

The chapel in St Patrick's was different. It had ten side altars where the other priests would say their obligatory morning Mass on a rota basis. These side Masses would go on as the Mass was being celebrated on the main altar.

At the end of Mass, Reverend President Father McCarthy mounted the main altar and repeated his cold, formal welcome back from holidays to all the students. He re-emphasised the procedure for the rest of the day. They were to leave the church in an orderly way, walk on the left-hand side of the corridor to the refectory; they were to maintain silence until after the communal Grace Before Breakfast.

Jack followed in the crowd though the door into the refectory. Wrinkles stood on the stage observing everything that moved – this height advantage gave him an unrestricted view. Jack went to his designated seat and stood facing the stage as instructed. A few other juniors were lost and found it difficult to find their designated chairs. One big raw soft boy was lost beyond his own reason. He blushed, fumbled and flustered around trying to find his seat.

Wrinkles spotted him and called him to come up onto the stage. He asked, 'What do you mean by moping around the place and holding up the proceedings?' The boy was too disturbed and too frightened to answer, and Wrinkles caught him by the lobe of the ear and pulled it viciously. 'Think, stupid boy. Think!' shouted Wrinkles. 'If you are lost what should you do?' shouted Wrinkles again.

As the public humiliation went on, the boy became even more disorientated. Wrinkles spotted the empty chair and while still holding him by the ear marched him down to the chair and shouted, 'That was easy. Will you forget it again?'

Wrinkles, like Father O'Sullivan, laid down early markers about the procedure he was going to impose consistently. He saw himself as the guardian of stipulated procedures. By God, he was going to make sure that they happened on a consistent basis according to this standard. He mounted the stage and said the Grace before Meals. All sat down and the silent period finished.

Breakfast consisted of a bowl of porridge, two slices of white sliced pan bread, a small lump of butter and the pot of pre-sugared and pre-milked tea in the large teapots with the two handles. The porridge wasn't like the porridge his mother made. It was thick, partly cooked and cold. Jack picked at it. Tim told him to eat up. Out of fear, he forced bits of it into his own mouth. He felt sick and cold.

The breakfast finished at 8.30 a.m., and Wrinkles said the Grace After Meals and dismissed them. They had twenty-five minutes of break-time to play in the quad yard. Jack didn't feel like playing. He just wanted to be back home and in command of his own little domain. Tim told them that the bell would ring at 8.55 a.m. to command them to queue up in predefined lines so that they could enter their classrooms correctly as the authorities defined it.

Jack felt that he was isolated and that everyone was looking at him during twenty-five minutes of break-time in the yard. He didn't realise that he wasn't alone in this sorrowful state. He had many colleagues who, in their own way, felt worse.

Most of the new juniors lined up as planned when the bell rang at 8.55 a.m. However, there were a few late laggards and lost souls. Father O'Keeffe, known to the seniors by the name of Sparks, was the dean of study. Hanging from his cassock was a brown thick belt known as the Strap.

Sparks was supervising and observed the laggards. He rounded them up into a straight line by the wall. He shouted that, because it was the first morning, he would be 'nice'. He commanded the line of lates to stretch out their right hands, palms facing upwards. He raised the Strap and pulled it down with force on each hand. He shouted at them to get back in line: 'I hope you won't ignore the bell again.' These public lessons were for everyone's consumption. They communicated what the priests expected, and they communicated the consequences of non-conformity. Clearly.

Sparks led Jack and his first year colleagues into a classroom. It was a large, deep room. The desks were in neat straight lines. He told the new juniors to fill the room from the back to the front. What Jack didn't observe was that there were two divides in the room, but the dividing partitions were currently folded back so that the three rooms became one.

Sparks stood at the front, said a public prayer and told the juniors to sit at their desks and to keep silent. He welcomed them to their classroom. He then told them that they would be divided into three classes known as 1A, 1B and 1C.

'The front section of the room will be occupied by 1A, the middle section by 1B, and the back divide of the classroom will be billeted by 1C. You will now sit a three-hour class-grading exam, to be completed at

12.30 p.m. The grades scored by the students for this exam will determine which class the individual students will get into.'

The new juniors could hardly contain their shock.

Three monitors then walked in and gave out the exam papers, which they placed face down on the individual desks. They then gave out foolscap paper upon which the new students were expected to write their answers. Sparks gave a signal: 'Now start. You have three hours to finish.'

The exam paper was in three sections: Irish, English and Maths. The sorrowful students struggled to cope with the bombshell. When Jack looked at the exam paper, his head was in a haze. He couldn't focus. Fear forced him to start writing.

He first tackled the English section and made some progress. The questions and composition were similar to those he encountered in the Primary Certificate. He then tackled the Maths section, but he couldn't remember some of the formulae. He put down the answers as best he could. At the Irish section, there was very little he could either understand or recognise. He recognised some words in the composition title, but he had no sense of the meaning of the title. Desperate situations require desperate responses. While he was a shaken country lad in foreign territory, he nevertheless had survival instincts. Based on the few words he recognised, he wrote the composition he had learned off by heart for his Primary Certificate and hoped for the best.

The bell rang at 12.30 p.m., and Sparks told the boys to stop writing and to turn their answer sheets over. The three monitors came and collected the answer papers. Sparks ordered the candidates to leave the extended classroom in an orderly way and go to the toilets to relieve themselves. They were to take a break in the quad yard and the bell would ring again at 12.55 p.m. for dinner. He warned them to observe the queuing code. It now dawned on Jack that his life was going to be regulated by bells and queues. Long gone were the free and easy days around Aunt Sheila's farm.

There were queues at the toilet. When Jack went into the cubicle to relieve himself and then to wipe his bottom, he saw that the toilet paper was shiny and was less effective than the fistfull of grass he used when he made his 'number two' on the farm. The torn-up newspapers his mother had in their own toilet at home were softer and more effective. Grass was smooth.

As in exams the world over, the post-mortem question was the first effort at cross-communication within this group of first year rookies. The reactive 'How did you answer that question?' facilitated the initial breaking of silences and physical isolation. Even though they had all been physically in close contact in such places as the refectory, dormitory and even the toilets, the new juniors were nevertheless, until now, a series of islands.

Even at this very early stage, a few cocky guys said that they did very well and that their mothers wanted them to be in the 1A class. They were from the town. They considered the country lads to be Culchies and therefore of lower intellect and ability. Jack had played club football against their likes. They had skills and were full of tricks and shaping, but they nevertheless fell and often cried when Jack and his country lads connected with them.

The bell went. A better queue formed this time and, on the signal from Sparks, they marched back into the classroom. Sparks stood at the front of the class and shouted the drill for the rest of the day. He said that the results of the exam would be posted on the notice board at 4 p.m. and that, based on these results, the students were to report to the correct classroom for that night's study and for classes from there on out. Jack had no ambition about which class he wanted to be in. He just wanted to be out of this place.

Sparks listed out more rules and regulations. He then went through the class timetable, the subjects and which teachers were assigned to teach them. It confused Jack. He sat there like a statue, neither observing nor resisting what was going on around him. He started to build a mental cocoon around himself and this was the defensive tactic for his immediate survival.

Survivors of long-term situations such as kidnapping and solitary confinement are not necessarily those who are physically strong. According to much evidence, the survivors are those able to build a mental cocoon around themselves and become immune to what has happened to them and around them.

Jack understood none of this psychology. But his natural survival instinct would play a big role for him in his future survival stakes.

The bell rang at 1.15 p.m. Sparks told the students to go in predetermined formation to the refectory. The drill for breakfast was again in place and would be in the future. The big chap whom Wrinkles had punished now stood by his chair like the other students waiting in silence for the Grace Before Meals. After, all sat down. Tim served the soup to himself and then divided the remainder among the other nine. By now, Jack and the lads began conversation. It was tentative. It was subdued. It was: 'Where are you from? What is your name?'

Dinner arrived in a big pot. It was a stew otherwise known as 'lucky dip'. You could find anything in it, and you would be lucky if you could find any lump of meat in it. That's how it got its brand name. Tim served himself with the best of it and then divided the remainder out among the nine boys. It smelled bad, was lukewarm and didn't have the same taste as his mother's stews. The students picked and shifted the lucky dip around their plates. They ate little.

Tim told them that this was the highlight meal of the week, which raised the question in Jack's mind, 'What is the rest of it going to be like?' The red jelly and yellow thick custard was welcome. The pre-milked and sugared tea in the big tea pot with the two big handles then arrived. Jack ate the jelly and custard but picked at the rest. He was still too overawed to notice his hunger.

Wrinkles called for attention to say Grace After Meals. He then told them that the college had been given a half day off from class and that the new students were to be taken for a supervised walk around the buildings, playing pitches and farm so that they could get their bearings regarding the facilities. It would also indicate to them which areas were out of bounds. The older boys were to go and tog out for games. He said that the bell would ring at 4 p.m. and that the new students were then to check the exam results on the notice board and find the class assigned to them. They were then to go to their assigned numbered desk in the appropriate classroom.

Father Molloy, who it later transpired was the history teacher, supervised the tour. He was caring and smiling and interesting as he explained the history of the college and, as his class followed him, he pointed out items of historic interest. In addition, he pointed out the locations that were out of bounds for first year students.

At 4 p.m., Jack and his colleagues went to the notice board. Jack found his name after a long search. He had been allocated desk 29 in Classroom 1C, the lowest grade in the college. The students sent to that class were considered to be stupid, and the other students and teachers treated them according to this low status. The significance of this floated over Jack's head. After the bell, he went into Classroom 1C and found his seat which was situated conveniently at the back left corner. He had now established an identity. He was Number 29. This applied to his bed, his school desk and the chair in the refectory. It was all structured and neat. In his own mind he thought that this was progress.

The heavy sliding partitions were now drawn, dividing the large deep schoolroom into three separate rooms of which Classroom 1C, the back section, housed thirty-five 'dunces' of the new crop of students. They were told to stand up when a teacher entered or left their classroom.

A tall priest entered Classroom 1C, stood in front of the blackboard and called for attention. He introduced himself as Father Hennessey. Jack and his fellow students would later learn that this was Browney, an appropriate nickname because of his desire to use his brown shiny strap to administer punishment. Browney told them straight that they were the dregs. He said that they were stupid and that it was his job to ensure that they acquired a basic education, even against the odds with which he was starting off.

Nobody dared dispute his analysis. He walked slowly around the classroom, got each student to call out his name and the school he had come from. This indicated that the lads were from a large geographical spread and were mainly from rural schools. When he arrived at Number 29, Jack said his name was Jack Cronin and that he came from the national school of Knockrue. Browney said that Jack was 'the first pupil he had from that school and here he was in 1C. Where does that leave the rest of the children attending Knockrue School?' Jack kept his eyes focused on the ground.

Jack reasoned that it was safer to stay within the shadow of the crowd. His leadership traits would later facilitate him to stand out from the crowd with its reluctant consequences.

Browney completed the introductions and passed out copies of the class timetables, which were broken down by days. Each class was to be 55 minutes long, except for the Double Science Practicals, whatever that was supposed to be. Jack looked down through the list and saw strange and frightening labels; Latin, Greek, Science and PE. PE was a big stumbling block as he wondered what the hell it was, but he dared not ask. A cheeky townie in the class might have put up his hand and asked. But not Jack or his rural colleagues. They were to be seen and not heard. He would later find out that, contrary to his initial negative reaction, it was a good subject. It stood for physical education.

Browney said that supervised study time was broken into two time slots. The first slot was from 4.30 p.m. to 5.55 p.m. to be followed by supper at 6.00 p.m. Study was then to resume at 7.00 p.m. and finish at 8.30 p.m. Then there would be a break until the bell rang for night prayers at 8.55 p.m. It was straight to bed after night prayers and lights out at 9.30 p.m. This was the drill from Monday to Saturday. They had half days from class on Wednesdays and Saturdays in order to facilitate the playing of games.

The timetable for Sunday was different, with the rising time 7.30 a.m. instead of 7 a.m. After breakfast at 8.30 a.m. there was a break until 10 a.m. There was reading time from 10 a.m. to 12 noon. Dinner was at 1 p.m., with games organised afterwards. Reading or study took place from 4 p.m. to 6 p.m. followed by supper. Night prayers were at 9 p.m. and lights out was at 9.30 p.m. Then it was back to the normal mid-week routine again. In Jack's mind, everything was about routine, bells and discipline.

Browney told them that they could write a letter home during the reading time on Sundays but that they should leave the envelope opened, so that he could read and check the contents. This gave a clear signal to these raw students that they should be careful what they wrote home about.

No visitors were allowed in the first month in order to allow them to settle down to the strict routine. Each student was allowed one visit per term. In order to receive that one visit, the student went through a process of first seeking and then receiving permission from Father O'Keeffe. Visiting time was from dinnertime to 4.30 p.m. on a Sunday. If they wished, parents could remain within the confines of the school for the duration of the visit. Or they could take their student out and have him back in the college by 4.30 p.m. sharp. If the student returned late, no permission for a visit in the following term would be granted.

Each student was entitled to one food parcel per term, with strict instructions that its contents be stored in the cupboards of the refectory. At 6 p.m. the bell rang for the Angelus. Browney called out the prayers of the Angelus and the subdued students answered. He told them to go to the refectory for supper. The menu of bread and a lump of butter was served, but on this occasion without jam.

Class proper started at 9 a.m. next morning. The first class was Latin. This was Double Dutch to Jack and his 1C classmates. The teacher was a young cleric who was studying for the priesthood and was very concerned to create a good impression with the dean of studies, Father O'Keeffe. He was not going to put up with any crap. In his own mind, he was going to make Latin scholars of this motley crew in 1C. He gave them the background to the importance of Latin as a core language and its association with the Roman Empire, which was of slight interest to a few of the class. He moved on to explaining the rudiments of Latin grammar. Jack was lost. He found it difficult to stop yawning.

Next teacher was Father O'Neill, the English teacher who had been around for a long time and who knew how to handle and mishandle these kinds of students. He made it clear from the start what he expected. He told of the punishment consequences for misbehaving or not doing homework. He distributed copies of a text book and *The Merchant of Venice*, by William Shakespeare. This would be the exam play for the Intermediate Certificate at the end of third year.

Teachers for the other subjects came in as Jack's timetable showed and set out their stall in their individual ways. The common thread going through them all was that punishment was going to be order of the day for Jack and his 1C colleagues if they failed to live up to the unrealistic expectations of these teachers.

The priest for Greek was an old man. He was in bad health and didn't show much desire to be in front of this motley crew. He told them that, in his opinion, most of this 1C class knew nothing and would continue to know nothing about the Greek language, but that they may as well try and enjoy the experience.

Jack had his first experience of formal supervised study that evening.

The first slot was from 4.30 p.m. to 5.55 p.m. It took place in the class-rooms which now had the two partitions folded back to convert the three classrooms into the larger one room. Study was conducted in silence. A senior monitor supervised. The senior monitor himself was supposed to be studying as well. But in this first night and for the early weeks, he seemed more intent on showing that he was the boss.

He looked around to find his first victim. He came down to Jack and wanted to know what all the shuffling and noise was all about. He suddenly hit Jack a slap across his face. While Jack's mother was a disciplinarian and prone to using a sally rod to administer punishment, this public slapping across his face was far more humiliating than her procedures. Jack couldn't see any link between his activity and this public slap. Jack couldn't settle down and had no interest whatsoever in starting to study. He watched the clock and counted the minutes.

The students had no homework to do this first night. They sat there and tried to appear to be gainfully occupied. This was psychological warfare as far as Jack was concerned. The bell for supper rang, and the students moved to the refectory for more of the same routine and food.

Following their post-supper break, the bell summoned them to enter the second nightly phase of study. The bell later summoned them for night prayers. Lights out was at 9.30 p.m. The bell summoned again at 7 a.m. for morning call. The routine was a boring process of around and around. Oh, for the carefree days around Aunt Sheila's farm where he was the centre of attention and praise was heaped on him. Here he was merely Number 29.

Days wore into weeks, weeks wore into months, and Jack and his class-mates started to act like the broken horse that no longer resisted its trainer. For ease of passage, they more or less fell in with the system. From time to time they tried, by carelessness or stubbornness, to test the system. In almost all such cases, they met the sting of a priest's strap.

A few of Jack's colleagues now assumed leadership roles. These were mostly lads from the town, or townies as they were known. Country lads like Jack lacked the brashness or confidence to come forward, or were too shrewd. The priests were the ultimate enemy, but the monitors and other seniors were often the immediate enemy. Some were bullies. These moni-tors drenched the young students in the toilets, stole their clothes, and planted stolen goods in their lockers. While it appeared to be great fun for them, it sapped the confidence of the targeted victims.

Bullies tend to sniff out weakness. They would identify the weak, shy boy who wouldn't fight back or who didn't have a bigger brother in the school to look out for him. Bullies are weak people. But again, as Einstein said, 'Everything is relative.' For bullies to inflict pain or to elevate their status or to show off their relative strength, they need even weaker victims.

Jack was not initially perceived to be the weakest link by these cowards. He had an initial try out when one of these potential bullies dropped a sweet paper and ordered Jack to pick it up. Except for orders from his mother, Jack generally reacted badly to being ordered. His spontaneous reaction to this order was to say, in his own mind, 'Fuck off.' He just kept walking, ignoring the bully.

We all have natural self-survival instincts. If we let nature takes its course, this instinct kicks in automatically. It is only when we stop and try to rationalise the options that we interfere with this natural reaction. In life, we need to understand the incidents we should let ride and those where we have to put a stop on ourselves and come up with a considered response. In the institutional world that Jack now found himself in, life became easier for those who suppressed their natural involuntary reactions and rationalised the responses acceptable to the priests.

A coward can be defined as a person who, in an emergency, thinks with his or her legs. By this definition, you could say that Jack was a coward. But if he were truly a coward, he would have picked up the sweet paper and shown weakness. In reality, his refusal to pick up the sweet paper was the first victory for Jack since he arrived in this drab and morale-sapping institution as he understood it.

As Jack and his fellow students became increasingly institutionalised, they went with the flow. Instead of resisting, they looked out, as they saw it, through the same window of desperation. A mutual understanding of self-survival was evolving within the group. It was 'Us against the World'.

Lessons for Jack from Being Alone in a Crowd

- **In a hostile environment the middle ground is perceived to be a safer place to be.** Jack and his fellow students rationalised that if the school or college authorities noticed you and saw that you were 'out at the edges', they considered you to be non-conforming to their formula. This often led to painful consequences for the identified student. Many otherwise brilliant students were destroyed by the conformance strategies and regimes of schools and other authorities. In the institutional world that Jack now found himself in, life became easier for those who suppressed their natural involuntary reactions and rationalised the responses acceptable to the priests.

- **In business you need to be perceived to be different in a meaningful way as your targeted customers perceive it.** How did your schooling and rearing influence you in this critical area?

- **Dinner arrived in a big pot.** It was a stew otherwise known as 'Lucky dip'. You could find anything in it, and you would be lucky if you could find any lump of meat in it. That's how it got its brand name. Is your life determined by the 'lucky dip' or are you taking responsibility and directing your sails irrespective of the wind direction?

- **A coward can be defined as a person who, in an emergency, thinks with his or her legs.** The survival instinct automatically kicks in and may be the correct tactic at that point.

- **In life, we need to understand the incidents we should let ride and those which we have to tackle.** Jack generally reacted badly to being ordered. His spontaneous reaction to orders was to say, in his own mind, 'Fuck off.'

  How do you react to orders?

Chapter 10

Sporting Chance

Sticky handpicked the captains for the eight football teams in the college junior league. His real name was Father Maughan, but Jack learned that he was known as Sticky because of his coaching tactic of shouting at the backs on the football field to stick to their opponents.

The authorities in the college organised a number of trial football and hurling games so that they could find out the stock of talent among the new students. They called a meeting after the completion of the second series of trial games. From that they arranged a school league for the different grades. The junior grade comprised the first year and second year students plus the tail of the third year students.

The eight captains drew lots in order to get the sequence of picking players from the total pool.

John, one of the eight, drew the longest straw and had the first option to choose the best player as he saw it from the pool. The process continued in sequence until all the students were on one of the eight team panels. The manager applied the same sequence for the hurling league.

No student had the option to opt out. This was hell on earth for those students who had neither the interest in, nor ability for, these games. They still had to tog out every Wednesday for football and every Saturday for hurling. For these, the meaning of participation was to stand out of the way as much as possible and hope that the ball wouldn't come their way.

The winters in the '60s were cold. These disinterested lads stood perished as the hailstones or windswept rain poured down on them. They had no tracksuits. Because of their lack of participation in the game, they generated little body heat and were thus frozen. There they stood in the cold. Some had snots running from their noses. Brown excrement ran down the frozen legs of one due to fear of the ball coming towards him. This was worse than the sting of the strap. It was psychological. Sticky's attitude was that this exposure would harden them up. For some, it left scars for life.

The eight captains picked the best of the second year players first. Then they handpicked any good first year players who were spotted during the trial games. John picked Jack for his football team and Gerry picked him for his hurling team.

A full listing of the teams plus the league schedule was put up on the notice boards. All the teams were given county labels. John's football team was designated the Down County team, with red and black jerseys. Down had won the All-Ireland in 1960 and 1961 and were the first team to take the Sam Maguire Cup across the border. They had a famous half-forward line made up of Sean O'Neill on the right, James McCartan in the centre and Paddy Doherty on the left. John tried to mould his team around this Down team.

Jack was considered to be built a bit like James McCartan, who was strong, big-bodied and had a low centre of gravity. He was renowned for his courage and ability to burst through tackles with the ball and create havoc in opposing back lines. This created the necessary space for the more skilful O'Neill and Doherty to clock up the scores. John placed Jack into this James McCartan, centre-forward position. This vote of confidence in Jack boosted him, and he was determined to grab the chance of a lifetime within the lifetime of the chance. He read any bits of paper he could find about the Down team.

In life everything is relative. Jack, in his own mind, was playing in Croke Park, while in reality he was playing in John's junior league team in the back college pitch over the cold winter days. Relative to the tail end of the third year's team, Jack was fantastic, but he was poor relative to the better second year students on the team. Nevertheless, he was now on the road to success. This was the first chink of light in his otherwise miserable existence so far in this college.

He had a good game, where he scored two good points and opened up the goal opportunity for his team captain, John, who burst through the centre from his number six spot. They won this first league game. They also won the next few games. People started to talk about them and spot the team. John led them from his centre-back position. He organised and reorganised his better players and instructed the tail of his team to keep out of the way, which they did in their continuing frozen, frightened state.

Football now became Jack's god. He spent his study periods writing out different formations for the team and the likely formation of their next competitors. John listened to him and encouraged him to have a go. This sports safety valve was critical. It gave Jack some recognition and status within his class and even among the second year students. He got on well with his two captains and dreamt of being a captain himself next year.

Down won the football league and were runners up in the hurling league. Based on Jack's performances, he was picked for the college junior football panel. They played an inter-schools league with six other schools. These games were played on a home-and-away basis every other year. During Jack's first year, they played three games at home and three games away.

These away games presented Jack and his playing colleagues with the rare opportunity to see outside the walls of the college. They travelled in a hired bus to the other colleges to play the away games. Although Sticky kept them under constant supervision, they nevertheless got some glimpse from the windows of the bus, of activity in the outside world. They also got a good feed in the host's refectory.

For these junior games, travel was restricted to the team panel members. Some sang on the bus on the way back. They sang more courageously when they won. This celebration was small fry compared to that which took place following victories for the seniors. Jack and his playing mates focused on analysing the game and how they could do even better the next time.

Jack was now becoming established and recognised, based on his relative achievement on the playing pitches, though he was still a laggard in the classroom and in other aspects of conforming to the repressive regime.

Some first year students settled in well. Others were in trouble. Pat, one of Jack's 1C classmates was missing. His desk was unoccupied and his bed was undisturbed. The priests conducted an aggressive search and enquiry to establish his last known movements. Rumours circulated. Did he jump into the river? Was he kidnapped? At the night prayers, Father Ryan prayed for his safe journey, but didn't say to where.

Two days later, a student saw Pat come into the main office accompanied by his mother. He overheard that Pat could not take it anymore and had thumbed his way home, but was now back. He reported this story to the class who wondered what the consequences would be for Pat.

At the night study, Sparks came in and stood at the top of the study room. He made a speech about how ungrateful Pat was to spurn this educational opportunity and how he had caused stress to the priests and to his parents who would be subjected to all types of gossip in their local rural parish. Pat stood there trembling. In order to ensure that there would be no misunderstanding by any of the rest of the class, Sparks said he was going to administer the punishment in public.

He told Pat to drop his trousers and to bend over. Pat cried and moaned as Sparks gave him twenty slaps with his strap. The rest of the class watched with disbelief written on their faces. Sparks then ordered Pat to stand up and stretch out his right hand palm facing upwards and with his strap, gave him ten slaps. He repeated this sequence on his left hand. To anchor the insult, he slapped Pat across the face with his open hand. He then ordered Pat to go to the sick room.

Sparks told the rest to get back to their study and to understand that there are consequences for all the actions they may take, both good and bad. Most of the class were scared. When scared, they fouled up their normal actions. Jack thought to himself: 'Oh, to be at home, or on Aunt Sheila's farm and be somebody.'

Jack had little pocket money compared with that of some of the other students. The tuck shop at the corner of the quad yard was operated by senior students on behalf of Sparks and opened for one hour per day. It was probably all part of the college financial business model. Jack knew that he had to save his limited money for the rainy day rather than splash it all on the first few days, as some of his classmates had done. Rather than admit that he had little money, Jack said that he didn't like sweets. His camouflage, denial of self and managing of scarce resources, were traits that Jack developed from this experience and which were to impact on his later life.

Mary Anne's letter to Jack said that, dependent on permission from the college, she and Mick Denny Bill planned to come and visit him 'on Sunday week'. They would be there at 1 p.m. sharp and they would drive out of the confines of the college and 'stop somewhere nice and have a picnic'. Mary Anne would prepare the sandwiches and the bottles of tea insulated in woollen socks. Jack was to write back confirming that he had received written permission for the visit. Jack was shy about going to the dean's office to request the permission, but the anticipated excitement about the visit was greater than the fear of asking.

As the designated Sunday approached, Jack walked with a lighter step and counted down the days on his calendar. Mary Anne and Mick Denny Bill and his brothers and sisters arrived on time. They had parked outside for some time before venturing into the college at precisely the designated time.

The priests and the educated elite held power over the timid people who were unlucky enough or not rich enough to have gone through the formal education system. The gap between the powerful and the powerless became fertile ground for abuse. Abuse by the powerful and by paedophiles in institutions was then rumoured but was not spoken about.

Mary Anne was confident and determined and rarely expressed emotion. However, when she saw Jack, her trapped dam of emotions burst open, and she hugged him tightly. It was public, but she didn't care. Jack looked sideways to see who might see this very personal display of weakness. Mick Denny Bill and Jack's brothers and sisters greeted Jack with restrained regard.

The Cronin family crushed into the car and drove out the front gate of the college. The air outside seemed to Jack to be so much fresher than the air within the walls of the college. The shyness and correctness and restraint in their communication within the car continued as Mary Anne asked all sorts of questions. Jack responded with grunts and with 'Yes' and 'No' answers. He was wound up. He had to uncoil himself over the first half hour before he was relaxed enough to be more forthcoming.

He didn't want to upset his mother so he painted a watered-down picture of life in the college. He adopted the defence mechanism that children have for their parents. He didn't tell her about the horrific beatings, the starvation, his inability to purchase anything from the tuck shop, the bullying from the seniors, the noises and smells in the dormitory, having to make his own bed perfectly every morning and other negatives. Instead, he spoke about his progress on the playing pitches and how he was friendly with David and Ron.

Even though Jack was young and selfishly didn't want to be there, he knew instinctively the sacrifices of his mother to support his formal education and that he had to energise her own vision. She planned to achieve her personal vision through her children.

As Jack saw it, he was paying too high a price, but he understood that he had no options. His own agenda was subsidiary to his mother's mission. Later in life he would understand the reason for her strategy. But that was then, and now is now. Jack was living and suffering in the moment as he saw it. Deferred gratification was not yet part of his philosophy.

They picked a scenic area on the side of the road with a view of the mountains and a river in order to have their picnic. The home-made brown bread, the lumps of bacon and the yellow mustard never tasted so good before. It reminded Jack of being in the bog and the mentally free and easy days he had there. He now wished he was back there, when even the tea in the bottles kept warm with the woollen socks tasted fantastic.

By the time he had chilled out and opened up his responses, it was time to go back. He hated it. They hated it. Mick Denny Bill said little but observed everything. He knew instinctively that Jack was putting on a brave face. Mick Denny Bill would like to have brought Jack home and let him cycle to The Tech. Knowing what life with Mary Anne would be like, if that happened, he couldn't allow himself the luxury of thinking this out loud.

There was little talk in the car as Mick Denny Bill drove it back to the college, in through the big gates, parking it in the quad yard. Mary Anne asked Jack how he was for pocket money. Jack responded that he was okay. In any case, she gave him £1. When they said farewells, out of sight of Mary Anne, his father slipped him a red ten-shilling note. This was an uncharacteristic expression of Mick Denny Bill's emotions. Jack appreciated getting this ten-shilling note so much that he decided not to spend it until such a time as he had no other option. Everything has a price, and the cost to Jack of holding on to this ten-shilling note were the sweets he had to forego in the interim.

For Jack it was back to bells, bad food, making beds and taking punishment from frustrated priests who felt that the use of the strap was the only available motivating technique. For some of these priests it was an ego trip. To have the reputation of being the most severe with the strap was in itself a differentiating factor. At the same time, it was a branding opportunity in their mundane frustrated lives.

When Jack's family got home they were sad. When the neighbours came in and enquired about Jack, Mary Anne, like most mothers, showed no weakness. She boasted about how well he was doing and that he was in line to become a great player. Most of the neighbours were happy for her. Some were envious.

As the school year slipped by, Jack became friendly with the lads in his class and especially with the better players in his football and hurling teams. Games became his passion. Classes in Latin, Greek and Irish just made life difficult. He hadn't a clue what they were about. Rather than apply himself to the necessarily hard work of trying to gain an understanding of these subjects, he prepared to suffer the consequences of the leather strap. He survived the long, quiet study periods by dreaming about a life far beyond his current prison sentence. He developed all sorts of exciting scenarios.

The Christmas holidays were a release. Jack, at first, found everything strange. He thought that all the rooms in his home were small and dark, which contrasted with the large dormitory and refectory he had become accustomed to over the first term. He was delighted to be home for the holidays and delighted to be back on the farm, but it took him and the rest of the family some time to adjust to the change.

Mary Anne instinctively knew how to handle it. She refrained from bombarding him with the questions which buzzed around in her head. She gave him space to chill out. He put on his old dungarees and boots and went to visit Aunt Sheila. The easygoing environment around Aunt Sheila's home and farmyard was the tonic required to facilitate his readjustment back to life on the outside. The freedom of the Christmas holidays was great, and his neighbours and cousins praised and gave their new celebrity recognition.

Freedom and pleasure has a price. This price was Jack's pain of going back to the college with its terror regime which would have to be suffered until the next holidays – the Easter holidays.

For the rest of year one, it was more of the same. Jack learned to survive on the playing pitches, but he did badly in class. He failed the dull subjects, as he saw them, but he did well in Maths. At national school, he struggled at all the academic subjects, especially Irish and Maths. But here he had achieved a practical understanding of Maths. The trigger point was Mr Ryan the Maths teacher. Mr Ryan was a football fanatic and had spotted Jack's football potential, so that he treated Jack in class with some respect. Jack grabbed this hook and focused on his subject. Jack ensured that he did his Maths homework correctly so that he wouldn't let Mr Ryan down.

He grew in confidence in his class. He was prepared to ask questions on angles of Maths he didn't understand. From the time Jack could work out the logic and sense of something that was foreign to him, he became receptive to it. Try and push something at him and his natural style was to resist it to the point of risking the lashes of the strap. An innate proud or stubborn streak in him cost him immense pain. In the long term, this trait was a vital ingredient in his passage through life.

One advantage of being in Classroom 1C was that there was no demotion possibility, but he wouldn't be lucky enough to be expelled for poor academic results. The college operated a business model based on a 100 per cent plus or minus occupancy. A student would be expelled only if the full year's fee was prepaid and only if he broke a major rule.

Some colleges operated a scorecard control tactic where the individual students were constantly scored on the left side of the page for academic performance and on the right for behaviour performance. These scorecards were on constant display on the class notice boards. If a student scored below a predetermined acceptable cut-off point, the priests triggered a menu of sanctions. These sanctions tended to be the withdrawal of privileges. This constant public scoring had severe psychological pain for many students. It was like the concept of the slow burner.

In St Patrick's, the punishment was emotional, spontaneous and sadistic. Many of the priests were themselves frustrated, but, because of their interest in the Church's teaching, they saw themselves as being there to save souls, and to accept their own self-sacrifice. This built up a human tension. The only obvious release was to lash out at the children and take a certain satisfaction from it. They dished out a disproportionate amount of punishment to the poorer and less confident children, who tended to be at the bottom of the hierarchy or their social class. Twenty per cent of the boys seemed to take 80 per cent of the punishment.

Within a week of his first summer holidays away from the college, Jack had integrated back to normal family life and work on the farm. He also spent time on Aunt Sheila's farm. Mary Anne and Aunt Sheila observed that he had lost weight. They wanted to make sure to build him up. He was growing up but he was not 'growing out'. Together, they agreed that he should take a tonic. The tonic was a raw hen's egg beaten in a glass of milk every morning, and two teaspoons of cod liver oil. A tablespoonful of Scott's Emulsion followed this in the evenings. Mary Anne supervised him until he swallowed each hateful lot in one ugly gulp. He had no option.

When Jack rejoined the local GAA club team, the selectors saw that he had improved his technique. The divisional team too wanted him. He enjoyed the praise and the recognition. He got the opportunity to play with the under-16 team too. Jack took a few heavy tackles, but his skill level more than compensated for his lack of physical strength against those mature sixteen-year-olds. As he scored freely, his confidence kept growing.

Jack had by now established himself and had gained the confidence to stand his ground. When Mary Anne organised the monthly Saturday trip to Confession, Jack put up a big fight not to go. He eventually relented under his mother's authority. He vowed that this would be the last time that he would participate in this monthly Saturday procedure. He knew that Father Curtin would recognise him in the darkened confessional box. He knew that Father Curtin would ask him about 'boy issues'- issues which he preferred not to be asked about.

As the summer holidays drew to a close, the household felt the same sinking feeling as they felt at the end of the Easter holidays. Jack got edgy. It had a ripple effect through everyone. Aunt Sheila was good for him, in that being once removed from the immediate family, she could say things to Jack which his parents would find more difficult. At the end of the day, she wasn't responsible for him.

When the postman delivered the bundle of letters among which was Jack's exam report that day in August, Mary Anne recognised it immediately, but she left the big brown envelope with the stamp of St Patrick's College large on the front until she sat down for her morning cup of tea to digest it fully. She saw that the results were far down the list from Bs or even Cs, but she had no benchmark against which to compare them. Jack was her first to go to College so he was able to fob off the poor results. His real tactic was to leave St Patrick's and its prison regime. His implied threat stopped Mary Anne's venting of her feelings. Instead of an all-out attack, she tried the tactic of coaxing him to continue on her predefined journey for him.

The family delivered Jack and his case back to the college on September 1st. The sight of the college gates in the distance brought the shouting, the beatings, the humiliations and the pain floating back into his head. He had two advantages this September versus last September. One was that he was going to be a captain of one of the eight football league teams. The second was that the new first year boys would be suffering more than he and would be feeling twice as lost. In comparison with them, he was now in a better space, but relative to his Primary school pals who were going to The Tech or in jobs, he felt that he was in a very bad space.

Second year progressed through the routine of bells, study, strap and humiliation.

Jack used his head to pick the best possible football team from the pool of first and second year students. He tried to keep the tail of the third years to as few as possible, since these would only be in the way on his journey towards victory. He had planned this selection strategy well beforehand.

He had picked six very good anchor players, which provided a robust spine to the team. They went unbeaten during the league and were crowned champions at the end. The smart tactic that Jack used was to observe the initial trial games for the new first year boys. He then identified three potential stars from that group. Being captain, he went out of his way to encourage these raw boys and integrate them into his team. He was selfish for himself, but it was also good for them. This was a win-win scenario.

Jack completed his second year at St Patrick's and returned home for the summer holidays. He slowly integrated back into the local scene, both on a work and social basis. However, he sensed that a distance was growing between himself and the other local lads. It was a slight feeling of a drift apart.

He worked on the home farm and on Aunt Sheila's farm. Mary Anne came home from town one day and told him that she had secured for him the opportunity of three weeks of summer work in the hardware shop. The job was to help the staff prepare the shop and store for annual stocktaking.

Jack now had a taste of employee status and of getting a weekly wage. He was the general dogsbody in the shop, but it reinforced his feeling that it was nonsense for him to put an opportunity like this on ice in order to go back to college which, except for the football, he continued to hate. There was an innate security in his mother's hard but consistent approach. His reality was that his mother's agenda would prevail.

What the Team Captain told Jack

- **There is a danger in living your life through others.** They may let you down in those areas you can't continuously control. Parents like Jack's mother can pay a high personal price to formally educate their children on the assumption that they, as parents, would benefit from it later. It leads to a kind of loving blackmail, and the cost to the child is often too high. This can be a dangerous strategy since the delivery of that mission eventually moves beyond one's control.

- **It's the sneak who represents danger to you.** On the football field, your opponent can be as tough and dirty as he likes and you will be able to handle him. The sneaky player who is nice to your face and then catches you unexpectedly when the referee is not looking, is the problem.

- **In life, everything is relative.** Jack, in his own mind, was playing in Croke Park, while in reality at that time he was playing in the junior league team. He was an excellent footballer relative to the poorer players and a poor player relative to the good players.

- **It is critical in life to be good at something.** Football presented Jack with the opportunity to be good at something. It gave Jack some recognition and status within his class.

- **People imprisoned in dreadful conditions have been shown to eventually adjust to their environment.** Jack learned through trial and error how to initially survive and then win.

- **The loud minority will always be jealous and criticise.** Many people will express sentiments such as: 'Where do they think they came from? Not too long ago they didn't have a seat in their trousers.' In order to succeed, one must ignore negativity and drive on in a planned direction.

- **Children learn to survive and are resilient.** Jack had little pocket money, but rather than admit it, he said he didn't like sweets. His camouflage, denial of self and managing of scarce resources, were traits that Jack developed from this experience and which were to impact on his later life.

Chapter 11

A Leader Emerges

In September, the priests and teachers of St Patrick's began preparing Jack and his fellow students for the State examination, the Intermediate Certificate, to be held in the following June. Three new, young, lay teachers replaced some of the burnt-out priests. They punished with the strap, but they balanced its usage. Instead of humiliating the students, they encouraged them. This change towards encouragement rather than strap-induced demand encouraged Jack to stop fighting against the subjects. In addition to Maths, he took interest in History and Science.

The three new teachers tried to create an interest and a hunger in the students, so that they could see the link between the subject matter and their daily lives. They encouraged them to ask questions and they responded in practical ways. An academic ray of light began to shine. Jack did well in Maths, History and Science. He did badly in the others. In one sense, the result snookered him. He passed the Intermediate Certificate exam, and he thus had a weaker excuse for not going back to do his Leaving Certificate.

The summer holidays were different from the previous two years. Instead of working on the farm, Jack got a summer job working as a labourer with a local builder. He had not previously been exposed to the rough physical work, the tough environment and the language and jokes of a building site. He nevertheless enjoyed the rough and tumble of it. His job was to make the tea for the tradesmen, run errands and clean their tools. He was contributing to the smooth operation of the business. He was also learning about the use of resources and how to manage them.

He was given a special job of recycling timber. The timber was in a big heap that the carpenters and brickies brought back to the builder's yard from demolition jobs. Jack's special job was to clean and extract the nails from each of the used planks of wood. When cleaned up, Jack restacked the planks into categories according to size and state so that they could be reused on other jobs. He had to cut waste and odd sizes into short lengths and split them so that they could be used for starting fires.

His hands blistered. There were no work gloves at that time. Seasoned tradesmen thought that Jack's blisters were great fun. They advised him to relieve the pain with the builder's cure of soaking his hands in 'maiden's water'. He was so innocent that he asked them and others around the building site where he could get this cure. His questions led to great amusement for his colleagues. This led to great embarrassment for Jack. But it was another part of his education for life.

The hard physical work of the building site built his upper body strength which stood to him on the football pitch. He was now a star underage player with his club and with the divisional team. The county minor selectors spotted him. The minor age category was under-18 years. When the selectors invited him to join their panel of thirty players, the parish priest came out to meet and shake the hand of the new celebrity in their midst. Mick Denny Bill and Mary Anne, now the proudest parents in the parish, walked around with a reserved sense of pride and their chests out. The recognition by the neighbours put Jack on a pedestal. He now also had an air of confidence and superiority.

He returned to St Patrick's on September 1st in a different frame of mind from previous returns. He had now found himself. The terrible college regime became less horrific as he moved up the hierarchy. He was now in the senior section with its added privileges relative to the juniors. He moved from the status of abused to the possibility of being an abuser of the new first year boys. In fourth year, the students were weaker relative to the fifth year, yet they were so much stronger than the first year students were. A culture had by now evolved within the college that the strap was used very sparingly on the senior students. The teachers would not use the strap on the senior-cycle students. The integration of the young lay teachers helped to neutralise the excesses of some of the frustrated priests.

The mission of many rural mothers, according to tradition, was to have a bull in the shed, a pump in the yard and a priest in the family. Rather than listen to a different calling, they initiated many religious vocations. Some religious were caught in a life sentence and its linked frustrations. They vented their feelings through the safety valve of the excess use of the strap. A few were paedophiles.

Jack and his mates had never heard the term homosexual. Neither had they heard the term paedophile. They nevertheless knew that they should avoid some priests, and indeed, some neighbours. They responded to their own instinctive defensive mechanisms. They also knew the people from the comments of informed schoolmates from the town and some neighbours back home whose cousins were teachers in the school. Jack learned that paedophiles tended to abuse their power positions in their quest for victims. Everyone in Jack's school knew of one suspect priest. Jack's friend told him that if you were isolated with him, you should try to escape.

This priest had sexually abused Pat, the student who ran away in first year and who was publicly flogged when his mother delivered him back to the college. The priest had befriended him at his lowest moments and had offered him protection. Pat was vulnerable. He had cried for help by running away, but neither the school authorities nor his parents protected him. Ignorance and shame can lead to terrible decisions which come home to roost later in life. After a very troubled and unfulfilled short life, Pat committed suicide at the age of twenty-three.

In the week after Christmas in the fourth year, Jack was again picked for the county minor football panel and also for the anchor centre-forward position on the college senior football team. The college team was good, but they were beaten by a point in the provincial final that year. The county minors went on to win the provincial final that year for the first time in ten years. Jack was toasted everywhere he went. The celebrations at county and at local club level went on for weeks.

Jack worked with the same builder as for the previous year's summer holidays. This time his job was to tend two brickies. As instructed by the foreman, he mixed the mortar and lined up the mixed mortar and a supply of bricks on the scaffolding for the brickies. He earned a fortune of £30 per week.

During tea breaks on the building site, the brickies asked him if he had got the *cosa trasna*. The *cosa trasna* was a reference to girls. Jack would later learn that it meant 'leg over'. The brickies teased him. Jack blushed, but internalised the full meaning of his sexual awakening.

On the building sites and in his socialising with his colleagues on the football teams, he learned more about girls and became more aware of them. But it was a complicated journey. Being an emerging local star, the girls flocked around him. Mick Denny Bill and Mary Anne, hearts in their mouths and fearing the consequences of what could happen in a moment of weakness, now allowed Jack to go to dances on a Sunday night during school holidays. Dancing and drinking were separate events. The old people went to the pub. The young people went to the dances.

Some people, who worked and had the money and transport, followed certain show bands around the country. Although Jack was musical and was a good dancer, he was shy in the company of girls. He tended to stand at the side or the bottom of the dancehall and observe what was going on. When a Ladies' Choice was called, he quickly withdrew in case some girl would ask him out to dance. While not actively participating, he was interested in and enjoyed the fun and the games they played, especially the shaping during the slow foxtrot dances.

Going back to college for the final year wasn't a big chore. He was now a monitor with its accompanying privileges. He was also honoured by being made captain of the college senior football team. This was a real privilege accompanied by a given level of status which Jack loved and took seriously. He now had many privileges relative to those around the school, and with that came increased self-worth. He now had an enhanced foundation rock on which to build the rest of his life. As a monitor he was tough but fair, and he empathised with the first year boys rather than sympathised with them. He had no discipline problems with them as they looked up to him. He was their role model.

Jack's college team took shape as the year progressed. Their early results indicated that they had the potential to do well that year. Sticky was the coach and being captain facilitated Jack to build up a good working relationship with him. They spent time in analysing the strengths and weaknesses of their own team. They also did their homework on their upcoming competitors. They did this by going to their matches and observing their tactics and team composition. From this, they worked out their individual game-plans in order to win their matches.

Team sport is different from individual sport. The team comprises fifteen individual players who have to be blended so that, as Gestalt Theory says, 'The total is greater than the sum of its individual parts.' This often means that certain individuals have to sacrifice their individual talents and adopt a predetermined team role.

The challenge was how best to get all these variables complementing each other in a consistent way over the entire course of a match. Teams often revert to their natural bad habits when they come under pressure. When the team is under pressure, the team members have to keep their shape and keep enough confidence in their game-plan to stick with it. This required strong leadership.

Jack was now forcefully demonstrating leadership both on and off the playing pitch. This was his whole focus. He had a very strong vision of winning the Colleges' All-Ireland that year.

Travelling outside the college to observe the competition playing their matches allowed Jack a degree of freedom. It allowed him to travel, with or without Sticky. Sticky gave money to him to have a meal which was a welcome diversion from the college food. He had time for some extra-curricular activities too.

The students in the college were jubilant when the team beat St Benedict's and won the senior provincial cup. Most of the students went to the match in pre-booked buses. For many it was like getting out of jail. In place of punishment by the strap, the priests denied some students the opportunity to go to the match. These students would have preferred a lashing of the strap to get it over with rather than being denied the opportunity of getting outside the walls of their jail.

Sticky and Jack had to work smart in order to bring the players down from the high so that they could prepare for the All-Ireland semi-final game against the formidable St Kieran's. They used the tactic of dropping two players who were still riding on past glory from the starting fifteen. This was a strong signal to the rest of the panel to pull up their socks and get back to basics. This was equivalent to fabulous business training for Jack and the others.

They won the semi-final by one point after extra time. Ron, who kept his head when others around him were losing theirs, was the star of the team. He held up the ball for that extra split second which allowed his teammates to restructure and focus. St Patrick's were now in the All-Ireland final for the first time in the long history of the college. The game was scheduled to be played on Sunday week at 3 p.m. The preparations and the tension intensified as the team members had their egos massaged in all sorts of ways.

One tangible indicator of this massage of ego was in the refectory. The cooks pulled the team members together at a special table. They had organised a special meal which included raw eggs floating in glasses of milk. The team members should drink this. They could eat as much red meat as they wanted. This was supposed to bring the adrenaline out in them.

Most of the teachers got into the spirit of the occasion and waived the normal rules and regulations. However, Father O'Keeffe saw this hype as a distraction from the core job of education and the necessity for structure and discipline. As the tide flowed in one direction, he rowed hard in the opposite direction. When he came in, one of the young teachers, angry but controlling his voice, said that he was 'a jealous spoilsport'.

Apart from his strap, Father O'Keeffe had a big stick. This stick was his shout in clear language to the team and supporters that any individual who did not conform to the rules or slacked in class would be punished by refusal of permission to go to the All-Ireland.

On the morning of the All-Ireland, a fleet of hired busses arrived in convoy and parked in a line at the front of the college. Breakfast was early. In addition to porridge, the cooks and kitchen staff wheeled out steaming plates with cooked breakfasts of two sausages, a rasher and a fried egg. The students hadn't tasted anything like it since their holidays. The team and Sticky boarded the lead bus, which had the special word 'Team' in large black letters on big white boards on the front, side and back.

The game was scheduled to start at Crory Park at 3 p.m. The buses carrying the supporters and the team of St Patrick's arrived at the pitch at 2 p.m. and parked close to the entrance gate. This was, on the priest's advice to the drivers, to ensure that none of the students sneaked away down town to smoke, buy dirty magazines, create trouble or meet girls. A teacher supervised each bus and was responsible for its numbers.

St Patrick's team moved into the designated dressing room and togged out in their new set of college jerseys. The team fussed about broken laces, cog nails coming through the soles of the football boots and engaged in dressing-room horseplay. Different players act differently in tense situations. Some are calm and take it in their stride. Others are tense and get physically sick. They get butterflies in the stomach.

Sticky said that if a player is so laid back that he doesn't get butterflies, he is unlikely to get the finger out in the playing field at the white-heat moments. Managing the balance between laid back and butterflies is the trick. This is where the leadership of the captain is so important. Jack was the captain and knew how to micro-manage the individuals so that he could be effective at macro-managing the team.

As the team got ready, a player said that he had heard a rumour. The rumour was that the opposition's St Munn's key county player, seriously injured in the semi final and not expected to play, was, in fact, going to play. Nobody could tell where the rumour had come from. In this dressing room the door was locked from the inside so that nobody from the outside could communicate with anyone inside. There were no mobile phones then. The rumour spread like wildfire and created fear within the team.

Jack showed his leadership. While Sticky panicked and those around him panicked, Jack stood up on the bench and addressed the team. He traced their journey to this point and challenged them. He asked, 'Are you happy just to participate, or do you want to win?' They yelled a feeble 'Ya! Ya! Ya!' Then he said, 'Are you all prepared to pay the price? You must win your individual battles and back up your teammates when they are in trouble.'

They yelled a stronger 'Ya! Ya! Ya!'

The he addressed the rumour that the star county player from the other side was going to play. 'I hope he is. Furthermore, I am going to take the responsibility of marking him. Now are you all up for it?'

Their 'Ya! Ya! Ya!' was now an animal roar.

Jack finished his address: 'Take pride in this jersey and ensure that your fellow students and your parents and neighbours out there can be proud of your achievement and go away after the match with their heads held high. Now let's focus and make this happen'.

Sticky then stood up on the bench. He seconded everything that Jack had said: 'Do it for yourself, your jersey and your local club.'

The reverend president of the college stood on the bench and muttered that he needed to say something. However, he was physically and mentally isolated from the journey to date of this team. Being the smart man he was, he didn't try to bullshit it. He just said a prayer, blessed all present and wished Jack and his team all the best over the following two hours.

The sap was rising. The officials threw, or rather flung, the door open and the team burst out onto the green pitch in the afternoon sun to an almighty roar from the hundreds of college supporters and hundreds more neighbours and friends.

Jack's parents, cousins and extended relations were in the roaring crowd. They too were riding on the coat-tails of St Patrick's achievement and reputation. Mick Denny Bill and Mary Anne allowed themselves to express a quiet and reserved pride with a smile and a nod to their neighbours. They now had a status within the parish as neighbours kept enquiring about the progress of Jack's team for weeks before this final. Jack's local football club organised a special bus to take the neighbours to the match. Some of the club's minors wore the club football jerseys as a statement of intent.

St Patrick's supporters used bugles, hooters and drums to keep the vocal support going and to give some structure and context to the songs. This was personal. They were directly competing with their counterparts on the other side. This involvement empowered them and gave them a direct and tangible part in this team effort.

The Sunday newspaper had devoted a half page with an article and photographs to this All-Ireland. The article analysed the pros and cons of both teams and concluded that it would be a very tight match between two good, competitive teams. The article called for a 'moment of magic' to divide the teams and decide who should win.

Jack got his hands on the first ball and shifted a heavy tackle. He was now into it. The game was tentative, lacklustre and lacked cohesion for the first ten minutes. David, the full back, allowed a high-dropping ball slip out of his grip into the back of the net for a goal for St Munn's. St Patrick's was down two points at half time, but that was okay as Jack saw it. They would have the wind to their back in the second half.

At half time, Sticky and Jack tried to refocus the team members using a combination of tactics. They included cajoling and threats to substitute some players if they didn't start winning their individual duels.

Early in the second half, Jack fielded a high ball around the middle of the pitch. Using his strong physique and skill, he soloed through the middle, breaking tackle after tackle with other defenders standing off him as they expected that he would pass the ball out. But, on and on went Jack. He then took an accurate rasping shot that went straight to the back of the opposition's net. This was, as the Sunday newspaper recorded, 'the delivery of the moment of magic'. The smiles on the faces of the supporters were smiles of ecstasy. St Patrick's was now in front for the first time.

One player from St Patrick's and one from St Munn's were put off for foul play. As the match entered the last five minutes, it was on a knife-edge. The St Patrick's boys renewed their support by knocking the utmost with all their energy out of their noisy instruments and their throats. They shouted at the referee to blow the final whistle. The opposition's last throw of the dice was to lob a high ball into St Patrick's goalmouth.

As the ball floated goalwards through the air, the tension and silence was dreadful. Jack plucked the ball out of the air and brought it to safety out of the danger area. Being smart, he held the ball long enough to draw in an unfair tackle. This resulted in a free out. It was the last kick of the game as the referee blew the final whistle. Jack and his teammates had made college history.

The college students and their parents invaded the pitch. Jack and his teammates were mobbed. The mob raised them shoulder high and carried them towards the stand for the presentation of the All-Ireland Cup. Jack and the team members made their way up the steps of the stand towards the presentation platform. The GAA President made a speech in Irish, praising both sides for providing a good sporting game and congratulating Jack and his team for making history for St Patrick's. Amidst a massive roar from St Patrick's supporters, he presented the cup to Jack.

Jack delivered his prepared speech which he and Sticky had previously prepared based on the assumption that they would win. He thanked the opposition for their stiff competition and also for the fact that they had reached the final for the second time in three years. He called for three cheers for them. He got a great response from his own supporters.

He thanked his teammates for their dedication and commitment, the college for their support and Father Maughan for all his guidance and support through this long journey. He thanked his club for nurturing the love of football in him and, in a special way, he thanked his parents for making him 'the man he is today'. Without his mother's vision and determination and his father's silent support, he would never have had this wonderful opportunity.

This was a proud moment for Mary Anne. Part of her dream had come true; but in her own silence there were other parts to this picture to be energised in the future. When Jack met his parents out on the pitch with the cup, his mother gave him a hug that was firmer than any before. This was special to him. His private, quiet, father, who said little and internalised everything and seldom before displayed emotion even in private, now hugged him with tears in his eyes. He saw his own private dream now happening through the medium of Jack.

Out on the pitch, the backslapping, the carrying on shoulders and the commotion went on for ages.

Jack tugged the cup back through the crowd and into the dressing room. The scenes of emotion were poignant. The price they had paid over the last five years as students in the college were, at this moment, worth it. This was an opportunity they couldn't have had elsewhere. The college president entered the dressing room. Someone called for silence. The college president congratulated Father Maughan and his team for doing the college proud. He announced that there would be special celebrations back in the college tonight and that there would be a half day from classes for everyone tomorrow. He announced, to hardly containable cheers, that the team members would have the full day off.

Sticky and Jack went into the competitors' dressing room and commiserated with their enemies. They got respect. And they gave respect back.

Their enemies were now friends. Down the corridor, the college president of St Munn's and Father McCarthy were in discussion with each other. Perhaps they were friends too.

After showering and dressing, the team members brought the cup out to their still-cheering supporters again. Jack spent some time with Mary Anne and Mick Denny Bill. He tried to make some sense of it all. He was so happy to make them so proud. Aunt Sheila was unable to make it to the match, his mother whispered to him. It was due to poor health, she said.

As Jack made his way back to the team bus, his mother had another whisper in his ear. She whispered that the Leaving Certificate examination was the next high mountain he had to climb. That was all. Her timing and her relative priority struck a subconscious chord.

Sticky joined in the cheers and singing in the bus on the way back to the college. He sang a number of rebel songs fuelling the mood for the rest of the celebrations. As they approached the college they saw a glow in the sky. It was the glow from a massive bonfire burning in the middle of the college quad yard. The students alighted from the buses and joined the crowd, the singing and the music around the fire.

The celebrations went on until 11 p.m., and then the bedtime bell, which hadn't been pulled at its normal time, gonged. The college president stood on a chair and addressed the students. He again said how proud they all were and congratulated Jack and his team for making history for the college. He officially announced the half day from class as a massive roar erupted. He asked for silence as he delivered the night prayers, which included of a prayer of thanks to the Almighty God for this wonderful event. Joe, the caretaker, took charge of quenching the fire safely as all departed for bed.

Jack twisted and turned all night. He couldn't wind down enough to get to sleep. Father McCarthy told him and his teammates to stay in bed until 10 a.m. the following morning and that Father Maughan would say a special Mass at 10.30 a.m. just for the team members. He said that there would be a special celebratory breakfast for the group after Mass. The rest of the students returned to their normal routine, except that on this Monday, they had a half day off.

Books, magazines and papers were strictly censored in the college.

However, on this occasion, the sports pages of the two daily newspapers were put up on the notice boards to be read by all students. The newspapers had photographs of the presentation of the cup and a full match analysis. The students formed a queue ten deep in front of the notice boards trying to read the analysis and who got special mention. Father McCarthy handed out individual copies of the full paper to the team and subs as a memento of the great occasion. He allowed them to bring them into the refectory and read them as they had their celebratory breakfast.

After the breakfast there were more speeches and back slapping. The lads were still on a high. As the celebrations tailed off, it dawned on Jack that, like disappointment, celebrations too are a passing event. The reality of life kicks in over time.

Mary Anne's post-match comment to Jack was telling. She was mentally preparing Jack for the time space past the victory celebrations where reality needed to be faced once more. As the days moved into weeks, the victory became a piece of history. The high mountain now facing the senior students was the Leaving Certificate examination.

Two big issues facing Jack were his participation with the county minor football team and his life after his exams. Because of his college football performance, his place on the county team was assured. They had a number of organised training sessions. This allowed Jack to get out of the college and start to adjust to life outside.

The county selectors and mentors were interested in ensuring that Jack would stay around for the good of the team and for their own ego enhancement. To energise this wish, they were prepared to offer him some jobs locally. Jack had yet an unclear vision of his future, but it was certainly bigger and wider than what they were painting for him. In any case, he played along with their agenda in the interim and enjoyed the football. They reached the All-Ireland semi-final, but were beaten by the eventual winners.

Running parallel with his involvement with the county minor team, Jack played a star role with his own club minor team and also played on the senior team. During the senior matches, some of the older opposition players tried to put a stop to his gallop. He shifted some very heavy tackles but, because of his speed, didn't sustain any serious injuries.

Back in the college all the focus was on the forthcoming exams. Father

O'Keeffe, better known as Sparky, tried to keep a shape to the academic year and get the desired exam results. The college prided itself on its academic results at any cost – this was the real measurement. What gets measured tends to get done. Football and other extra curricular activities were down the priority scale within the traditional culture of the college.

Jack did what he wanted to do and saw this formal education process as a means to an end. The students in the higher grade classes swotted to a dangerous point as they viewed the exam, and its results, as an end in itself.

The exam start date arrived. The study and sports' halls were laid out in neat, numbered rows of desks suitably spaced far enough apart to prevent copying. The tension around now, while intense, was of a different type to that which was present prior to the All-Ireland football final. It was more of a cloak-and-dagger type. Various rumours and tips went around. If you were adequately prepared to answer the range of tips, you would have the whole curriculum covered and then there would be no need to be worried about tips. It was like a horse-race meeting where you are given a range of tips. Put money on every tip you get and you will have all the horses in the race backed. This wouldn't be logical.

Jack was bored with the whole focus on the exam. He decided that he had to make one last imprint on the college before he finally left. Since the All-Ireland, he walked on air and, in the eyes of the authorities, he could do no wrong. On the night before the last exam he organised the other less academic lads like himself to gather up their text books and notes on Latin, Greek, Irish and the other subjects that they hated. They then organised a march from the quad yard to outside the front gate and made a bonfire of the lot.

As the literature of ages burned, they danced around the fire and adopted the ritual of spitting into the fire. This was their statement about how they really felt about both the methodology of the teaching and the impracticality of the subject matter as they then saw it. The college authorities were shocked but they were smart enough to resist their natural reaction. They just ignored the incident.

On the following day, the exams were over. Parents, including Mary Anne and Mick Denny Bill, arrived in their cars. Jack and his schoolmates of five years drove out the front gates of the college and over the ashes of their formal learning.

Jack was home for some days when it dawned on him that the door he had come through was now shut. He needed to move on to the next station, the next milestone of his life. The football kept him going. He took up one of the job offers arranged by one of the county selectors. This was an office job. The money was good, but the job itself was confining and boring, although the girls working alongside Jack interested him. The girl with the large, smiling blue eyes interested him more than the others.

Mary Anne had driven the education agenda to provide an alternative option for Jack and his siblings. Emigration was the traditional normal release valve in this rural area. In her own mind, Mary Anne had earmarked Jack for a nice pensionable job near home.

Jack wanted to kick the traces and find space to clarify his own vision. At eighteen years of age, the last thing a high-testosterone lad was interested in was a nice pensionable job near home. When he was in Dublin after the All-Ireland semi-final, he decided that he would go now rather than return home and have to battle the expected resistances. Joe, a playing team-mate, also decided to accompany him.

They went to the North Wall and purchased two one-way tickets on the cattle-cum-passenger ship to Holyhead. Jack had last week's wages, the clothes on his back and his football gear as he stepped onto the ship. The ticket cost £3, which was the same price as the train ticket from Dublin to Jack's local railway station.

They set sail with adrenaline pumping due to a combination of excitement, expectation and fear. Jack wrote, stamped and posted a letter to Mary Anne before they boarded. In his letter he tried to explain his vision and the decision he had made. Mary Anne read the letter with shock, disappointment and disbelief.

Jack's departure devastated her on the inside, but she played a game on the outside. She informed the neighbours that Jack had received an offer to play with a team in England and that they had organised everything. In any case, if he didn't like it, he could always come home and get a good job. Mary Anne dumped the blame on Mick Denny Bill. She made him suffer in silence in subtle ways for a long time.

This was the closing of another chapter on Jack's journey. Like the security double doors going into a bank, you have to close one before the next one will open.

What the Priest told Jack

- **Yesterday's victory is history.** Jack, like all sportspeople, knew that he could not live the rest of his life based on past victories. The next challenge had to be faced. Taking the boat to England was a manifestation of this.

- **John F. Kennedy advised us: 'We should not let our fears hold us back from pursuing our hopes.'** Fear is one of the biggest barriers to our forward journey. Uncertainty about the future fuels this fear.

- **People in authority have a greater influencing effect than they often realise.** The three new teachers teaching Jack's class tried to create an interest and a hunger in their students so that they could see the link between the subject matter and their daily lives. They encouraged them to ask questions and they responded in practical ways. An academic ray of light began to shine for Jack.

- **Individual sports have fewer variables to manage than team sports.** The team comprises fifteen individual players who have to be blended so that, as Gestalt Theory says, 'The total is greater than the sum of its individual parts.' This often means that certain individuals have to sacrifice their individual talents and adopt a predetermined team role.

I do not hesitate to say that the road to eminence and power, from an obscure condition, ought not to be made too easy, nor a thing too much, of course. If rare merit be the rarest of all rare things, it ought to pass through some sort of probation. The temple of honour ought to be seated on an eminence. If it be open through virtue, let it be remembered, too, that virtue is never tried but by some difficulty and some struggle.

– Edmund Burke (1729–97)

Chapter 12

Emigrating to Uncertainty

Jack stood on the ship's deck that dark night as it moved away from the pier in the North Wall, leaving the streets of Dublin behind and sailed out from the harbour. As it hit the rough open sea, the ship rocked from side to side and the wooden benches on deck moved. This was a new experience for Jack. The shifting ground under him made him sick. It was worse than some of the heavy tackles he took from senior players who took pleasure in shaking the bones and stomachs of new and rising football stars.

This ship carried live cattle for the UK market on the lower deck and passengers on the upper deck. The cattle drovers were distinctive in their leather leggings and leather boots with their trousers tucked inside the leggings to keep them clean. Most wore long gabardine coats and all wore hats. They drove the cattle from the rail wagons onto the ship where they were held in cattle pens which had a good thickness of fresh straw and buckets of water.

In their normal environment of grazing away in their fields, the cattle had nothing to disturb them other than a few foxes, badgers, crows or a stray dog. Since the cattle fair they had been loaded onto the cattle wagons and transported to the North Wall on the overnight train. From the confines of these cattle wagons, they were now driven down the ramp to the holding pens in the lower deck of this ship. The drovers shouted and beat these frightened animals with sticks to force them onto another unfamiliar space for them.

It reminded Jack in a stark way of the horror of his early days in the college where the priests used the leather strap to beat the new boys into shape as they tried to come to terms with their new environment and culture.

On this ship there seemed to be more accommodation for the cattle than there was for people. Some passengers seemed to permanently occupy the wooden benches on the deck. This forced Jack and Joe to stand by the railing. From here they observed the city fading into the background. Some people around Jack and Joe vomited, leaving the contents of their stomachs on the deck. The sickly sight and smell of this vomit and the swaying of the ship moved Jack and Joe to get sick over the side. They had no mother nearby to comfort them. They felt sorry for themselves.

They noticed that the seasoned travellers were lying down rather than standing up. They later learned that you need to lie down and go with the sway of the boat rather than resist it. The resistance upsets the equilibrium in the stomach.

The crossing was scheduled to take seven hours, but because of the stormy night, it took nine. A woman on the ship felt sorry for them and advised them that the important thing about seasickness is that it disappears as you walk onto dry land. She asked them questions about where they were going and whether they had jobs. These were the questions that Jack had on his mind, but was too afraid even to ask himself. He emigrated on impulse. He was really running away from something rather than running towards something. He had no plan. He hoped that it would be okay on the day.

Dawn broke and they saw land. As the ship drew nearer to the coast of Wales, it hit calmer waters and eventually glided into its docking position. A team of sailors lowered the foot-step rail and the passengers walked off. As they disembarked, customs officers in their black uniforms and white shirts stopped Jack and Joe. They had few possessions, and they allowed them pass through easily.

The border police in blue uniforms were their next barrier to entry. Jack and Joe had no passports. When the police questioned them about their identity they showed their student cards. The police asked where they had come from, where they were going and for what purpose – and quickly saw just two raw young fellows coming to the mainland with stars in their eyes. They matched none of the profiles for subversives.

Now that they were through these entry barriers, the big question facing them was where to go from here. Jack decided that they would take the bus to Liverpool as he knew that there was a large Irish population there. He had also heard about the Liverpool football team. They bought one-way tickets to Liverpool with five pounds sterling and boarded the bus. They now felt better. They were on dry land and they were going somewhere, even if they had no idea where Liverpool might lead them.

On the bus they fell asleep. Their next conscious moment was when an inspector entered to check the passenger tickets. Jack had thought of chancing the journey without a ticket in order to preserve his limited cash, but decided to be honourable and honest.

As the bus went through Birkenhead, they entered the connecting tunnel with Liverpool. They had never been in a tunnel before. They were excited to see the double lane of traffic, each vehicle with lights on and each lane going in opposite directions. When the bus emerged on the other side it took a few seconds for their eyes to adjust to the intensity of daylight. The bus pulled into the central bus station, and all the passengers disembarked.

Jack and Joe were now at a new crossroads. They had no map and no plan. They needed to get somewhere to stay and needed to look for jobs. They were the blind leading the blind, but they took comfort in each other's company, figuratively and literally. They walked aimlessly – their stress and panic leading them to exhaustion. They drifted from the station towards an old residential part of the city where they spotted a number of signs for digs. They went to the first landlady and booked two beds for one night.

The landlady was well used to this scenario – she asked few questions. The rate was one pound sterling per bed per night. When they took out their money, Jack and Joe remembered that it was Irish money, but they had £2 sterling, the change from the bus tickets.

The dormitory-type room reminded Jack of the unpleasant times he spent in dormitories at St Patrick's. As she showed them the room, the landlady told them that the third bed in the room belonged to John, another Irishman who would be home at around 8 p.m. She showed them where the nearest bank was so that they could change their Irish money into sterling.

Down the street was a café. There they had a feed of fish and chips and mushy peas. They had nothing else to eat as they were watching their money. They returned to their digs at 7.30 p.m., went to bed and fell into a deep sleep. They didn't hear John coming in from work and later getting into bed.

John's cursing and farting wakened them as he got out of bed for another day's work. Jack and Joe pretended to be asleep until he was gone. They both got up at 8 a.m. and, after a quick lick of water on their faces, came down for an Irish breakfast of porridge and a fry. Serving them breakfast, the landlady asked if they intended to stay longer or if they were vacating their beds this morning.

They told the landlady their embellished but sanitised story and added that they were looking for work. They asked her if she knew of any. She had been through this many times over the years. She said that there was a lot of building going on at the far side of the city and that they should go to the sites and ask for a start. She looked at them carefully and told them that a prospective employer would likely regard them as too clean-cut and raw to be taken seriously. The only way they were going to survive was to start somewhere. They decided that they would book the beds for two more nights. Based on the success of their job hunting, they would then decide whether to stay or go.

After breakfast, they left their battered suitcases on their beds. They walked in the direction the landlady had indicated and came to a building site. They stood outside the gate wondering what to do and whom to ask for. The more they thought about it, the more frightening the task seemed to become. Feeling the pain of the harsh reality they had manoeuvred themselves into, they forced themselves to tiptoe into the site and ask for the foreman.

The tea man pointed him out at the far end of the site. Jack and Joe walked over the rough site ground through the foundations. Just as they neared the foreman, Joe stumbled over the plumb-line being used to mark out the foundations. The foreman saw this and shouted at them to get off this building site before he would kick them out. They retreated as quickly as they could.

Over the course of the day, they went into six other building sites. They returned to their digs, hungry and dejected. The landlady's food was poor but plentiful. Hunger transcends all niceties.

John, their cursing and farting roommate, returned from work and sat down to eat his dinner. Contrary to their first impression, he was a personable type, aged about thirty-five years. He told them his life story. He had been married in Westmeath and had one child. He had married into his wife's farm. He could not get on with her mother who lived in the house with them. They had many rows. One day he just walked out and never went back. He didn't know what the situation was there now. They had no contact with him either. He fell on bad times when he first came over to Liverpool. He drank a lot of alcohol. He moved around from digs to digs and from job to job. He just existed.

When he had got his story off his chest, the lads got a chance to say something. They gave him a brief scenario of their predicament and said that they were looking for work. John told them that the foreman on the building site where he now worked was looking for labourers. The project had to be completed over the next two weeks while the factory was closed for its annual break. He told them that it was all jackhammer work, operating in a very narrow and dusty space, but that the money was good and there was lots of overtime to be had. He offered to bring them to the site the following morning and introduce them to the foreman.

On the following morning, same time as John, they got up at 5a.m. They had breakfast together and accompanied him to the pick-up point, where the company bus collected them at 6.30 a.m. The bus drove through the Mersey Tunnel to Birkenhead and eventually pulled into a large industrial complex. All the lads, many of them with Irish accents, went to the entrance to clock in. John took the lads to the foreman and told him that they were looking for a start.

Aby was Irish. He questioned Jack and Joe to see if they knew anything about building. Jack spoke up and told him about his experience. By implication, Joe was riding on this too. Aby said he had this very dirty contract which had to be finished within two weeks, and he was putting together teams to cover two twelve-hour shifts starting that night at 8 p.m. He said that they should be at the bus stop at 7 p.m., and he would start them then.

They were elated and, as a reward to themselves, they took the shuttle boat from Birkenhead back to Liverpool. It was such a nice day that they walked into the centre of Liverpool for a look around at the streets and the sights.

They came back to the digs at 2 p.m. and told the landlady that they had got two weeks' work operating night shifts which were to run from 8 p.m. to 8 a.m. They needed dinner at 6 p.m. and breakfast at 9 a.m. when they got home after working the night shift. She agreed. They went to bed to get some sleep before the night shift. The landlady called them at 5 p.m. They had their dinner and then made their way to the bus stop at 6 p.m. The bus, with thirty men on board, arrived at the site at 7 p.m. All except Jack and Joe, who were still in their travel clothes, were dressed in old working clothes and boots.

On arrival, Aby gave them their time cards and took down their basic details. He then took the team into the depths of the building. This was a huge paper-manufacturing factory, and the project to be completed was to remove a concrete compression chamber to make way for new machinery. There were thirty men on each shift. Aby divided the men into pairs at random and told them to hold this pairing for the next two weeks.

He paired Jack with a weather-beaten man from Galway. Their job was to cut channels on the concrete walls so that the reinforcing steel could be exposed. This would allow the steel cutters to use gas torches to cut the reinforcing steel. In turn, this would allow the sections of the wall to be lifted off by crane. The job that Jack and the other crew members had to do was to jackhammer away the concrete in straight lines so as to expose the reinforcing steel. This compression chamber was in the depths of the factory with no natural light or air circulating. The job involved fifteen jackhammers cutting five vertical channels in the wall. Treble-deck scaffolding was built up against the wall. Five teams of two operated on the top deck, five more on the middle deck and the other five at ground level.

Aby told Jack and his Galway partner, Matty, to go to work on the middle deck. The dust and debris from the deck above fell continuously down on and around them. One of the pair held the jackhammer horizontally and tried to make an impression on the hard concrete wall while his partner tried to hold and balance the hammer. This horizontal position was difficult. The jackhammer is designed to operate in a vertical mode with its natural weight providing the resistance for the compressed air to operate and provide the hammering effect. This was not naturally available when using the jackhammer in the horizontal mode. The operators had to constantly apply their body weight against the jackhammer in order for it to work effectively. Jack felt his insides being shifted from their sockets from the vibration, but on and on went the process.

Jack and the others had no ear muffs, dust pads or eye goggles to safeguard them from the massive noise and dust of working all these jackhammers in such a confined space.

Jack and Matty sweated in this hostile environment as they tried to hold their jackhammer in the horizontal position and apply the necessary body weight so that the hammer bit could make an impression on the tough concrete wall. The drill bit kept slipping off the wall so that they had a mighty effort to keep it on track.

Aby and his ganger kept a close watch on the teams. He measured their progress by the length of the chase cut during the twelve-hour shift. While Jack was physically fit for football, it was no preparation for this slavish job. Matty had a lot of jackhammer experience and told Jack that this was the most difficult and dangerous job he had ever been on. In reality, that's why this job was available to Jack and his likes.

When the hooter sounded, the jackhammer noise stopped and the men got down from the scaffolding, going to the toilets and the canteen. Jack's muscles twitched. He had a ringing in his ears and his eyes watered. He felt he was in a mess. This was the decision he made when he succumbed to the rush of blood to his head and made the impulsive decision to take the cattle boat to England.

They got what appeared to be good food and drink in the canteen. Then the hooter went off and they were ordered back to the job. The noise and the dust rose again. Later, one of the jackhammers slipped and fell down on to the second deck and hit one of the crew members. He was knocked out and was quickly taken by ambulance from the scene. The rest of the crew were ordered back to work immediately as there was a tight deadline to be met. Jack later heard that the injured man died on the way to hospital. He was an Irish man and had worked on building sites for years. He seemed to have no family connections. To Jack, this was sad and distressing. To others, it was just life. Injury or death could not be allowed to delay meeting the deadline.

The hooter went at the end of the shift and they made their way out into the open air. Their hair and faces and overalls were covered in a grey dust. The bus arrived and they crowded in and made their way back to Liverpool and their digs. The landlady looked at them and wondered how long they would last. She told them that they could have a warm bath on Saturday night. They ate their breakfast, went straight to bed and slept deeply. She called them at 5.30 p.m. for dinner. Their heads were ringing and their muscles ached. They battled with their bodies to get out of bed.

They went to the bus stop, and the cycle started again. In the evening, an officer from head office came around to check their time cards. Jack noticed a number of the men asking for a sub. Matty explained that a sub meant that you could get part-paid on Tuesday and not have to wait until the following Thursday for your pay package. Being short of funds, Jack arranged with the officer to get a sub of £40 even though he didn't know when he would have time to spend it. Joe did likewise. He replicated every move that Jack made.

The cycle went on night after night with no letup. Jack and Joe were afraid to call a sicky and not turn up for work. They won the debate in their own minds and kept going on the bus, clocking in, swallowing dust, stretching their muscles and putting their health at risk for the sake of money and pride that they had done the right thing in coming to Liverpool. On Thursday they got their first pay-package. When they looked at the payslip, they were pleasantly surprised to find that there was a bonus called 'dirt money' and a special bonus for night-time shift work. It didn't make the job any easier. But at least they had £100, less the £40 sub, now in their pockets.

It was strange for Jack to have to work the first Sunday. At home he would have gone to Mass and probably have played a football match while the rest of the family and neighbours just relaxed and punched in the day.

Here they went to bed after breakfast and caught the bus to go into work at approximately the same time that back home in Ireland they would be looking for a lift into town to attend the dance with just enough money to get in the door. This was a different country and a different scene. Here, they had money.

Over the two weeks Jack found that he got on well with Matty, and they worked out a system to get the work done. Aby was pleasantly surprised as he didn't expect Jack and Joe to last the pace. Aby was from Wicklow and had played a lot of football with his local team. He had been in England for twenty-five years and had kept up his interest in the football championship.

He always got the Monday Irish newspapers and listened to Michael O'Hehir's broadcasts of the big matches whenever he could get good reception on Sundays. When he found out that Jack was a footballer, he spoke with him at the meal breaks about the old players and the current games. He was a great admirer of Kerry football, and Mick O'Connell was his hero. He said that O'Connell gathered the ball so high in the air that there was often ice on it on his way back to earth.

Jack stopped fighting the hard work. Instead, he got stuck in and decided that the sacrifice for two weeks would be worth it. It would give him money to get working clothes, it would give him experience and it would give him time to get settled in.

At the end of the two weeks, Joe had enough and decided to go back home to his mother. Jack was tempted to go home with Joe, but his pride prevented him from doing so. He defeated the urge.

He worked the fourteen nights without stop. By then, he was shattered and decided that he needed to take a break. Aby told them that he was moving to a more regular contract the following week. He offered him a job which Jack was delighted to accept. With the two days' break, Jack had time to have a good long bath and buy some suitable working clothes. He paid the price for initiation into the life of a navvy. He survived, and he succeeded.

One of the lads on the job told him that he should go to the Irish Centre in Liverpool. He ordered his first beer to try and wash down the dust that was stuck in his gullet. He had broken into another dimension of the life of an Irish navvy in Liverpool.

As agreed, he went to the designated bus stop at 6.30 a.m. and mounted the bus for his new job. Aby was there and booked him in and got his job card. The building site was an oil storage depot in which massive silos stored the oil from the shipping tankers which came and went in the nearby port. This was day work, and it was out in the open air. They finished at 5 p.m., allowing Jack to be back in his digs with his landlady at 6.15 p.m. for dinner.

Their main job was digging trenches and pulling cables. All the trenches had to be hand-dug using picks and shovels – no mechanical diggers were allowed on site due to fire-safety precautions. Because of that, the crews were bigger than for the previous job, and there was less focus on meeting deadlines.

The crews were mature. Jack was the only newcomer. He was the youngest on site, and as such they tended to adopt him. Many of the older crew had perfected the art of appearing to be busy, but at the same time doing little. Jack found this a very difficult art. He was forever watchful in case he would be caught idle. He feared being sacked.

To Jack, the mental torture of trying to appear busy was more stressful than working hard.

Tim was a boxer at weekends and a ganger by day. He was Jack's immediate boss. He was a champion in amateur boxing in his local Dublin club, and when he came to Liverpool, he found there was a niche for professional boxing around the drinking clubs at the weekends. Many of the men's drinking clubs had makeshift boxing rings. They matched up the boxers who fought for small purses and ran unofficial betting scams with the winning boxer's team taking all.

Tim was a wiry fighter and carried a photograph of himself in the ring with an ex-British Commonwealth champion whom he had beaten at a pub brawl. He kept inviting the lads to certain fights. He had a betting scam whereby he would let the lads know which night he was prepared to throw the fight so that they could win money on their bets. They gave him 10 per cent of their winnings for this insider information. They didn't yet know enough about Jack to trust him and invite him to participate in one of their betting scams.

The cable-pulling gang, of which Tim was in charge, comprised ten to twelve men dragging heavy electric cable through pipes in the ground from electric substations to connection points out at the oil silos where the electrical power was required. It was heavy work. It required good coordination from the pulling team, who used the scientific techniques employed in Tug-of-War. Tim was the master, and when he got tired of shouting, he used a whistle to indicate when the team should pull and when to slack.

As the distance from the substations grew longer, the resistance friction between the cable and the surrounding pipes grew, and therefore required greater pulling power to get the cable to its designated point. The gang discussed this resistance at length and tried all sorts of practical tricks, techniques and tactics to reduce it. Their best tactic seemed to be to scatter gritty sand along the pipes so that the cable would roll along easier on the grit.

As Jack listened and watched, he suddenly recalled his science lessons from school. His teacher had talked about friction resistance and had used various mathematical formulae to calculate it. None of it made any sense to him at the time. Here he was, in the middle of an oil storage depot with a gang of Irish and Welsh navvies talking naturally about how they made their job easier by using gritty sand to reduce the friction. This was another lesson for Jack – he now saw that education is about learning how to formulate and apply practical solutions to real problems.

The navvies' hut was an eye opener for Jack. The walls were plastered with newspaper pictures of Page 3 girls in different poses showing off their breasts. To Jack, the funny thing was that nobody seemed to notice. Nobody seemed to notice either the course language of the navvies laden with sex, jokes, cursing and swearing. The intensity and detail both excited and shocked him. This all-male environment was all talk about sex and probably little follow-on action. Jack later learned in life that those who talk most about sex do less of it. He recalled from Shakespeare in his studies for the Leaving Certificate a quotation which said 'He protests too much,' and he recalled his mother's saying: 'Empty vessels make the most noise.'

Jack used the opportunity to work seven days per week, since he had no agenda or facilities to spend his spare time and the landlady didn't want her tenants hanging around during the day.

On one Sunday off from work, Jack went to the new cathedral to attend Mass. From there he went to the central station and picked a strategic seat so that he could watch the crowd come and go. He let his mind wander and imagined stories about the people he observed. He tried to match people to jobs and roles. He was probably wrong most of the time, but his hobby, which he picked up while in St Patrick's, helped him to fill in time. His mind wandered to wondering what life and work was all about. There must be more to life than this, he thought to himself.

Jack remembered what Mary Anne had said. When you seek clarity, let your mind wander. Then write your thoughts down quickly on paper. He wrote his thoughts with a stub of pencil on two or three sheets of paper that he always kept in his pocket. Every evening he transcribed his notes into a notebook that he kept in the locker beside his bed.

He wrote that the navvies living in the lodging houses lived their lives around work, for six to seven days per week, and around the pub. He wrote that he observed that their routine was bed to work, then into the pub, and eventually back to their digs and to bed, and work, and the pub again. As the years passed, they became institutionalised into this routine and lost most of the linkage they had with home and their other interests.

Jack learned, by observation and by listening and asking questions as he got to know more and more of the lads on the site, that many were running from their past and were now on the road to nowhere. Some had been married and had families, but had left in rage over some issue, always meaning to retrace their steps. As time went by, it became more difficult, and their dreams just became dreams. Some men came and worked on the building sites in winter and returned to their little farms and families in Ireland in the spring. They had a mission to make as much money as possible. They worked all the hours available and saved their money to send home. As time went by, some stayed longer and went home to Ireland for shorter periods.

They went home to attend the christening of a child, to experience love and affection again, or to impregnate their wives with another child. Many were troubled and relied on the temporary euphoria generated from alcoholic drink to help them through. Their temporary problem became permanent. During drinking sessions, they socialised with others who had failed or were on the treadmill and would be comforted by pulling others down to their level.

Jack observed and interacted with them. He wrote in his notebook that they were basically good people, but they were the victims of certain circumstances as they grew up. He put them into categories:

> Those who were over just to make money and go home;
> Those who were running away from the courts and family commitments;
> Those who were victims of industrial schools;
> Those who were victims of the formal education system and abuse of all sorts.

Jack had cut off all contact with home after posting that letter to his mother from the North Wall informing her that he was going to England. Now that he had adapted to the navvy routine, he wrote a letter to her, using what was known at the time as a letter card. This was a pre-stamped package which he bought at the post office. There was room to write his message. He licked the sides to seal it up on three sides.

Like many emigrants writing home, Jack varnished the truth in his letter. He described how well he had settled and that the job was going well and that he was very happy with the digs he lived in. He enclosed a £10 note for his mother to go and buy a watch for herself. She never had a watch but often hinted that someday, when the children were reared, she would buy one.

Parents of the time, especially mothers, did without their little pleasures of life so that they could put together enough money to pay for their children's educations. They were prepared to pay the necessary price in order to make this happen. Mary Anne was just such a woman.

Now Jack was giving her some token of reward for her sacrifice. She was delighted to get his letter card and its contents. However, Jack's address was missing. She saw from the postmark that the lettercard was posted in Birkenhead. That was as close as she could get to know his whereabouts. Because of pride and self survival, she didn't make her feelings known to the inquisitive neighbours. She played the games that all people play to keep face.

As the weeks moved into months, Jack got restless and felt that he should advance beyond being a navvy. He observed that there was a hierarchical structure within the building site. In priority order there was the boss, the engineers, the architects, the wages' officer, and then the site foreman. Then followed the gangers.

At the bottom of the hierarchy were the navvies who were used and abused like slaves. If it suited the boss, they could be sacked at a moment's notice or forced to work inordinate hours, often under horrifically dangerous conditions. The more Jack reflected on this, the clearer his vision became. He knew he didn't want to finish up at the bottom rung of this ladder. That was a big decision. As of yet he had no plan or strategy to climb the ladder.

Working in a drain on a building site one wet November day, he sweated as he cleared the muck and the stones left behind the JCB digger. He saw that the digger driver sat in dry conditions working the machine's hydraulics in the protection of his cab while Jack himself stood in the hole shovelling muck, wet to the skin, for much less pay.

Jack worked it out in his head that the majority of the lads were stuck working in wet drains and holes shovelling muck, while the minority were up on dry land looking down on them. To those working in the drains, those above just seemed to swagger about.

One day the foreman instructed Jack and three colleagues to take the site van and go to his home. Their task was to complete a job on his garden. It was a beautiful home and the plan for the garden was attractive. They worked as instructed for a number of days until the job was completed. The foreman's wife passed in and out without recognising that they existed. In Ireland, Jack reflected, each would have been welcomed personally and offered a cup of tea.

Some of the lads said that this work was being done at the expense of the company and that the time and material used was charged to the oil depot. The foreman told them not to mention this work if there were any enquiries from the wages' officer. He told them they should fill up their timesheets as if they were digging drains in the oil depot building site. Nobody questioned this. They knew the game they needed to play in order to survive. The game was: 'You scratch my back and I'll scratch yours.' Jack learned that the further people were up the hierarchy, the more options opened for them.

Jack was now fully integrated into the gang and was getting on with the usual daily rows over small things created by people with sore heads from the previous night's drinking. He was now being institutionalised into the system of work to bed to work. This was attractive from a wage viewpoint, but it had its price. At nineteen years of age, it was dawning on Jack that there had to be more to life than this vicious cycle.

The building site closed for three days over the Christmas holidays. Aby wanted an emergency team on duty. It was an eye-opener for Jack that a number of navvies wanted to work over Christmas. Jack put himself forward voluntarily for the work. This was going to be his first Christmas away from home, and his landlady didn't want him hanging around the digs for the three days. Aby picked him and two others to cover the three days. There was no work planned to be done – they were just to be there in case of an emergency. They were to cover three eight-hour shifts between them. They were paid treble time for the three days – just to be there.

The time he spent alone in the hut gave Jack an opportunity to look at where he had come from, where he was at and where he wanted to go. The more he reflected on this, the more he knew he needed to get out of this rut. He built up an impetus in his mind and decided that, after the holiday period, he would give Aby notice that he would quit.

When the site reopened after Christmas and the weather was very poor, the mental impetus that Jack had built up was gradually neutralised. His problem was that he knew he had to break, but he had no roadmap planned for himself. It is very difficult to change when you are faced with a vacuum. He settled back into the rut. Because he was in the vicious cycle of work to bed to work, he had enough activity to allow him to avoid the issue.

At Easter, Aby got seriously ill and was predicted to be to out of work for a number of months. Tim assumed his role. Tim was a reasonable club boxer and had a limited ability to manage the cable-pulling gang while under the supervision of Aby. But when the covering management of Aby was gone, he turned out to be a disaster. In management terms he had been promoted not just to the level of his competency, but beyond it. One day Tim came down to the building site and accused Jack of failing to complete his work. He then sacked him. He accused Jack in the wrong, and Jack looked to his colleagues to defend him and to stand up for him. Their own self-preservation was more important to them and instead they nodded agreement with Tim.

Having a series of witnesses does not, in itself, prove anything. They may have had apparent respectability, but the motivation for self-preservation can outweigh honesty.

Jack had no choice but to go.

What Jack Learned about Uncertainty

- **Are you running from something or towards something?** Many of the navvies that Jack met were running from some personal historical event, but were now more or less institutionalised in their role of digging the streets of England.

  Do you want something different?

  What is it?

  What is your game plan?

- **Uncertainty is very stressful.** Jack and Joe were now at a new crossroads. They had no map and no plan. They needed to get somewhere to stay and needed to look for jobs. They were the blind leading the blind, but they took comfort in each other's company, figuratively and literally. They walked aimlessly; their stress and panic leading them to exhaustion.

- **People learn to survive in their environment.** There is a management concept known as group think. It means that as a group settles down, the individual members get comfortable with each other irrespective of their dire circumstances. They tend to look out through the same window of life and see the same picture. In these circumstances, the group tends to sink together, since no one is prepared to stir it up.

Nothing is as it appears from the outside. 'You Westerners think you know it all. You come here with your fancy ideas and judge us through your own set of eyes. But, I'm OK as I see it from where I am sitting.'

– An old beggar woman to the author on a visit to Tula, Russia

- **Everything has a price.** Jack stopped fighting the hard work. Instead, he got stuck in and decided that the sacrifice would be worth it. It would give him money to get working clothes, it would give him experience and it would give him time to get settled in.

- **Having a series of witnesses does not, in itself, prove anything.** Jack's colleagues may have had apparent respectability, but their motivation for self-preservation outweighed their ability to stand up and be counted.

Chapter 13

The London Experience

He gathered his tools and clothes, went to the office to collect his cards and outstanding money and left the building site without saying farewell to anyone. He came back to his digs and told the landlady he was leaving immediately. He paid her for his outstanding bill, packed his bag and walked to the train station to catch the next train to London. He had accumulated £1,500 and felt that he was rich in comparison with the other navvies he worked with. They worked for money generally from week to week. By Monday, they were broke and had to look for a sub to carry them through to payday.

As he sat in the train carriage as it made its way down through England on its way towards London, Jack again had time to reflect on his situation. He was proud of his £1,500 and how he had survived on his own over the last nine months, but he knew that it was naught but a shallow victory. Something inside him told him that he could do better – what that better was he had no idea yet. Stories he had heard and ballads he had listened to about London told him that it would be all there to greet him when he arrived at Paddington Station.

When he got off the train, the sway of the crowd pulled him out through an exit and onto a London street. He had no plan or idea where to go from that point. While he was smarter than when he arrived in Liverpool, the reality was that he had lived the last nine months in a cocoon of work to bed to work. The goings on of the outside world had just passed him by. He was conscious that this cycle needed to be broken. He decided that he needed to get a job other than as a navvy.

Instead of plodding the streets in hope, he headed for the Crown Bar in Cricklewood. This pub provided an even more important service than beer and a place to stay. It was a focal point for social networking and the gathering of knowledge about who did what, where, when and with whom. At the bar he ordered a beer, his second beer ever, merely using it as a prop to engage with the barman and get some information. He told the barman a sanitised version of his story. The barman gave him the name and address of a landlady, advising him that work wasn't that good in London at that stage, but if he enquired around, he could get a start.

She was a motherly Irish lady and, lucky for Jack, she had a vacant bed. Jack booked it and paid her for a week in advance. The deal was bed and breakfast with dinner in the evening between 6 p.m. and 9 p.m. If he was later than that he could reheat the cooked dinner in the oven himself. This was more homely than his Liverpool digs. He put his clothes in the locker and rested on the bed until 2 p.m. He got up, washed his face at the cold tap and went out to buy the evening newspaper to see what jobs were advertised.

He sat on a park bench near a public phone box scanning the newspaper for jobs other than jobs on buildings. He looked at jobs such as hotel porter, cleaner, security guards and driving jobs. Jobs as a van driver were of no use to him since he had no driving licence. He marked five possible jobs and called the relevant phone numbers to test the water. The first three calls were of no use, since the jobs had already been filled. In the other two cases he was invited for interviews over the following few days. Jack had never done an interview other than walking onto building sites in Liverpool and asking for a start. This interview process was a new experience for him, and the results indicated that he was ill-prepared. He didn't get either of the jobs. He repeated the exercise over the next few days with the same negative results.

Rather than have nothing, he reluctantly took the offer of a kitchen clean-up job in a hotel for Friday, Saturday and Sunday nights from 5 p.m. until 1 a.m. He reported to the hotel at 4.45 p.m., and the receptionist pointed him towards the kitchen. A manageress gave him an apron and told him that his job was to wash the pots and utensils as soon as they were emptied, so that they could be recycled back into use by the chef. No matter how hard he worked, the heap of dirty pots and utensils never seemed to get less. He sweated over the hot water and suds, and if the pots, knives, forks, plates and glasses weren't sparklingly clean, the chef shouted at him and told him to repeat the washing. This was Jack's first experience of working in a job that was a never-ending conveyor belt of work.

By 1 a.m., Jack was exhausted. He wondered if he could face it again the following night. Being resilient, and with no other immediate job options, he reported for work the following evening and repeated the same routine.

On Sunday night a large function in the hotel caused the kitchen to be stretched and the head chef to become an antichrist. Around 10.30 p.m., the chef looked for a utensil in the middle of Jack's heap of dirty pots. As he roared for it, Jack tried to retrieve it. But as he did so, the other dirty pots slipped and fell making a mess on the floor.

The chef shouted at Jack to 'fuck off out of my kitchen and go back to the bogs in Ireland where you came from!' This was Jack's second sacking in a week. He returned to his digs questioning himself and doubting his confidence. But like his mother, he had a stubborn streak and just wouldn't let these disappointments defeat him. He went through the newspapers every evening, made phone calls, did interviews, but he still didn't get a job.

He returned to the Crown Bar, ordered a beer and talked to another fellow who was drinking there. He gave Jack some local information about jobs and who was who. He told him he should go in the mornings to a recognised pick-up spot and join the queue there. The contract builders' trucks would pull up and hire men from the queue for the day. He needed to be dressed for building-site work and to appear fresh. This was a worse scenario than he had in Liverpool, but desperate situations require drastic actions. He did not want to fall back to this option.

He joined the queue next morning and, at 6.30 a.m., a convoy of builders' trucks and vans pulled up and hired men from the queue. Murphy's were large digging contractors in London. Jack got into the back of the truck with the rest of the hired crew. The truck took them to

Wimbledon, where Murphy's had a contract to lay electrical cables under the street. This was familiar work for Jack, but in a different environment. Instead of the oil silos, there was continuous traffic and the constant flow of pedestrians. This unnerved him at first because he was afraid he might be spotted by someone from home who would get the word back to the locals that he was now a navvy in London, digging holes in the street like the rest of them.

The attitude of the gangers was far more aggressive than that in Liverpool. Men here were paid by the day and were as disposable as snuff at a traditional Irish country wake. No tax or social insurance was deducted from their pay so that anybody injured was just thrown aside and replaced. This was equivalent to slavery.

Jack was disillusioned. He went to the pubs more often and became involved in drinking bouts with other navvies. This tactic just drowned his sorrows rather than provide a solution to solving his hazy ambitions. At least his visits to the pubs, and then to the dances, put a more rounded structure on his life compared with his one-dimensional life in Liverpool. Because the work here was more slavish and degrading, he felt that he needed this antidote more than ever. Most of the navvies were going nowhere except to the hiring lines again in the morning.

He recalled the words of wisdom of his old football manager: 'People with a purpose can break from the pack. You must remain unsatisfied with your present conditions in order to unlock your gate to change. The lock to this gate must be opened from the inside. You have the lock combination, but are you prepared to pay the price?'

No one can persuade you to change. You guard the gate to change which can only be opened from the inside.

Jack met Mary at the dance in Cricklewood. She was originally from Clare and was a student nurse in the local hospital. She lived in the adjoining nurses' home and had passes to go to the dances on Sunday nights. They struck a chord. Jack became aware of a side of himself that he didn't previously know existed. Their dates became the highlight of the week for Jack. As they danced well together and became more comfortable with each other, they started to court. Their courting was mild compared with the version that Jack heard about on the building sites.

Jealousy can be a motivating factor for either good or bad. Jack became jealous of the job of the engineers. They seemed to be well-dressed young fellows who swanned onto the building sites late in the morning, did some measurements and were gone early in the evening. While they were on site, the foreman and the gangers fawned attention on them and seemed to be over zealous in trying to please them.

The gap between Jack's perception of their job and his own job of digging hard ground with a pick and shovel was painful to him. The challenge for Jack was this: Was it painful enough for him to do something about it, and was he prepared to pay the necessary price?

His life currently followed the pattern of hiring queues, digging, digs, pub and Sunday dances with Mary. Over time it became more solidified – the resulting rut became deeper and deeper. The general talk among the lads in the digging gangs was about sex, football and their grand plans to return home to Ireland someday to settle down and have a family. In reality, the majority of them only talked about it. They failed to do something positive about it.

Jack now worked six days per week with Sunday free. He had time to go to Mass and meet people other than his fellow ditch diggers. He still had his football gear in a bag back in the digs, but because of the work rut he was in over the last few years, he didn't think about it or even miss it. It looked like another life when he thought about it. Jack observed that many other Irish people in London were not digging ditches or washing pots. During Mass he saw many well-dressed couples who he knew from listening to their accents were Irish. He longed to be at a similar stage. But how?

He recalled the words his mentor had told him: We become what we think about, therefore be careful what you wish for. Whatever you expect with confidence becomes your own self-fulfilling philosophy. Expectations come from our fundamental beliefs about ourselves.

The hiring became routine. The same lads were put together daily. One day, Jimmy joined Jack's normal gang. Jack could see that he was different from the rest of the gang members. He seemed to be focussed single-mindedly on getting work done. Jimmy wasn't the strongest or loudest man in the gang, but he produced more output in the day than anyone else. Because of this, the ganger liked him. He had a better way of doing the job.

Jack befriended Jimmy. They talked together about everything. As they became more trusting of each other, they divulged more and more of themselves to each other in their evolving safe environment.

Jack discovered that Jimmy was very intelligent, educated and articulate, and that, because of a family row, he was disinherited of his share of the family business. Jimmy told Jack how he reacted angrily to this and attacked those he felt were the cause of his misfortune. He left Ireland in a hurry without any assets before the law caught up with him. He went through a period of depression and slept rough in the streets for a number of years. This gutter existence brought him to the point of suicide a number of times, but, as he explained to Jack, he flunked it. He was afraid of living, but he was also afraid of dying.

Over the years he regained his composure and, like the rest around him, worked on the lump system. The ganger knew that Jimmy was capable of more, but every time he tried to take the next step of the ladder, he fell off again. Navvy work was his sustainable level at the moment. He spotted that Jack, too, was different and, based on his own experiences, began to mentor him. He challenged Jack about his life going forward. Where did Mary fit in? Was he going to work on the lump for the rest of his life? Was he going to live in digs, get drunk and go back over the same cycle week after week?

Jack started to value Jimmy's advice and challenges. He confided in Jimmy that he envied the job the engineers had and that he would love to have their cushy job. Jimmy challenged him to think, 'Why not me?' This challenge was the equivalent of today's brainstorming, where management try to focus their hazy vision into a more transparent roadmap for their business future. Jimmy was conditioning Jack over time to check on himself. He used the carrot-and-the-stick strategy. The carrot was this: 'Do you want to be digging this shit under the shouting supervision of that ganger there for the rest of your life? Or do you want to be like Joe Murphy there, with his good clothes, flashy car, good job and high salary?'

This stark contrast played on Jack's mind over time. Jack decided that Joe Murphy, and not his fellow digger, was to be his role model.

Jimmy kept challenging Jack with tests: 'Do you want to be like me? Go back while you can still make it happen.'

Jimmy told him, 'A friend knows all about you and still cares about you.

A friend is someone in whose company you can be sincere. You can think aloud in their presence and let your guard down completely – the ultimate sounding board.'

Jimmy certainly satisfied this criterion for Jack, and through him he could think aloud in a safe environment.

Jack kept juggling around in his head the price he would have to pay to make it happen. Debates in his own head about whether it was worth it kept annoying him. Jack shared some of these debates with Mary, who listened intently to him, but because she was sure of her own career path, she didn't want him to potentially mess it up. She liked Jack. Their current relationship was convenient for her in the short term, but he didn't feature in her long-term vision of her own life. She believed that Jack's talk was just that – talk – and that he would be still talking about what he was going to do in ten years' time. She had seen too many other Irish navvies walk the road of theory.

Jack started to investigate what was involved in getting qualified as an engineer. He wrote to the university in Dublin for their prospectus and devoured its content when it arrived. There was no points' system in place at that time and, since he had passed Maths in the Leaving Certificate, he seemed to fulfil their entry criteria. The other big entry barrier was the cost of the college fees and the cost of living in Dublin. He calculated what the fees and accommodation would cost him over the four years of the degree course. This was the money figure he needed to earn and save if he was to make this career move happen.

There was no question of getting money from home or from the banks, so he felt that this was his own personal challenge. He had to have this amount of money in place before he could make his move. This was the monetary price he had to pay in order to energise his dream. There were obviously other non-monetary dimensions to this price. Based on his potential net savings per week, he estimated that he would build up the necessary fund by September twelve months.

He recalled a prayer by St Francis of Assisi that his mother had taught him: 'God give me the serenity to accept the things I cannot change, the courage to change the things I can and the wisdom to know the difference.'

He discussed his challenge with Jimmy. Together, they worked out the financial plan. Jimmy advised him not to mention his plan to any of the other navvies. He told Jack they may appear to be supportive on the surface, but some of them would be jealous and would nail him over the intervening period. They would see their own lost vision being stolen by this young upstart.

Jack now saw his planned further education as a means to a better quality of life.

What Jack Learned from the London Experience

- **Everyone is supposed to have a value.** Many of these navvies seemed not to have a value in the eyes of their gangers. Men here were paid by the day and were as disposable as snuff at a traditional Irish country wake. No tax or social insurance was deducted from their pay so that anybody injured was just thrown aside and replaced. This was equivalent to slavery that just had a wage at the end of the day.

- **Always begin somewhere; you cannot build a reputation on what you intend to do.** People with a purpose can break from the pack. You must remain unsatisfied with your present conditions in order to unlock your gate to change. You have the lock combination, but are you prepared to pay the price?

- **Jealousy can be a motivating factor for either good or bad.** Jack became jealous of the job the engineers had. They seemed to be well-dressed young fellows who swanked onto the building sites late in the morning, did some measurements and were gone early in the evening. While they were on site, the foreman and the gangers fawned attention on them and seemed to be over zealous in trying to please them. The gap between Jack's perception of their job and his own job of digging hard ground with a pick and shovel was the catalyst for him to consider changing.

- **An ounce of brain is worth more than a ton of muscle.** It's not the load that breaks you down; it's the way you carry it.

- **Real generosity is doing something good for someone who will never find out the extent of your influence.** Jimmy was generous to Jack in that he challenged him to 'Get out while you still have the chance.'

- **It's never too late to become what you might have been.** Every great journey starts with one small step. To get to the top, start climbing off the bottom.

- **Wishing for something to happen is one thing.** Making it happen is a different thing. This is your challenge.

Chapter 14

Break-Up and a New Horizon

Mary didn't believe that Jack would make money and help her realise her own dream. He was 'all theory,' she said. She was selfish for her own career as a nurse and consciously decided that Jack was a hindrance rather than an enabler of her own agenda of buying a house, getting married, creating a home, keeping her in the style to which she was accustomed and having three babies. She told him she wanted to move on without the burdens of Jack's issues. Her rational reasoning countered her hormone-driven feelings and her care for him.

Jack cared for her. He agonised for weeks on a future without her. He could not afford her dream just now, and he had his own dream to follow. The sparkle and the fizz had gone out of their time together. He agreed with her and thought it best for both to end their relationship. He phoned Mary and told her their love relationship was now over. She knew and he knew. From now on, their communication would be purely civil, if at all. He wrote a letter of thanks to her for their sharing of good times and wished her well. They had clearly communicated the end of the relationship to each other – there would be no unfinished business for the rest of their separate lives. They would go on their separate life journeys.

Although Mary continued to occupy his thoughts, she no longer shared his time and his life. Jack used his new found freedom on Sundays to write his plans on numerous sheets of paper and refine his roadmap for the future. He put together doodles and notes as he tried to rationalise the variables and the links between them to manage his time and money to achieve his own dream. He didn't have a label for it, but he was unwittingly building his career plan, not by long scripts, but through the process of mind-mapping.

Drawing these mind-maps demonstrated his natural focus for creating linkages between variables. He didn't have the typical, left-brained engineering mind. He had a lot of right-brained creativity. This profile type was to prove useful in his later career.

As the transition period to September and entry to the university moved closer, Jack's main interest was to accumulate money to meet his target as documented in his plan. In addition to his navvy job on the building sites, he got a job working in a local pub on the weekends. This achieved two things for him. First, it earned him enough money from which he could live for the week. He was thus able to save all his navvy wages. Secondly, he now operated from inside the bar counter rather than from the outside. The counter top was the difference for him between earning and spending. Serving behind that pub counter gave Jack a different perspective on immigrant life.

The view from inside the pub counter allowed him to read people's body language, see who was feeling down and who didn't have the energy to camouflage it. He could see the exploiters in positions of power who played games with people's lives. He could see the pretenders and liars. He saw them exploit those at the bottom and use their relative power and authority to hire or sack biddable, disposable men.

The picture evolving from outside the counter was an eye opener for Jack. He was intrigued by it. But on reflection over time, it horrified and angered him to see people exploited. This acted as a further stimulus to differentiate himself from those on the bottom rung of life and manage his way up the ladder. Jack could not have bought this realisation. Not only did he learn this critical lesson at the pub customers' expense, he got paid for it too. It was a win-win situation for him.

One critical variable of his transition roadmap that he needed to manage was to re-establish contact with home in Ireland. He had left home three years before without any farewells. He had merely sent home a letter card posted in Birkenhead. At the time he climbed into the cattle boat out of the North Wall in Dublin Port, he was of the view that if he had gone home and asked their permission to go the UK, his mother and Aunt Sheila would have talked him out of it. They would have encouraged him, now that he was educated, to get a permanent and pensionable job.

Whether he was right or wrong, he went to England – what was done couldn't be undone. He had no direct contact with Ireland or home. He picked up bits of news from Irish newspapers and listened to the stories from new immigrants coming into the pub. He had written to his mother and had included a few pounds three times since he arrived in England, but he had never given her a forwarding address.

Now that he had the next major step of his life's journey rationalised and planned, he wrote to his mother outlining his plan. On this occasion he included a forwarding address. He felt that this regeneration of communication was best done through the written word. His mother would get an awful shock if he appeared unannounced some day at the kitchen door.

By writing this letter, he started the reconciliation process. He redrafted the letter many times. He tried to explain to her that he had done what he did, not to cause pain to her and the family, but to give him space to rationalise his thoughts, to prove to himself and everyone else that he could fend for himself, get a job and make his own mistakes. He had been the school and local football team hero. All had watched his achievements and raised expectations to suit their own agendas. From this high, a low was bound to come. He didn't want to appear low in front of those who loved him or who held him as a hero.

The final version of the letter set out his proposed journey. He would register as a student in university and do a degree in engineering. He would have the necessary amount of money saved up by the middle of August. He would then come home for a couple of weeks' holiday and catch up on all the comings and goings of the local scene. He would go back to college as a mature student, now in his twenties, in the second week of September.

He finished off the letter enquiring about the rest of the family and Aunt Sheila. He also told his mother that he really appreciated all her support, vision and efforts to get him to today's decision. He said he loved her.

He expressed hope that she would be proud of him as he travelled on his new journey.

He read and reread the letter several times. He worried about it. He was stressed about posting it. He held on to it for several days and spoke with Jimmy about his worries.

Jimmy listened to Jack and empathised with him. He told Jack of his own situation. He too had written a letter to his aging mother, whom he had walked out on after the row about inheritance and thus hadn't seen for years. He didn't post it, and then it was too late. He got word indirectly that she had died. He would never get the chance to try to make peace with her. This personal insight hit Jack. Jimmy told him to bring the letter to work the following day, that he would post it for him. As the letter slipped from Jimmy's hand into the red post-box on his behalf and couldn't be retrieved, Jack described the relief to him as 'heavenly'.

The postman cycled up to Jack's home and said to Mary Anne, 'I have a letter from Jack for you.' The local postmistress, postman, priest, teacher, shopkeeper and others know about each other in local communities, almost know each other's innermost thoughts and know their handwriting. Mary Anne's heart jumped. She looked at the envelope several times and instinctively knew that this letter was different from the previous three letter cards she had received from Jack.

Mothers know these things intuitively. She was too afraid and too excited to open it. She left it there, leaving it until dinner time when Mick Denny Bill would come in from the fields. She would get him to open and read it. If the story was bad, at least he would screen the news and would be there for her to lean on. As the morning wore on, she became restless in anticipation of the news contained within Jack's letter sitting on the mantelpiece.

Joan, her next-door neighbour, called into Mary Anne for a cup of tea. She updated her on all the local gossip. She asked Mary Anne how Jack was doing. She enquired if he had any notion of coming home. Mary Anne played the game of neighbour politics, self-survival and protection of her family with the instinct of a lioness. Internally, she wondered what was in Jack's letter. Her instincts told her the news from Jack was good news, but life had toughened her to keep a door open so that, in the event of it being otherwise, she wouldn't get caught out. She fobbed off her next-door neighbour's enquiry, politely telling her that he was busy on a new construction project for the government in London.

The morning dragged on to dinner time. Mary Anne went out to the farmyard and blew the whistle to call the lads into dinner. The church bell, the whistle and the train were the benchmark time indicators of the '50s and '60s. Most farmers didn't carry watches. Some of the older men had pocket watches and chains which they wore with their suits and waistcoats to Mass. The watch chain laced through the button holes of the waist coat gave the owner a certain level of decorum or propriety. Mick Denny Bill had no watch.

When Mick Denny Bill came into the kitchen, Mary Anne, with trembling hands, gave him Jack's letter. Mick Denny Bill had learned over many years of trial and error how to survive their relationship. He would not panic and reinforce her tensions. He was the ideal counterfoil to her naturally high-tension personality. He went over to the dresser, got his glasses, put them on and, with a knife from the table, he calmly and neatly slit open the envelope. He silently read Jack's letter without expression. Mary Anne observed his body language to gain a signal about its message. She noticed that no money was included. This was different from the previous letters from Jack.

Mick Denny Bill looked up solemnly and said, 'I don't believe it.'

'Believe what?' she spouted, not knowing whether it was good or bad news. She saw his eyes mist over. He asked Mary Anne how she would feel if she had a son qualified as an engineer. 'What?' she said as she grabbed the letter and read it herself. In an unusual demonstration of emotion and love, she caught Mick Denny Bill and hugged and kissed him.

Hugging and kissing was then confined to the darkened bedroom and was, as the priest advised, for the purpose of procreation and not for celebration or self-pleasure. When she disengaged from Mick Denny Bill, they sat down and tried to talk it through. They wondered if it was true. Could it be happening to them, a poor rural farm family, that their son was coming home to go to university? They oscillated from peaks of elation to troughs of disbelief, all the time coming back and reading and re-reading Jack's letter. It was definitely his handwriting.

They sat together and reminisced about all the events, good and bad, from the time they first made love, to guessing when and where he was conceived, to Mary Anne discovering that she was pregnant, to his birth, his time at national and secondary school, his football days and then that fateful lettercard posted in the North Wall announcing that he had emigrated to England. They reflected that communication was in only one direction over the following years. All was now forgiven. They were joyful.

Their instinct was to avoid blowing from the tree tops about Jack's return, just in case it might not happen. They adopted a strategy of letting the word out obliquely, understated and locally. 'Did I tell you that Jack said he hopes to come home to go back to university?' said Mary Anne with a tact worthy of a trained diplomat knowing well that she hadn't told Joan and the neighbours already. It was now April. Jack said that he planned to come home in August. He still had more funds to build up.

Now that she had a return address, Mary Anne pulled out her notepaper and composed her letter. When he was in secondary school, she wrote with words of stern advice from her head. This time she wrote from her heart. She told Jack how she and Mick Denny Bill loved him, how elated and proud they were of his plan, and that she had full confidence in him. She told him that she was mad with him over his spontaneous break off of contact, but that this was only natural for a concerned mother.

In a postscript, she thanked Jack for the watch which she had bought with the money he enclosed in the envelope with his second letter. 'I can't wait to show it to you,' she said. She finished by asking Jack to write again soon and to keep them updated about his planned return. She promised to write again next week when she would give him more details about the rest of the family and exciting local events.

For her, the most exciting local event was that Jack was coming home and that she herself was going to be the mother of a university-qualified engineer. She noted in her mind that Jack was going to be the first university graduate to have gone to the local national school.

This first was big stuff as far as she was concerned, and it would solidify the relatively elevated status she always thought she had within the parish. She always knew she was better than the rest, but she always kept that to herself. Her original stretching vision for Jack and her other children was now taking its next logical step after the interruption of the last three years. She rationalised that the pain of the last three years was the price she had to pay in order to get to this new big prize.

Back in London, Jack got his mother's letter and treasured it. He read and re-read it as he tried to visualise the emotional impact his new plan was having not just on himself, but also on others – especially his mother.

Jimmy was aware of this emotional moment for Jack. He gave him space to work it out in his own head, while at the same time he was there to support him. Jimmy asked him many open-ended questions and allowed Jack the licence to fill in the detail to the extent that he was comfortable with.

Jack continued to work his plan and monitor progress against the money benchmark he had set for himself. He marked off on his calendar the days left to his return to Ireland.

The manager of the pub asked Jack if he was interested in giving up the navvy job and becoming a shift manager at the pub. It would pay well. This was attractive, and for a while Jack wondered if he should change his mind and accept it. The opportunity cost of following his plan to do an engineering degree in university was now his refusal to take up this attractive offer.

He spoke to Jimmy about the offer. Jimmy advised Jack to stick with his plan. He told Jack that other opportunities would come along when he is fit to take them up and optimise them.

He thanked the pub manager for his kind offer. He told him he had to reluctantly refuse it on this occasion as he needed to return to Ireland to complete some unfinished business. He asked the manager to consider him again if he returned back to London. This safety net was now useful for Jack in the event that his proposed career change fell foul at any point.

One morning, Jack wasn't in the hire line queue. Nobody other than Jimmy noticed. Men were always coming and going and, in any event, in this building firm, men were disposable. Jimmy didn't make management any the wiser.

Jack gave Jimmy a box on the evening before his departure, but told him not to open it until the weekend. In the box was a thank you note from Jack to Jimmy thanking him for his valued mentoring advice over the years. Jimmy was a heavy pipe smoker who had been using his burned out pipe for too long, so Jack had put a new pipe in the box. This new pipe was very welcome. It would remind him of Jack every time he prepared the tobacco and lit up.

Jack also included his Irish home address and promised that he would return the compliment, in what way he didn't know, but that he was sure that he would. This piece of recognition and gratitude meant so much to Jimmy. He cried himself to sleep that night and mourned for all the missed opportunities in his own life.

When Jack took the cattle boat to Holyhead on his way to England three years before, he dreamed that one day he would return home to Ireland by plane. He went into a travel agency and bought a one-way ticket from Heathrow airport to Dublin. Aer Lingus, the national carrier, had a monopoly on this route between Ireland and the UK. They charged massive prices in order to pay for the inefficiencies which tend to follow monopoly operators. In turn, they prided themselves in their smiling hostesses in their green national type uniforms. Irrespective of price, Jack planned to return home in luxury. He wanted to start this phase of his life the way he meant it to continue.

He got the train from Paddington to Heathrow. It was his first time to enter an airport. The size and seemingly complicated systems operating within the airport completely disorientated him. He gave himself plenty of time so that he could suss out how to get through the gauntlet of airport checks and customs' procedures.

He had spent the previous Saturday shopping for gifts for his mother, his father, his siblings and Aunt Sheila. For his siblings he bought bright, coloured polo-necked shirts, the likes of which were never before seen in rural Ireland.

When he booked in at the airport, he followed the signage towards the departure gate and after a further two-hour delay he, and about sixty other passengers, boarded the waiting aircraft. He went to his designated seat and the hostess told him to put on his safety belt. The plane was full and the captain announced the flight to Dublin. The cabin crew demonstrated basic safety procedures to be followed by the passengers in the event of an emergency or drop in cabin air pressure. The engines shuddered noisily as the huge propellers gathered speed and shook the plane, readying it for take-off. Jack marvelled at his first flight as the plane lifted from the runway and climbed into the clouds.

Jack was amazed at the sight from his window seat of the airport below him and the city of London fading behind him into the distance. The plane went above the clouds and he saw the blanket of cloud below and the sun setting in the west.

The man in the business suit sitting beside him folded his *Financial Times* and turned to Jack. He asked him if he was returning to Ireland on holidays, where he was from and what he did for a living. Jack told him during the meal served by another smiling air hostess that he was returning so that he could go to university in order to study engineering. He told him that he had been working in England for the last few years doing various jobs in order to build the fees to finance his university studies. This man of obvious great education, experience and wisdom congratulated Jack on his decision, giving him further affirmation that he had made the correct decision.

The captain announced that they were approaching Dublin airport and would be landing in minutes. As the plane dropped its cruising height, Jack's ears clogged and pained him. He thought his head would burst. The man beside him advised him to hold his nose and to blow out against this resistance until his ears popped. His ears popped to his pleasant relief.

The plane landed with a shudder. The passengers disembarked, and he followed the crowd through immigration control and baggage collection. He followed some of the crowd through customs but didn't see the red and green signs. In his innocence, he put his bags on the inspection table where the customs' officer asked him, 'What have you to declare?' Jack didn't know what he meant. It took some explanation for him to realise that the few presents he had bought were clear of tax and the customs' officer waved him through. Jack was confident enough to create fun with the customs' officer quoting Oscar Wilde of his schooldays saying, 'I have nothing to declare but my genius.'

On the shuttle bus to the train station he reflected on how wonderful it was to be back. During a two-hour time space to his train home, he bought a newspaper and ordered his first pint of Guinness in Ireland. It definitely tasted better than the Guinness served in London. Jimmy had told him the taste was different because of the water drawn from the River Liffey. It helped Jack to relax and reflect on his impending journey home.

He hadn't given an exact date or time, but Mary Anne, reading between the lines of his letters, had worked out the most probable day and time he would arrive. She arranged for herself and Mick Denny Bill to go quietly to the railway station to meet her targeted train. If she guessed the wrong train, no one would know the difference.

As the train pulled into the railway station, Jack recognised various landmarks and his mind raced back nostalgically to associated events of his younger days. He reflected on how his parents and siblings would be feeling, especially his mother. He knew her well enough to know that she wouldn't expose her inner emotional feeling in public. He knew her governing principle was that when you allow yourself to get into a high, the only way you can go is down. Based on her own series of downs in life and their associated pains, she adopted the strategy of avoidance. She knew that present restraint saved later pain.

As the train came to a stop, Jack collected his bags and got out onto the platform. He assumed that he would need to secure a lift home from some other people going in his direction. To his surprise, there was his mother running down the platform toward him, her arms open to embrace him. Her body language indicated to Jack that all was forgiven. He was the prodigal son being welcomed home by his very proud and happy parents.

When they met, they hugged each other. His mother whispered into his ear how much she loved him and how proud she was. The strength of her embrace conveyed to Jack the intensity of her feelings for him. Typical of fathers of the rural Ireland of the '60s, Mick Denny Bill kept his true feelings under check and, with an almost indifferent handshake, quickly asked Jack if he needed a hand with his bags.

In the car, the moods of father, mother and son swung from outbursts of questions to moments of awkward silence. This readjusting process could not be driven ahead of the readiness of the various parties.

Jack asked his mother for the low-down on his siblings and old friends and neighbours. As this stunted discussion went on, Mick Denny Bill kept his eyes on the road and his ears listening intently. He was observer rather than participant.

The roughness of the car journey and the efforts of his father to avoid the potholes reminded Jack that at least the surface of the roads hadn't changed in three years.

As they pulled into the yard, Spotty jumped up on Jack and licked his face agitatedly. Dogs know that sometimes you have to go away and make yourself scarce in order to be appreciated. As Jack went through the yard of his childhood and into the house, his head flooded with thoughts and emotions that had lain dormant for years.

Word quickly filtered out to the village and townland that Jack was back. His brothers and sisters quickly gathered from their different locations and welcomed him home.

He managed his own shyness and the shyness and uncertainty of his brothers and sisters, but as a few neighbours came in, they, as outsiders, helped to smother these normal moments of initial awkwardness.

Jack was back home and nothing much had changed there except the greying heads of the older people, and the time that had passed while he was in a different world.

Lessons for Jack from Break-up

- **During life, we are faced with many watershed points.** Watershed points are like the roundabouts you encounter when driving along the road. Take one exit from the roundabout and you'll end up in Ballydehob; take another and you'll end up in Belfast. The decisions we make about which exit to take from these roundabouts have a massive bearing on our lives.

- **We rise to the level of our own and others' expectation of us.** Jimmy expressed his higher expectations of what Jack was capable of. He didn't treat him as he was, but rather as he could be. Over time, he influenced Jack to raise his expectations of what was possible for him.

- **We are where we are based on the decisions we made or avoided in the past.** Jack was now digging holes because of his past decisions, which were made in haste and based on escaping rather than on achieving. Jimmy influenced him to now make better decisions which would determine his future.

- **People either enable or hinder us on our journey.** Mary was selfish for her own career as a nurse and consciously decided that Jack was a hindrance rather than an enabler. Her rational reasoning countered her hormone-driven feelings and her care for him.

- **We get a different view of the world by standing on a different spot.** When Jack started working inside the pub counter, it gave him a different perspective on immigrant life. The view from inside the pub counter allowed him to read people's body language, see who was feeling down and who didn't have the energy to camouflage it. He could see the exploiters in positions of power who played games with people's lives. He could see the pretenders and liars. He saw them exploit those at the bottom and use their relative power and authority to hire or sack biddable, disposable men. This acted as a further stimulus to Jack to differentiate himself from those outside the counter.

- **Mothers know these things intuitively.** Jack's mother instinctively knew that his letter contained exciting news, even before she opened it.

- **Nothing happens until you do something.** The incremental approach to change is effective, when what you want is more of what you have already got.

Chapter 15

A Leadership Experience

At the railway station, Jack bade farewell to Mary Anne and Mick Denny Bill, his neighbours and Aunt Sheila, and climbed onto the train for Dublin. When he found his seat on the train, he focused his mind on his two main objectives. The first was to register for his place in the engineering degree programme in the university in Dublin. The second was to find accommodation for his time there.

He was shocked at the size of the university campus. He had visioned that it might be similar to his former secondary school, St Patrick's. A university porter told him to join the long queue of other young men and women at the registration office. Here he stood in the queue feeling older, more mature and superior to the new first year students, many of whom were accompanied by one or other of their parents for this big day in their lives.

When his turn came, the girl at the registration desk asked him to present a copy of his application form, a copy of his Leaving Certificate results and a long version of his Birth Certificate. She asked him to sign some administration forms and gave him an invoice.

He faced another first. He had never written a cheque before. In England he deposited his savings in the post office and filled in and stamped his post office book whenever there were transactions in or out of the account. Now he took out his new bank cheque book. He fumbled trying to understand how to use it. The girl at the registration desk guided him how to fill it in and sign it – she had seen thousands like him. She gave him his receipt, then gave him a student number and told him to go to the next room where a photographer would take his photo so that it could be inserted in his student card.

He would need this student card, she told him, in order to gain access to the library and other facilities around the campus. The good news, she said, was that the card would allow him to get student discounts in named shops and the student bar, and it would allow him into student dances. She told him to return to her and submit his Dublin address when he secured his new accommodation. She wished him the best and moved on to serve the next applicant.

Outside the registration office stood groups of students trying to convince the new students to join debating, GAA, rugby, soccer, historical, geographical and other societies and organisations. Jack agreed to join the football society, even though he hadn't kicked a football either in love or anger since he played in the semi-final of the minor championship four years ago. In Jack's mind, that was another world.

He wandered around the university campus trying to comprehend its size and its facilities. He pinched himself at his good fortune. This was real, and it was happening to him. He reflected on his wild journey from Classroom 1C in St Patrick's some nine years ago to this point.

The notice board on the wall outside the registration desk listed digs, flats and bedsits. It listed also that the college had some accommodation on the campus. He asked the official at the desk about accommodation on the campus. The official told him that there was no vacancy, as it had all been pre-booked. That was good, in another sense, as he thought back to unpleasant memories of his school dormitory days. He realised too that he had enough of inquisitive landladies with their peculiar mannerisms and rules and regulations. He decided that digs was not an option for him. This reduced his options to either flats or bedsits.

He recalled the squalor of bedsits in London, often occupied by depressed and drunken immigrant navvies. He knew no other students with whom he could share a flat. The bedsit was the only option. He got a listing of bedsits from the accommodation office and then made phone calls from a nearby public telephone box.

Landlords understood the dynamics of supply and demand; at the opening of the college year, they looked for premium prices from students for hovels. Jack made ten phone calls and agreed with the landlords to view two bedsits at 2 p.m. and 3 p.m. When he arrived at the first, just off South Circular Road, he saw a queue of like-minded students there. He moved to the next in his list. Another queue.

Rather than queue anymore, he bought a copy of the *Evening Herald*, sat down on a bench and marked off likely places from the 'To Let' section of the paper. He worked his way through this list, using the public phone to contact the landlords and agents to make arrangements for viewing. They were mostly in Ranelagh. They were residential houses which had been converted into a series of bedsits. You wouldn't put pigs in some of them, he thought.

Jack's standards and high expectations were quickly eroded. A bedsit in Ranelagh was his last option. Each room of the original residential house had been converted into single bedsits. He chose a bedsit which consisted of a single bed, a small table and chair, a wardrobe, a small kitchenette with a sink, a cold tap, a two-plate cooker and a two-bar electric fire. He and the occupants of the other bedsits shared the lone toilet on this floor, which was entered from the landing. The model for rearing battery chickens must have been hatched here, he thought to himself.

It was on par with some of the hovels he saw in London. He had to pay the rent one month in advance. In addition, he had to pay one-month rent equivalent as a deposit or bond which he would get back at the end provided he left the bedsit in as good a condition as he got it. All of these transactions were conducted in cash – the landlord must have operated outside the tax system. He was a wiry man and reminded Jack of his mother, who could have done this business in her stride. A telephone with a black coin box in the front hallway catered for the ten bedsits in the house.

Now that he had an address, Jack took the bus for the university to tell the girl at reception of his accommodation address. She told him that his student card would be ready for collection on Friday.

He saw on the timetable that his first lecture was billed for 9 a.m. next morning. There was time to kill, or time to use. He wandered around the campus. First he went into the restaurant for tea. Then the music beckoned him to the campus bar where he ordered a pint of Guinness. He was surprised at the price – the drink suppliers subsidised the prices they charged so as to build brand loyalty among students. He walked from the campus back to his bedsit and calculated the time it took to walk this journey. This would allow him to more accurately plan his mornings so that he could attend his lectures on schedule. His travel options were to go by bus or bicycle or walk.

He called to the corner shop and bought milk, tea, bread, butter, jam and some cheese. When he got back to his bedsit, he put the food in the cooker oven for safe storage. There was no fridge in the bedsit.

He tried to put some order on his limited living space. There were no sheets, no pillowcases and no towels. He decided that since he would be going home on Friday, he would get a supply from his mother, so there was no need to be spending his scarce money on such items. He would be okay for these few nights with what he had.

Working as a navvy in London had taught him how to handle scarcity. He boiled the kettle and made tea and a cheese sandwich. This meal was well short of the dinner he got from his landladies when in Liverpool and London. He nevertheless felt the freedom at being lord of his own manor. It was worth it. He had no radio and no television. Few residences had television at that time.

After tea, he rinsed his cup and plate and left them drip on the sink. The trade mark brown stains on the poorly-washed cups had built up over time.

He sat down and reflected on the events of the day. While he had a certain questioning of his own sanity, he was, nevertheless, excited for being in this space. He took out the literature he got from the college and reread it. It was so inviting that he was in a hurry to get going.

To break the night, he went out for a walk to suss out the area and see what was what. While he had lived in Liverpool and London for a number of years, he had, for the most part, lived a sheltered life, which was a cycle of work to the digs and back to work, with frequent visits to the pub intruding into this cycle. In the latter time, he spent his pub time working inside the bar rather than drinking on the other side of the bar.

As he walked around, he saw that most of the houses had been converted into bedsits and flats. These were occupied mostly by students who didn't seem to have a worry in the world. They moved around in groups, laughing, singing and play-acting. Many of the local pubs were full of students. Jack sensed that he was opening up another door in life for himself. All he needed was the code to unlock that door and become part of the student scene. He felt happy but apprehensive.

He twisted and turned in his bed during the night and got up at 7.30 a.m. He prepared and consumed his simple breakfast of tea and bread and walked to the university. He allowed time to arrive on time for his first lecture. This was another watershed point in his life.

Because he was not yet familiar with the landscape of the university, he went astray in his attempts to locate the lecture hall.

Unlike the serried rows of desks in St Patrick's, the seats were arranged like the stand at the county GAA football pitch, but above eye level. The students sat on tiers of benches that arose up into the sky in a horseshoe shape that surrounded the lecturer's desk. Jack reckoned that in excess of one hundred students were seated by the time the lecture started. He assumed by the number of empty seats that some students didn't make it on time.

The lecturer looked like a judge in a courtroom. Dressed in a long black robe, he stood looking around and up to the layers of new students on the gallery of benches before him. He welcomed them and then made a roll call. He then put the whole engineering department in context for them, detailing the subject options they had available to them. He told them of the various specialist streams they could follow, depending on their exam results at the end of the first year.

'Look at the student sitting next to you. Look into his or her eyes and decide which one of the two of you will fail your first year's exams. Statistically, only about half of first year engineering students pass their first year exams. Now the choice is in your hands. You are no longer in secondary school. You are now adults and you must decide your own destiny.'

Some of the students were frightened. Others pretended they didn't care. Like the swan sailing serenely on the river, they held their heads up high, but they paddled like hell underneath.

After the first introductory lecture, the next lecture wasn't until 12 noon; the third and final lecture was at 3 p.m. Jack soon observed that the number of hours of formal lectures was small and that there were large spaces of time between them. He later reasoned that his success would depend on how smart he was at utilising this framework of time commitments.

Jack saw on the notice board that there was an initial kick-around and 'getting to know you' football session planned for 5 p.m. – that evening. He still had his school football gear which he never got to use during his time in the UK. He went back to his flat, or gaff as the students called it, and collected his playing gear. He would take this opportunity.

At the football pitch, he was surprised to see the number of potential footballers. He was surprised too to see that amongst the officials was Barry, who had played on the minor county team with Jack some years ago. Barry expressed delight. Why had Jack vanished from the face of the earth after they were beaten in that All-Ireland semi-final four years ago? Jack told him his story about going to Liverpool and then London.

Barry introduced Jack to other students and said that when he did some training he should be certainly good enough for the freshers' team; over time he may have bigger opportunities. Jack's body was as hard as nails from his time on the building sites, but this was a different fitness from that required to play football at a higher level.

During the kick-around session, Jack felt his sap rising again as he reacquainted himself with football. He now realised the void it had left in his life over the last few years. After the first practice session, Barry gathered the group of players and gave them information about the history of the football in the college. He also said that it was a great opportunity for the students to socialise.

Jack and Barry went to the students' bar and had a few pints of Guinness. Barry gave Jack a run-down on what was what and who was who around the campus. Barry was in third year medicine. He told Jack that he loved the college scene. He advised Jack that getting over the first year exams was the real trick and that the wind would then be to his back. He introduced Jack to other students. Jack's integration process had begun. He committed himself to a tough training regime in order to get match-fit and see how he could resurrect his football career.

Jack loved the first few days of college life. It was such a contrast from the drudgery and negativity he had lived with for the last few years. Here there was life: laughter, sport, time and an air of unreality. In reality, he had just substituted one bubble for another. This campus bubble facilitated a balancing of his life between pleasure and the possibly serious work of passing his exams.

When Jack took the train home that first Friday night, he was ecstatic. He wanted to tell his mother everything he now knew about life in the university. Unusual for Jack, he couldn't stop talking as he described his experience of the different events and activities of university life. Mary Anne was delighted. She was living her dream through Jack.

Aunt Sheila had aged greatly since Jack last saw her, and she was ill when he visited her. She now had dementia the doctor said. She was not tuned into the reality that he was home again in Ireland and that he was now in university. Jack reasoned that if she only had her full faculties, she would have been in awe of his achievement.

On Saturday, Jack met with some of his old club football friends. He told them that he had broken the ice in the college and was getting back to playing football again. They invited him to rejoin their club's senior football panel. They offered to pay his travel expenses to come home for their matches.

Jack noticed that some of his national school classmates were not as friendly towards him as they had been when he lived at home. He was unsure about the reason. In reality, both sides had grown away from each other – each had gone in a different direction. Some had gone to the local technical school and now served their time in the trades. Others had taken local jobs or were working on their home farms. A few had emigrated. These strained relationships eased as Jack played football again with the local club's senior football team.

On Sunday night, Mary Anne made a parcel of bed sheets, pillowcases and food for Jack to take back to Dublin. She showed Jack how to do basic cooking and advised him to keep away from the frying-pan because, as she said, 'the frying-pan and stomach ulcers are close bed mates'.

When Jack arrived in Dublin, he went to the students' clubhouse.

There he had a few drinks, and, as he quickly integrated into the group, they discussed the upcoming All-Ireland football final to be played the following Sunday in Croke Park.

Groups of girl students hung around. The lads wondered what the best tactics might be to break them up, so that they would have a better chance of shifting one. A shift involved some kissing on the lips and touching, but nothing more. Their mothers had warned their daughters of the danger of letting boys put their hands beyond their knees. Mothers of the time forgot or were too shy to tell their daughters of the feelings and actions that might result from this activity.

Lectures were starting, but Jack didn't see any need to wonder how he might adjust to the arduous work of study. He knew that his previous track record in study was less than encouraging. He was determined to enter this process here in a completely different frame of mind. Even though the content of the lectures was new to him, Jack wasn't worried by it.

Some girls in the class always sat at the front and took down every word the lecturers gave out. They did it irrespective of whether or not it made sense. At the other extreme, some of the lads sat at the back and attended the lectures only to ensure that their presence was recorded in the roll-call. They assumed that they could cover the subject territory in a big burst of study towards the end of the last term – they didn't want to stretch their brains so early in the academic year.

Jack was older than most of his class, the majority of whom had come directly from secondary school into university. There is a theory that age should bring maturity and smartness. But the theory is only true if one has had stretching experiences. In Jack's case, the main stretching experience was learning to survive in difficult circumstances. He had been exposed to the results of bad judgement by various navvies in the trenches in London. His major advantage over the younger students was that he was in university because he wanted to be here, and he was prepared to pay the necessary price to get what he wanted.

Jack quickly found that most of the lecturers were poor communicators and merely went through the motions of lecturing. He understood that there was, at best, only one real learning point per lecture – the rest was just filling. He resolved to make a note of this key learning point from each lecture.

When a lecturer announced to the twenty students sitting in the fourth row that they had just been appointed project leaders, they were shocked. The lecturer gave them the responsibility of selecting five other students from the group to form a project team of six. Jack sat in row four that day, so he automatically became one of the appointed project leaders.

Although he didn't have a label for it, Jack already understood from experience how the project team process worked. He moved fast. He invited the five brightest in the class to join his project team. He had many offers, but he had an entry barrier: 'What will you bring to this team?' Because of his first-striker advantage and his smart criteria, he finished up with a bright and balanced team, much like the football team he had during second year in St Patrick's. He copied the methodology of the good foreman he observed managing jobs on the building site in London.

He saw himself as the project manager and delegated pieces of the project to the various team players. He agreed with each what their output contribution was going to be within specified time frames. He then pulled the individual team members together into a cohesive whole. This was a live example of good project management. Project management was a term Jack hadn't yet come across, although he had been involved in projects when he was digging trenches and pulling cables from the power houses to the oil silos in Liverpool. He knew that some gangers were better than others at getting results from their teams of navvies. As a project manager here, he now put this experience, now an innate intuition, to good use. He adopted the project management tactics naturally energised by the more successful gangers.

Jack showed his maturity by understanding the dynamics of going for gold in the smartest way possible. He spotted the opportunity this team offered to him. This was a resource he could use as leverage for issues other than just this designated project. His principal objective was to pass the first year exams the first time.

He thought out this smart objective carefully and then pulled together his project team of the five brightest for a special meeting. There was one item on the agenda: how the six could pass their first year exams with the least input. This led to a brainstorm session in which each member of the group gave opinions and ideas and engaged with each other in intensive debate, lateral thinking and discussion.

Jack and his team now had the elements of a simple but, potentially, very effective plan. It required each team member to specialise in one subject and become an expert in that subject. The team member would then make good notes on the key learning points, research the past exam papers and then present an idiot-proof version to the group. Between the six of them, they would have perfect answers worked out for each subject with the minimum of effort. It was just one-sixth of the effort they would have to exert if each worked solo.

Jack allocated the subjects. The team agreed to meet on Mondays at 10 a.m. and Thursdays at 2 p.m. when each had available time according to their diaries. Each would then present their precise notes and worked answers to the rest of the group. As the project manager, Jack had his choice of subject. He picked Pure Maths.

Jack joined the debating society in the university. Some of his football colleagues joined too. He was fascinated with how the debating teams tore strips off each other and how the judges awarded points and decided the winners. He said to himself that he would like to perform as a debater some day.

As he trained with the footballers, his dormant talent started to come through. Because of his age and hardened frame from the digging of the trenches, allied to his football prowess, he emerged as a star fresher. He was invited to join the extended panel for the senior football team, which would compete in a number of competitions and, most importantly, the Sigerson Cup.

There were many senior county footballers on the panel. Thus, the competition for places was keen. Being on the senior panel was a privilege for a first year student and challenged Jack to get into a fitness regime and hone his skills against the best. They started at a gentle pace, but the intensity of the training quickly increased. Mick, their head coach, was an ex-county, All-Ireland-winning manager who was paid a retainer fee to get the job done. Because of this and the importance of preserving his reputation, Mick wasn't prepared to take prisoners.

The more intense and demanding the training became, the more united the group became both on and off the field. From this Jack built a social network which allowed him to quickly integrate into college life.

His wanderings around the campus and his visits to the library to read interesting quasi-subject-related books and publications, contributed to opening his mind to a new world he did not know already existed. Yet his rural poor background had a benefit: he could appreciate better than most the riches and the opportunities that were available.

Jack had his own money. He had eaerned it earned by the sweat of his own brow in London and wasn't now beholden to anyone. Another benefit. Knowing that he had money and where it had come from allowed him a degree of mental freedom and know-how that his other classmates didn't have. He didn't spend money foolishly. He had money if he needed it. He could pay for photocopying and typing of lecture notes.

As the social culture gathered all around him, Jack attracted the attention of young women. One told him to his amazement that he was more manly than the normal, immature first year students, that she loved how easy-going he was and that he had leadership traits. At the student dances he would easily pull a young woman for the night. But he resisted the temptation of this trend in anticipation of developing a more permanent arrangement. Life was potentially too good to allow him to get hooked by a young woman who might have possessive instincts as soon as she got her claws well dug in.

Lessons for Jack from Leadership Experience

- **It's the start that often stops you from getting ahead.** You will remember the first time you did lots of things. Just stop for a moment and reflect on some of these events.

  Did you feel awkward?

  Can you remember the hundredth time you did it?

  What is the message here for you?

- **Commerce is determined by the dynamics of supply and demand.** Jack learned that landlords understood this dynamic at the opening of the college year. They looked for premium prices from students for hovels.

- **We all have scarce resources relative to what we need in order to achieve our objectives.** Therefore we have to make choices. Working as a navvy in London had taught Jack how to handle scarcity. As he boiled the kettle, he boiled his egg in the same water.

- **Life is competitive and for every success there is the opposite happening in parallel.** Jack understood this dynamic better than the other raw students when their Professor advised them to 'Look at the student sitting next to you. Look into his or her eyes and decide which one of the two of you will fail your first year's exams. Statistically, only about half of engineering students pass their first year exams. Now the choice is in your hands. You are no longer in secondary school. You are now adults and you must decide your own destiny.'

- **It matters not so much what happens but how you react.** Some students were frightened. Others pretended they didn't care. Like the swan sailing serenely on the river, they held their heads up high, but they paddled like hell underneath.

- **Life is a series of bubbles and you have to learn how to succeed against the prevailing backdrops.** Jack loved the first few days of college life. It was such a contrast from the bubbles of drudgery and negativity he had lived with for the last few years. Here there was a new bubble of life, laughter, sport, time and an air of unreality. In reality, he had just substituted one bubble for another. This campus bubble facilitated a balancing of his life between pleasure and the serious work of passing his exams.

- **As you develop, you naturally move forward at a greater pace than for many of your colleagues.** This manifests itself in emotional responses ranging from jealousy to fear. Jack experienced this with his former club football colleagues. They were stuck and he was moving forward.

Chapter 16

Home for Christmas

The first term went quickly, and the college closed for three weeks of holidays at Christmas. There were continuous assessment exams, but Jack's project-team methodology was working well. So far so good. He decided that he needed to keep his cash balance topped up, so he applied for, and got, a three-week holiday job with An Post sorting Christmas mail. This was shift work, which still allowed him to complete his college and football commitments. He came home on Christmas Eve. Mary Anne was so delighted to have her full clutch of children together again for the first time in four Christmases.

Christmas in rural Ireland is about family, time to relax, renewing friendships with the neighbours and getting back to basics. Christmas Eve night was always exciting. The main focus was the lighting of the candles in the windows by Mick, his baby brother.

Mary Anne and Mick Denny Bill made a large fire. Some neighbours wandered in to welcome Jack home. They were anxious to know the details of his experiences of college life, which were far outside their own experiences of life and living. Jack illustrated and embellished his stories, generating a sense of excitement and jealousy among his listeners. His brothers and sisters were in impressionable awe of the scene their big brother, now in his twenties, painted. He was becoming a role model for them. Jack didn't know that being a role model carries responsibilities.

Jack started a custom in his family by exchanging small Christmas presents which he had bought with some of his An Post money. He distributed the presents to the family members after the last of the neighbours had left for home.

Christmas Day routine hadn't changed in Jack's house in his years away in London. His mother had the whole family up and washed early so that they could all go to the 10 a.m. Mass as a united family. This was always a special Mass. A full choir, accompanied by the organist, would sing their hearts out. After Mass the neighbours wished each other 'Happy Christmas'.

Mary Anne was particularly pleased this Christmas morning because Jack was back, having missed so many Christmases. She had another reason for happiness: she now had a son at university.

Jack was so contented to be back within his family bosom. He compared it with how he had spent previous Christmases working and only having sandwiches to eat.

Christmas dinner was traditional. A roasted, home-grown turkey was the centre piece. In addition, there was a stack of trimmings. Much of the discussion around the table focused on Jack's exploits during the previous Christmases in Liverpool and London. He said that it was 'touch and go'. He described how he was lonesome and how he had to work through the experience of going away from home to gain independence so that he could get it out of his system.

As Jack told stories and related his reasoning for going to Liverpool and London, Mary Anne found it difficult to hide her emotions. She felt personal guilt that she hadn't trusted both herself and Jack to understand that the core foundations she had built in rearing her children and managing her family unit would result in a good output, even if she couldn't visualise the now emerging picture. She wasn't confident enough through the years to dare think that big.

After dinner, she delegated to Jack and his brothers and sisters the jobs of washing the dishes and cleaning up. Mary Anne was showing her natural management skills.

The combination of the excess eating, alcohol, heat and a congenial atmosphere all added up to marvellous sleep. When Jack and his siblings completed the wash up, they joined their slumbering fellow family members to sleep off the excesses of the day and the reality of the year gone by.

On St Stephen's day, known to Jack as Boxing Day when he was in England, farm families throughout rural Ireland did the least amount of farm work possible. Other than watering and feeding the farm animals, it was a day to laze around and meet with the neighbours and whoever else might visit or pass along the road. Most of the family didn't rise until midday. Mary Anne cooked what is now known in more sophisticated circles as a brunch. This meal was partly salvaged from the leftovers of the previous day. She added fried pieces, and the entire meal acted as breakfast and dinner for that day.

Jack visited his aged Aunt Sheila who was ill. He sat with her for a while, but he wasn't sure whether she recognised him or not.

When he returned home, some of Jack's cousins had arrived to make their Christmas visit. They were so anxious to hear his stories of his exploits in England and at college. They listened to his stories of his mundane and slavish jobs of digging drains, pulling cables, and working a jackhammer.

Jack embellished these stories to suit his audience. He embellished them further for his aunts in particular, to shock them. Whether they were really shocked he didn't know, but they appeared to be shocked. They were defensive in their stances and their blushes. In later life, Jack reasoned that his aunts 'knew all the time', but they merely played a game that was culturally acceptable in those darker and more innocent times.

Rural farming life was mundane for most of the year. Farm families tried to forecast the weather in efforts to grow crops, save hay and cut turf. They tried to outguess nature with intensive work through nights and weeks at calving time or lambing time. High points of their social life were attending Mass, going to town and watching football derbies where half sides of the parish were pitted against each other in the local league or championship. It was a big treat to attend the annual horse races at the nearest race track.

Jack's life in England and at university was exciting to the locals as it contrasted so greatly with their rural lifestyle. Jack thought to himself that all the hardship and sweat he had gone through in England was worth it for these moments of adulation from his neighbours. He didn't realise that these moments pass by so quickly.

St Stephen's night was the night of the biggest dance of the year in rural

Ireland. Every young person felt peer pressure to be out that night. Few had cars, but some borrowed the family car if there was one. Jack and his friends thumbed a lift to Town Hall. The Royal Showband usually drew large crowds, but on St Stephen's night, it drew multitudes. Jack led his friends to the fish and chips restaurant, where they stocked up on calories for the night's fun ahead, and then into the pub for pints of Guinness.

His friends didn't yet associate drinking with going to dances, but this was now normal practice for an England-experienced Jack. At 10 p.m., they made their way to Town Hall. Inside, all the girls sat in a line on the right-hand side of the ballroom and the lads sat on the left-hand side. A local support band played to warm up the crowd. A few engaged and married couples and those doing steady lines tended to do some early dancing while they had space to move and show off their agility and timing.

At 11 p.m., the Royal Showband burst onto the stage. The crowd went wild as the Royals raised the octave level and got them moving. The dance process was such that a young man would spot a young woman on the opposite side of the hall and build up enough courage to walk over and ask her to dance. Shy lads tended to stand back and observe what was happening. Others, more intent on creating havoc, added to the male mass as it approached the female trenches. This heaving and shoving often resulted in a Hobson's choice for the lads, their glazed eyes laden with grim intent. In the swing of the heave, they were pushed away from their targeted girl. A lad would, in desperation, just grab any girl's hand and mutter, 'Would you like to dance?' A smile of acceptance or a stare of indifference dictated his fate.

Ballroom owners had little regard for health and safety even though most people smoked cigarettes within this potential fire time-bomb. The numbers per square metre was well above the safety figure. Because of poor ventilation, the temperature inside was hot and humid. Everyone sweated and eventually stank. Personal hygiene levels were low, but because it applied to everyone, no one really noticed. In life, everything is relative. Many houses of that time had no bathrooms. Toilets were organic and green and consisted mostly of the sheltered sides of ditches. Toiletries were fistfuls of nettle-free grass.

Although few understood, the accepted code at dances was that, if a lad asked the girl he was dancing with for a second dance, and if she accepted, she understood that they would be together for the night and that, later on, he would get a shift. A shift involved taking her out to her car or laneway or, if he had his own car, taking her home. The young man sought to get her into a quiet, dark space so that he could use his persuasive tactics to get his shift. The young woman had her own agenda too.

The young women saw Jack to be different from the other young men. He was thus a target for the more confident young women, who deployed all their feminine charms to get his attention. During the ladies' choice dance, a number of young women approached him. He hadn't much of a say as one dragged him onto the dance floor. Jack was always stubborn. He reacted negatively to being either commanded or left with no choices. This upfront grabbing of Jack was the wrong tactic adopted by these over-eager young women, so that nothing stirred after the dance was over.

Jack picked his own girl coming towards 1 a.m. After a couple of dances he took her to the mineral bar and bought her a bottle of Coaxeyorum. She was from town and worked in the office of the large drapery shop there. After the dance, he walked her the half-mile to her home, where he got what he described as a half shift – a kiss on her lips and a feel of her breast. After that, he walked back to the town centre, alone.

At 3 a.m., he and his friends walked towards home and thumbed a lift. A neighbour, whose girlfriend had rejected him, stopped his car and drove them to the crossroads from where they walked the rest of the way home. Jack got to bed at five in the morning. He arose at noon and his mother quizzed him about the events of the night, asking him if he had met any nice girl. Jack was vague in both his memory and his answers.

He spent the rest of that Christmas week visiting cousins and neighbours, playing cards and relaxing.

The ringing in of the New Year was another emotional night for Mary Anne. She organised it so that this year she had the whole family around her. Jack enjoyed it. He was clear on both his wishes and his ambitions for the New Year. His resolutions were to pass his first year exams with the least effort possible, enjoy college life and hold his place on the Sigerson football panel.

Jack enjoyed being home for the Christmas holidays, but he decided to get back to Dublin straight away. He packed his bag and his mother took him to the train station. She kissed him goodbye and hugged him very tightly as she whispered to him how proud she was of him and that she hoped the New Year would be good for him. She told him that he had to grab this opportunity during the lifetime of this opportunity.

Jack went straight to his now damp cold Dublin bedsit, which had no evidence of the passing festive season. This was in stark contrast to the warm Christmas atmosphere his mother had created at home. It reminded him of the navvies in London living lonely, meaningless lives. He unpacked his bag and thought about his London friend, Jimmy. He decided that he would write him a letter and wish him all the best for the New Year. He put on the kettle and had a cup of tea and a slice of his mother's brown soda bread. The two-bar electric heater warmed the room.

He sat down and drafted his letter in which he poured out his heart to Jimmy. When he read it, he tore it up – it was an unfair effort as it was all about his own issues and showed no concern for Jimmy and his issues. He rewrote it from Jimmy's perspective, put it in a stamped, addressed envelope and then posted it in the nearest post-box. He felt better now that he had done this necessary task.

He met some fellow students on the street. They went to their local students' pub and recounted their experiences of the Christmas period and how they felt that they needed to come back to this student environment earlier than normal. Jack now empathised more with his fellow students than with his friends with whom he had gone drinking and dancing on St Stephen's night. He had grown beyond them. His focus was strategic and on world-wide opportunity. Their focus was traditional, local and parochial. This was great in the short term, but, over long periods of time, it would depress Jack.

Over the next few days, the students drifted back to their flats and college. The timetabled lectures started at the university on the following Friday morning. The process quickly settled down to a pattern. Jack was determined to pass his first year exams at the first go. He quickly reconvened his project team, and they agreed on the action plan and timetable for the new academic term. It was difficult to get the engine cranked up, but Jack, as captain and project manager, was determined that it would happen. Within a week, this engine purred nicely.

Now that the core academic strategy was in place, Jack was both time-free and mentally-free to indulge in his other interests. He was now on a strict fitness regime with the football panel, and while he didn't expect to make the senior starting fifteen this year, he was laying the foundations for the following years. That year the university was hosting the Sigerson Cup finals, so a number of other functions and activities needed to be put in place. Jack actively participated in a number of these events' committees, which allowed him to get to know a wider range of students and the policies of getting things done.

Although he attended the debating society events, he hadn't yet taken part in a debate. He got vocally involved in the two debates that the first year students in engineering organised. Now that he had the ice broken, it was only a matter of time before he got vocally involved in the main debates.

As this second term moved along, Jack built a balanced college life between smart-work, football, debating and socialising.

During the Easter holidays he got a job as a helper with a furniture removal firm. This gave him some top-up funding and also gave him the opportunity to see inside the homes of the rich as he collected and delivered furniture. This stretching exposure opened his mind to wider possibilities.

The hosting of the Sigerson Cup football finals went smoothly. As he expected, Jack didn't make the first fifteen, but he was, nevertheless, one of the togged-out subs. The glorification of their football heroes by the fans drove Jack to make sure that he would be the centre-forward on this team for the next three years. He felt that this adulation was better than food to nourish the body and mind.

Lessons from Home for Jack

- **Society is made up of a series of family units.** Jack's parents, like their neighbours, would die in defence of their family unit. Mary Anne was so delighted to have her full clutch of children together again for the first time in four Christmases.

- **Stories are narratives delivered to the advantage of the teller.** Jack illustrated and embellished his stories, generating a sense of excitement and jealousy among his listeners. He embellished them further for his aunts in order to shock them. Whether they were really shocked he didn't know, but they appeared to be shocked. They were defensive in their stances and their blushes.

- **We are all influenced by role models and we, in turn, are role models to others.** Jack's brothers and sisters were in impressionable awe of the scene being painted by their big brother. He was becoming a role model for his siblings. At that stage, he didn't know that being a role model carries responsibilities.

- **We become what we constantly think about and follow it up with deliberate action.** Mary Anne had her clear vision and was confident and determined enough to drive through the obstacles to energise it. Even her relative stretching vision was confined by her experiences within her environment. She couldn't yet visualise the bigger picture that Jack was now on the road towards achieving.

- **Without the benefit of contrast, we wouldn't know how well or how badly off we are.** Jack's new journey was providing a contrast with his former local football club players. Unfortunately, it seemed to be forming a barrier rather than a stimulus to them. Their focus continued to be traditional, local and parochial. They were not grabbing the opportunity for themselves within the lifetime of the opportunity.

- **Everyone at the dance sweated and eventually stank.** Personal hygiene levels were low, but because it applied to everyone, no one really noticed. In life, everything is relative.

Chapter 17

Summer in New York

Jack planned to go to New York straight after his exams. He applied to the Department of Foreign Affairs for a student visa to allow him to work in America for the summer. To his delight, he received it a month later. He booked his return flight and told his mother about his plan after it was all arranged.

The final academic term was only five weeks long. Tension built around the college as exam time approached. Even the lazy students who swanked and swanned around the campus during the year now swotted, panicked and looked for sympathy and help. Jack stood back from this. He better understood the dynamics which were evolving. His project team had worked well and they were confident that together they had covered enough to get honours.

In the week before the exams, they took a subject per day. That specialism approach took the team through the critical points. They challenged each other in question-and-answer sessions. Over six days they covered the territory in a smart way. Many around them depended on black coffee to keep awake so that they could work around the clock. These others worked off the wrong assumption that there was a direct relationship between their exam results and the number of hours they could stay physically awake in the April and May period. The correct assumption should have been that there is a direct relationship between the quality of their outputs, namely good results in their exams, and the quality of their inputs of smart study.

For Jack and his project team, the exams went as planned. By mid-May, they had completed them. They were confident that they wouldn't have to repeat them in August.

The celebrations of the last night of the exams were built on the excessive consumption of Guinness chased down with glasses of neat Irish whiskey. The celebrations resulted in many sick heads.

Jack finalised his account with his landlord next morning. He gathered his clothes, his toilet bag and equipment into two heaps. What he didn't need in America, he packed into a big box which he put on the train at Heuston Station for delivery home. The rest he put into a gunny sack which he slung over his shoulder and made his way to Dublin Airport for his flight to New York. He had his passport, student visa and buffer spending money. A number of other students were making the same trip.

This was a chartered flight for students. The schedules for niche operators who organise chartered flights were rarely on time, and this flight was called some twenty hours after the scheduled time. Jack and the other students had to spend the night at the airport. They slept wherever they could lay their heads. This was Jack's second time on an aeroplane, but it was his first long-haul flight. Because it was a low-budget flight, the services on board were minimal. Jack slept for most of the journey and awoke to the captain's announcement that they would land in John F. Kennedy International Airport (JKF) in thirty minutes.

Jack was nervous and excited. He had no idea where he was going to work, but he felt that he was probably better prepared for the evolving scenario than his more vocal fellow students scattered throughout the aeroplane.

When they landed at JFK, they went through immigration and then customs. Jack's feet were now on American soil. Standing outside the exit door of the airport, he wondered which direction to take from here. It was now a case of the blind leading the blind. If you went in one direction, the herd followed. Jack decided that the best place to head for was central Manhattan and see where to go from there.

As he went to get the train, a number of students he knew and others followed him. Now a group of ten, they decided that they needed somewhere to stay that first night. Jack announced that he and John would book a hotel room, and the others could then sneak in and sleep on the bedroom floor. They agreed to split the costs.

Jack and John booked a room in a hotel in downtown Manhattan. Over the next hour the other eight made their way quietly one by one up to this room. Jack collected their contributions, and a ten-way split became an eight-way split so that he and John had the room for nothing. They had sub-let the room to the other eight. They lay down where they could get floor space and went to sleep. Early next morning, still suffering from jet-lag, they slipped out quietly; they agreed to hold the room for another two nights in order to give everyone a chance to make alternative arrangements.

Brian, who was captain of the university football team, had given Jack a contact number for Paddy Joe Long. Brian had told Jack that Paddy Joe would get him fixed up with a football team and, out of that, a job would be arranged. Jack rang Paddy Joe and explained who he was and arranged to meet up with him in front of Madison Square Garden at 6 p.m. on the following evening.

In the meantime, Jack walked around Manhattan and tried, without success, to get a start in some pubs and restaurants. Next evening he went to Madison Square Garden and hoped that Paddy Joe would recognise him as a fresher from Ireland. It was a warm, humid evening. Jack sat on a low wall surrounding a flower bed on the shady side of the building. He observed the comings and goings. He was excited to be at Madison Square Garden, famous to him through commentaries he had heard on radio of heavyweight boxing title fights, especially those of Cassius Clay versus Sonny Liston.

As Jack sweltered in the humidity, another young man sat on the low wall beside him. Jack didn't know why his own defence mechanism told him of danger. A cold shiver went up his spine. Jack observed painted finger nails, dyed hair and peculiar head and body movements. As advised by one of his teachers about the approach of strangers in New York, Jack moved away without making eye contact. Jack was twenty-one and had spent four years in Liverpool and London. However, he had never heard of homosexuality. This introduction shocked and frightened him.

An athletic guy with an Irish accent asked him if he was Jack. They had

never previously met, but Jack instinctively knew that this was Paddy Joe
Long. Paddy Joe shook hands and said that he was involved with the
Limerick GAA club and that they would welcome good footballers for the
summer championships. He explained to Jack how the football clubs were
organised in New York and that each senior club adopted a county name of
convenience. That didn't mean that you had to be from that county to play
for the designated club out here. He said there were only two players in the
panel from Limerick. The rest were drawn from other counties.

Jack told Paddy Joe about his captaining of the school football team to
All-Ireland victory, that he hadn't played for the years he worked in
Liverpool and London, but that he was now on the Sigerson Cup panel and
expected to nail down the centre-forward position on this team for the next
three years. Paddy Joe asked Jack where he was staying. He invited Jack to
come with him to football training. Jack collected his football gear at the
hotel and they drove in Paddy Joe's car to Van Cortlandt Park.

Paddy Joe pointed out various landmarks to Jack. He was fascinated at
seeing iconic structures he had previously heard about in story and song.
When neighbours came home on holidays from America, they boasted
about the size of everything in America and how small and parochial
Ireland was in comparison. Paddy Joe was anxious to get the latest news
from Ireland and quizzed Jack about the latest events happening back
home. Jack got a gut feeling about Paddy Joe. In his view, this was a sincere
man. Initial gut feeling is generally correct. Paddy Joe and his friends
demonstrated their sincerity to Jack by their later acts of kindness to him.

Van Cortlandt Park, on 1,146 acres in the ridges and valleys of the
northwest Bronx, is New York City's third-largest park. A major supplier of
recreation space, this green retreat has dozens of playgrounds and ball
fields, and miles of beautiful trails. The set-up in the Van Cortlandt Park
was interesting. Each county-labelled team had their own recognised patch
in the park which they used for training. Paddy Joe introduced Jack to the
other Limerick club members and invited him to go out and train with
them.

Jack was still fit from his Sigerson Cup training and quickly dug into
the task on hand. While there were heavy hits coming in, this did not
bother him as he had a frame of iron built up from his navvy days. After

the training session, Paddy Joe took Jack aside and invited him to join the club for the summer in order to play in the championship. In addition, he invited Jack to come and stay in their apartment, where four others of the team were also staying. They would also try to get him a job, although Paddy Joe said jobs were hard to get in New York.

Jack booked out of the hotel the next evening and took the subway as instructed by Paddy Joe. Paddy Joe had told him to get the train going north and named the station at which he should get off. He had drawn a map giving Jack a pictorial view of the route from the station to his apartment. Jack lost his bearings and in his panic made the wrong train connection. When he got off the train, it was dark. He had no idea where he was. He feared appearing lost, since he realised he was in a 'black' area. His vision was that, as it got darker, he could see the whites of their eyes. The stories he had heard about the gangs in Harlem came back to him. He was lost and afraid. He walked on in the hope that he would meet a white person so that he could ask for directions.

In Jack's case, his panic, fuelled by his vision of the worst, stimulated him to walk faster. But to where? As it got darker, the whites of their eyes seemed to get brighter. Jack was spinning around but getting nowhere.

Jack's brain clicked back to more rational thinking and now understood that he needed to retrace his journey to a known starting point. This was the subway station where he had got off the train sixty minutes ago. Unlike a dog, he hadn't marked his territory and had few landmarks to guide him on his route back. He found himself going in one direction, but often finished up back from where he started. This looping back drained him as he suspected some of the street hangers-on would sense that he was lost and that he would be easy prey. He avoided making eye contact. While he was terrified inside, he camouflaged it in his external body language. The quiet, safe environment of his home back in Ireland became more attractive by the minute.

When a subway train passed below him, he walked following its sound until he got to the next subway station. Once inside he went to the map on the wall and tried to fathom out where he was. He tried to identify the station he needed and work out what line it was on. By now, he had an idea of his bearings, and he cross-checked them with the ticket seller. Now on the correct train going north, he watched the names of the stations as they passed and followed them on the route map. He got off at the station which Paddy Joe had instructed him and used the drawn map to guide him from the station to Paddy Joe's apartment.

They thought he had changed his mind. Paddy Joe welcomed him and reintroduced him to the other four. He gave Jack a single bed in Paddy Joe's and Peter's room. They had finished dinner, but Mick, the eldest, rustled up some food for Jack. They settled back, had a few beers and quizzed Jack on the latest gossip from back home in Ireland.

They spoke about employment opportunity and all agreed that they would enquire from their current employers if there was any possibility of a summer job for Jack. They gave Jack some ideas of where he might look for work and the best local newspapers for summer jobs' advertisements.

Next morning, the apartment was buzzing from 5.30 a.m. onwards. Today, Mick had the role of Bean an Tí. He cooked the breakfast, which they all ate quickly. Each washed his cup and plate and rushed out the door to get to work on time. Mick gave Jack a key to the apartment. When Jack asked about paying rent, he told him not to worry about it, until he got a job. If he played well for the team, then there wouldn't be any rent. There would be just his contribution to the weekly shopping bill.

Mick was from North Kerry and had been in New York for twenty years. He had a supervisory job in a large factory and was very structured in his job, apartment duties and in his life generally. He went back to Ireland every Easter to visit with his mother and family. He was unmarried. He was the anchor tenant in this apartment, with others coming and going, even though Paddy Joe and Peter had been living there for three years. Peter was a policeman, a native of County Laois. He told Jack that both the police and the fire services were full of Irish, of either first or second generation. He liked his job and told stories of the robberies, violence and murders they dealt with on patrol in the city.

Jack walked the streets and worked the paper advertisements as advised by his friends. They told him to adopt the strategy of survival in this city. 'You have whatever trade is required at that moment in time.' The manager of a decoration company offered him a job as a painter. The manager instructed him to report to paint an apartment the following morning at

7.30 a.m. He was delighted with himself and told the lads his good news.

Out of bed early next morning he made his way to the address. He met the ganger who asked him about his experience. He passed that hurdle. The ganger gave him light white overalls, a paint brush and a large tin of paint and told him to go with Roger, so that they could work as a pair. Roger seemed to Jack to be uncertain. They took the internal lift to the roof from where they were instructed to work from the top down painting all the window sills on the outside of the tall, thirty-floor-high apartment block. When he looked down, the distance to the street below frightened Jack. He suspected that Roger was no more comfortable than he was.

In his naivety, Jack wondered where they would get ladders long enough to reach these window sills. Back home, Jack would use two wooden ladders tied together with a rope in order to reach the top of the hay-barn. This was different. They were not to use ladders. They were to use the swinging platform regulated by a flimsy motorised pulley system. Roger and Jack were to climb out onto this swinging platform and regulate its height to suit the different levels of the window sills they were to paint. 'Come on, Paddy,' said Roger as he walked out onto the platform.

Although he had a number of years' experience of working on the building sites in Liverpool and London, Jack had worked mostly in holes in the ground. A swinging platform dangling thirty stories up from ground level was altogether different. He froze and couldn't unfreeze himself. He pulled back and sat on the ground. When he regained a sense of himself, he stood up, trembling and weak at the knees. He took off his overalls, dropped the tin of paint and the paint brush on the ground, ran down the thirty flights of stairs and out onto the street below. He had started and quit his first New York job within one hour.

Back on the street and feeling bad that he had flunked this first job opportunity in New York, Jack wondered how his friends would react to his decision to quit. He couldn't tell it as it was. He knew that he had to build a reputation for himself both on and off the football pitch. He would tell a lie. He would say that there was a mix-up with the numbers and that there wasn't a role for him. When he regained his composure, he went back to the advertisements in the specified newspapers and pounded the streets in search of a new job.

The manager of a shop-fitting outfit offered him one week's work where his job was to service the tradesmen. At least this would be work on firm ground. He was to report for work the following Monday morning. As they made their way to football training that evening, Jack told the lads his version of the events. Paddy Joe said that kind of thing happens all the time.

Limerick was scheduled to play Roscommon in the first championship match to be played on Sunday in Gaelic Park. Jack had made a good impression during training – he was picked to play at centre-forward for Sunday's game. He was excited about seeing and playing in Gaelic Park. It brought back memories of home with his father, listening to Michael O'Hehir's radio commentaries on football games played there. The big perk for the winners of the national league in Ireland was to go to New York to play the local team for the League Cup. A free trip to New York was a big achievement.

Jack's mental image of Gaelic Park contrasted with reality. When he arrived with the lads on Sunday to prepare for their 12 noon match against Roscommon, Jack saw dressing rooms made of corrugated iron and many brown bare patches on the pitch. The weather had changed the patches into dust bowels. Every time a player slid or fell on these patches, a ball of dry dust rose up. The team assembled and togged out. Team manager Thomas gave a pep talk and spoke about the star player on the Roscommon team. He said that there were rumours that they had also imported two county players from Ireland in order to strengthen their team.

The game started on time. In the first ten minutes there were many heavy tackles. Jack eased himself into the game and laid the ball off, without going for glory himself. At half-time the scores were level, and Thomas made some technical changes for the second half. He told the midfielders to channel the ball into the inside forward through Jack. Jack himself cut through for two early points and became the centre of attention from both the Roscommon team and the Limerick supporters. As the game entered the final minute, Limerick trailed Roscommon by one point. Jack collected a good pass and cut inside the Roscommon backs, who were expecting him to lay the ball off. Using his head and his physique to his advantage, Jack kept possession and unleashed a shot that thundered to the back of the Roscommon net. This was a carbon copy of the goal he had scored in the

All-Ireland final many years ago. Limerick won by two points, and Jack became an instant hero among the Limerick fans. He was the focus of attention at the celebrations in the bar.

As the day wore on, Jack grew to like Gaelic Park more and more – the poor conditions of the fixed assets were irrelevant. It was the interaction of the people and the atmosphere they created which gave the place its great character. This was the Holy Grail for the Irish in New York. It was their home away from home. They could be themselves here. Most of them spent all day Sunday here, interacting with fellow Irish. Here they lubricated their relationships in the bar. A new game was played every ninety minutes so that, over the course of the day, six or seven games were played.

Here were Irish immigrants who lived rounded lives between their work, recreation and building of stable families. He compared and contrasted them with the navvies he worked with in the trenches of Liverpool and London. They had a completely different view of their world and how to live it. Why the difference, he wondered.

It became more and more obvious to Jack that his football capabilities would be his meal ticket in New York. The officials from the club refused Jack's offer to pay for his drinks or meals or tickets. They said he was not to put 'his hand in his pocket'. Mick told him that his lodgings were completely free and that there would be no more discussion about it.

The officials spoke to him about work. Jack told them about the week's work he was starting in the morning with the shop-fitting crew. Thomas brought over another man and introduced him to Jack. Tim O'Neill was a manager with United Parcels. He told Jack that he would fix him up with a job the week after next. He gave him a small card with his contact details on it. This was Jack's first time seeing a business card. He was so struck by it that he decided that he would have one for himself some day.

Jack got up early next day and reported for work at 8 a.m. The foreman asked him to service two tradesmen who were installing a hanging ceiling in this new shopping complex. It was Jack's job to bring the aeroboard slabs from the storage area and hand them in rotation to the two men operating on the scaffolding. They were light in weight, but the consistency of keeping the two men supplied kept Jack busy. New York is humid in June and, like the rest of the people, Jack sweated in these working conditions.

One of these tradesmen was from County Mayo and the other was from County Tyrone. They were interested in Jack's opinion about the emerging political troubles back in Northern Ireland. While Jack didn't know it at the time, they performed this screening exercise to find out if he was a sympathiser with the subversives. Jack was then politically neutral. He wasn't a threat to anyone. Based on this, they were pleasant to him.

Jack worked for the week and was paid. He now had money in his pocket.

On Monday he called Tim O'Neill, who invited him to come in at 5 p.m. for induction. Jack and five other new employees were shown a short video explaining the history and structure of United Parcels, a business like the post office in Ireland but confined to delivering parcels. An official took their photographs and their fingerprints for their security cards. He took them into the sorting department where Jack was assigned to conveyor belt number three.

The massive conveyor belt ran from the entry loading bay right through to the sorting bags. Nick, a huge black man, was Jack's supervisor. He showed Jack what to do: turn up the parcels coming along the conveyor belt so that the addresses faced up and could be read from the left-hand side of the conveyor belt. This was a no-brainer to Jack. He just kept turning up the addresses of the parcels. But they kept coming. He soon learned that there was no beginning or end to this movement. Nick advised Jack that he had been told by Tim O'Neill to put him on the day shift, as he was needed in the evenings for football training up in Van Cortlandt Park.

Nick moved Jack from the menial job on the conveyor belt to the more mentally-challenging job of sorting. This involved sorting the parcels by postal area. Any parcels not for Jack's six postal areas were left on the belt to continue to the next sorting station further down. This process required active alertness. Jack had to learn to quickly scan the stream of parcels passing by and to make instant decisions to pull relevant parcels and place them in the appropriate trolleys. Staff wheeled full trolleys to the out-loading bay and to the postal area delivery vans. These vans were already backed into their respective loading bays and were scheduled to move out within tight time frames.

Nick told Jack that an incorrectly sorted parcel could end up anywhere in the country and the end client would have to wait until the system rectified itself over a three-day cycle. It was often tempting to throw these parcels into the trolleys at random, but, in a quality-assured system, the inspectors selected trolleys at random and checked that the correct parcels were in the correct trolleys. The corporate target was to have 98 per cent accurate delivery within twenty-four hours of receiving the parcels in the first place.

In order to achieve this stretching corporate objective, all the critical variables had to be managed efficiently. Jack, with his engineering mind and project management experience, visualised the whole process in sequential steps. He was intrigued about its efficiency. He was to utilise this experience to good effect in his later professional life.

The job was boring, but the pay was good. Having this job and his football life and associated social life, Jack enjoyed his time in New York. His one gripe was the humidity, especially while travelling in over-crowded subway trains. These sweating bodies created an overpowering stink on the trains during rush hour. When the lads came back to the apartment in the evening, they had a shower and Mick cooked the evening meal. They tended to have their evening meal together, except for some who were caught to do overtime work.

Jack wrote to his mother as soon as he got his permanent address so that she could post him his exam results. When her letter arrived, Jack was happy to learn that not only had he passed his exam, but he had achieved second class honours. His mother expressed great pride. Jack had planned this result. It was a good output from the smart input methodology he had organised his project team to achieve. He hoped and expected that the other five members of his project team did just as well.

Most socialising took place at weekends. Jack used Saturday to explore the sights of New York. Some of the lads took him on exploratory trips outside the city so that he could get a feel for the place.

Sundays were occupied with Gaelic Park and football. It was a networking day if no games were organised. The Irish in New York went early into Gaelic Park on the day and had breakfast. They loved their Irish Breakfast of bacon, sausages, white and black puddings and fried eggs. All of these products were imported directly from Ireland and tasted much different from the American-produced fare. Because of the heat and its accompanying thirst, everyone drank lots of cool beer. This lubricated the brains and tongues of the drinkers and it often led to singing of Irish rebel songs and sometimes fights.

On the Sundays on which they played matches, they went to a booze-up in the pub and then to the Irish dances at the Irish Centre. Jack was popular and attracted the attention of many girls. He found that they were more daring and more sexually-liberated than the girls back home. They had fewer inhibitions in their physical attention to him and taught Jack to lose some of his own shyness in his relationships with girls.

The work, the money and the social life in New York combined to create an eventful and exciting time for Jack. However, the totality failed to fulfil his dream. He was not self-actualised. He wanted more from life.

What Jack Learned from New York

- **Be careful of your assumptions; they can make an Ass of U and Me.** Many of Jack's fellow students worked off the wrong assumptions. They assumed that there was a direct relationship between their exam results and the number of hours they could stay awake in the April and May period. Their correct assumption should have been that there is a direct relationship between the quality of their outputs, namely good results in their exams, and the quality of their inputs of smart study. It's an input/output model.

- **Opportunities must be recognised and then exploited.** Otherwise they are merely dreams. Jack showed his early entre- preneurial traits when he and John sublet their bedroom in the hotel in Manhattan to their fellow students.

- **Be slow to go against your gut feelings, as they are generally right.** Jack used his intuition to good effect in New York and else- where. He was street wise.

- **You will have a more successful journey if you build in balance between your personal life and your business life.** Football provided Jack with this opportunity. What is your football equiva- lent?

- **You will grow only by having stretching experiences and learning from them.** You are achieving no traction if you are merely travelling around the same circle but at a faster pace. Jack was stretching himself and building his capacity which underpinned his later journey.

- **Are you experiencing stretching experiences?** Identify them and optimise your return from your investment in these difficult first-move spots.

Chapter 18

Catalyst for Change

Jack answered an advertisement for the job of night cleaner in a 'club' in Times Square, the entertainment area of New York. This was for two nights per week and didn't interfere with his football training. His job was to go around the club, clean the toilets and empty the bins. Each of the ladies in residence in this upmarket brothel had her own room to entertain her clients. The Madame of the brothel vetted and organised the clients in a professional manner. This was a new experience for Jack, but he saw it from the commercial-model perspective rather than from the sexual-exploitation perspective. Paddy Joe had told him that the banks make no moral judgement on where money comes from.

Part of his job was to power hose the street both at the front and back of the club. The back of the club faced onto 40th Street, at the back of Times Square. From 11 p.m., the trucks came and backed into the loading bay of the *New York Times* distribution depot to collect the newspapers for delivery. Jack was hosing the street one night when he saw a truck backing into one of the loading bays. As it swung around, its light dazzled a deranged man who was walking along the sidewalk. The man walked up to the truck, took a gun from his jacket and shot the driver dead. The truck lights had annoyed him.

During the commotion and police sirens, someone said to Jack that the man with the gun was on drugs. With a power hose it is difficult to regulate its flow and difficult to avoid sprinkling passers-by on the footpath and street. Now shocked from witnessing the random taking of this life, Jack feared that, as he hosed the street, he might inadvertently sprinkle someone and be shot.

Jack was cleaning the footpath at the back of the club on another night when he saw a young man in the shadow of a doorway shivering and shaking all over. His fellow cleaner told him that this young man was suffering the withdrawal effect of drugs. The young man was shaking so much and was so sick that Jack thought he was dying. Jack's knowledge of drugs was those prescribed by the doctor or the Aspro one took for a headache – he was unaware of other types of drugs which destroyed life.

While hosing down the footpath on yet another night, he saw on the opposite side of the street a fight between a girl and a man. The man hit and kicked the girl, who was now lying on the ground. The lads had warned Jack to ignore any fights he might see and move away. He felt dismay to see this brutality and to see that people just kept walking by as if the terrible event had not happened. His colleague told him that it was a row between a prostitute and her pimp.

While cleaning the footpath on another night, he saw a lady of the night walking towards Times Square. A homosexual walking up the opposite direction shouted out, 'Goodnight, prostitute!' She looked at him in disgust and shouted back, 'Goodnight, substitute!'

Jack was, up to now, unaware of this subculture of society, or indeed of life. Witnessing murder and the effects of drugs and brutality were stretching experiences for him. He thought how ill-prepared he was for this life. He thought, if only his mother could see him now.

The football championship was going well. Limerick was in the quarter finals for the first time. Then they met a strong Kerry team which was backboned by a number of imported Kerry county footballers. Kerry beat them by just two points. Jack had a solid game and won his fight against the imported Kerry county player. The Limerick club officials were happy with their year's progress and with Jack's contribution to it. On the night of the quarter-final defeat, Jack and all the team celebrated and retired to a dance in the local Irish Centre.

As the lads came out to the car, Paddy Joe saw a prostitute offering her services and called her over. She looked into the car, and Paddy Joe said: 'How much for the lot?' She said that she would handle just two. She then hopped into the car after he negotiated the price.

Jack and Mick got out of the car to let the others have their space – they got the train back. By the time they had walked the remainder of the journey to the apartment, Paddy Joe's car was already parked on the sidewalk. In the apartment Paddy Joe was steeping himself in a hot bath impregnated with Jeyes-Fluid. This, in his opinion, would kill any germs he might have picked up from the prostitute. The beer and the elation of the football game had reduced Paddy Joe's resistance, and he had surrendered to the temptation.

His experiences in New York crystallised for Jack his need to go back to Ireland and complete his university degree course. His experiences dispelled any doubts he had about continuing the course.

Jack's flight home to Ireland was fixed for September 28th, and Paddy Joe took him to the airport. Just as he was about to say goodbye, Paddy Joe put a brown envelope into Jack's pocket and told him not to open it until he was airborne. On the plane, in the privacy of the toilet, he opened the envelope and found that it contained $500 and a note from the club thanking him for his services.

The note also invited him to come back the following summer to play for them and that they would cover the flight costs. They said that they would have a better-paying job waiting for him as well. In one sense, this made Jack a professional footballer, which was against the pure amateur code of the GAA. But Jack didn't care. He felt very touched by this gesture and all the other hospitality they had lavished on him over the last three months. He had learned a lot in a friendly environment. Moreover, he had plenty of money to cover his college fees and accommodation for the following year. For security reasons, he carried most of this money inside his socks – he pinned the rest to his underwear.

When Jack flew into Dublin, he went straight to the bank and lodged his money. With that secure, he went to the train station for the next train home. During his last Saturday in New York, he bought a special gift for his mother and some smaller bits and pieces for his brothers and sisters. He got a taxi home from the railway station. Mary Anne, Mick Denny Bill and his brothers and sisters were surprised to see him and greeted their returned hero with shyness, awe, and a new respect.

Jack gave them a sanitised, positive version of his experiences in New York. He left out bits about his traumas in front of Madison Square Garden and Times Square. He told his parents that he had enough money to cover his total college fees and accommodation for his second year in college. He also told them that he had an invitation from the Limerick football club to go back to New York and play football with them again next summer and that they would cover the cost of the flights.

When the news got out that Jack was home, more neighbours called to see the 'returned Yank'. Jack had brought bottles of Irish whiskey and a bottle of sweet sherry from the duty-free shop at the airport. His mother shared this with the neighbours and celebrated and toasted Jack's return and his exam results. They asked him if he had met anyone over there with local connection. Jack said he hadn't.

He stayed at home for a few days in order to get rid of his jet-lag and refocus for his second academic year. Over the next few days he integrated with his local football club and came on as a sub in two matches. The mentors said that he played out of his skin, but they had to be careful that they didn't drop any of their current players to open a place for him. After all, these players were available for the whole year while Jack was following his own life's agenda, of which commitment to his local football club was only part.

On October 1st, Jack went to Dublin and then to the university to register and pay his fees for his second year of the engineering degree programme. He had made arrangements with his previous landlord that he could have first option on his bedsit, his single room with its shared toilet and bathroom, again for second year. He now contacted the landlord and took up the option. He collected the keys of the bedsit and decided that, since he was going to be living here for the next nine months, he should cheer it up. He painted it, bought readymade curtains and put them up. This gave the place a fresh clean feel. In addition, he purchased a second-hand fridge and TV, and a new, small electric radio. In order to give himself some comfort, he also purchased a better heater.

His investment in cheering up the place made it possible for Jack to invite girls back to his gaff if the occasion arose. He had previously found it a hindrance to start by apologising to girls about the conditions of his temporary home. Instinctively, Jack knew that our external environment is a reflection of our internal mindset. Jack had got a taste for the company of girls during his time in New York and didn't intend to let it become just a pleasant memory. He planned to indulge more in this pleasurable possibility.

Students drifted back to the college over the next few days. Jack now learned that each member of his first year project team had done well in their first year exams. Two of his original team had decided to specialise in electronics and were thus of less use to the remainder of the team since they would be doing many different subjects. They now knew the success formula; it was up to them to follow the study methodology Jack had energised during their first year.

As the new academic year entered its second week, Jack called the remainder of his first year study project team together for a strategic review of where they were, where they wanted to go and how best to get through their second year exams. They brainstormed their opportunities and decided they needed to invite two new members onto the team so that they could cover all the subjects. They worked out the entry criteria. They agreed that each existing team member would submit two names for consideration at the next meeting. They agreed that the shortlisted candidates would be formally interviewed and that the final choice would have to be a unanimous decision. This structured approach was a good experience for the lads and would be useful to Jack later in his career.

As they went through the selection process, the interviewees gave them some angles they had not thought of. This challenged Jack and the lads to refine their methodology to good effect.

Jack was now a fully integrated player on the Sigerson Cup team, and the selectors expected him to hold down the centre-forward position. Their team coach had a planning meeting with the football panel, and they agreed that their smart objective for the year was to win the Sigerson Cup. He asked for 100 per cent, honest commitment from the assembled players and said that if any players weren't in a position to give that commitment, they should be honest enough to leave the panel now.

Jack was fit after his experiences in New York and committed himself to this exhausting task with energy and zeal. His local newspaper at home commented that he should get a run with the senior county football team. A selector called and invited him to attend the planned county trial game to be held on the first Saturday of the new year. Jack felt elated, honoured and privileged. He was determined to grab this opportunity while it was there. This gave him another incentive to focus more on his fitness and football skills.

He adopted a new motto for this coming year: 'Work smart and play hard'.

The study project team with its two new members settled in well. With good delegation and monitoring by Jack, they covered the academic pillars of their college life. They were all on their own in relation to the other pillars of college life. Jack got himself onto the engineering debating team and participated in the internal debating contests among other faculties. Some of the motions for debate were both weird and wonderful, as they should be.

He recalled the words of a professor who said that part of the value of university life is to stretch the boundaries, see what snaps, see what breaks and see what springs back to hit you.

They organised debates with the engineering faculties of other universities in Ireland and Jack got more comfortable at speaking in public. The tougher the opposition, the more he liked it and the better the debater he became.

The inter-college faculty debate was held at Galway University. Jack and his three team colleagues hired a car in Dublin and drove to Galway. The debate was scheduled for Saturday night at 7 p.m. Jack and the lads arrived on Friday evening, so they had the opportunity to suss out the place and be refreshed for the debate on the following night. Like all students socialising together, they enjoyed the night and slept late the following morning. After breakfast they went for a long walk out along the sea-front to clear their heads.

The methodology and structure of these debates was that each university had a team, and the motion for the debate was only made available to the teams one hour before the start. This required the team to have a balance of expertise on a wide range of issues, supported by raw debating capability. At 6 p.m., the debate chairman officially delivered the motion to the assembled teams. The motion was: 'What will be the impact of pollution on our economy over the next twenty years?'

It was the first time for Jack or any of his teammates to hear the word pollution. They had to look up the word in the *Concise Oxford Dictionary*. The team members of the other colleges didn't know either, as they too rushed for their dictionaries. There was pollution, but it was not an issue. Smelly water and brown water were spoken about, but not acted on. People got on with their lives as best they could. They were indifferent to pollution – they had more critical issues to tackle in the '60s.

The factories around the country were built near waterways so that they could discharge their waste directly into these waterways. In rural areas, sometimes dead animals were thrown into rivers as it saved digging holes in the land to bury them. The critical issues were immigration, jobs and trying to have enough money to pay for food and shelter. Rural parents tried to put enough money together to educate their children to secondary school level. These parents regarded formal education and recognised qualifications for their children as a viable solution to combat poverty.

Lack of specific knowledge of the motion seldom stopped good debaters having a go and putting on a superb performance as they challenged their competitors putting them on the defence.

The debate was called at 7 p.m. The three adjudicators comprised a representative of the sponsor, whom they regarded as a very important person since he sponsored the beer, a representative of the university and a captain of business. The debate was serious, competitive and fun. Jack's team won the debate by just one point.

They celebrated and commiserated with the losers in the student bar. They raised a toast to the sponsor, who covered the beer tab, making the celebrations more pleasant. Meanwhile, the girls from Galway tried to find out what the lads from the winning Dublin team were like.

Jack's academic project team continued to deliver their planned outputs and eventual exam results. On the football front, the Sigerson team had a bad run of injuries. Jack himself was now the anchor centre-forward, but too many around him were falling.

Jack received a letter from Paddy Joe in New York just before St Patrick's Day confirming their previous invitation to play with the Limerick team again this summer. He told Jack to purchase the flight tickets and that he would be reimbursed for it when he arrived in New York. Jack made his arrangements with the student travel company for his return flight ticket. He completed a stack of necessary forms to satisfy immigration and customs.

He continued to play with his home club team in the league and was included in the county senior squad. His agenda was divided about his participation in the county team. On one hand, he was anxious to make the grade and be on the starting fifteen. On the other hand, he wanted to go back to New York this coming summer and recommence where he left off the previous September. If he was on the starting fifteen of the county team, he would have to delay his departure to New York until such time as the county team was beaten in the football championship. This was a play-off between dollars and county glory. For a student who had to pay his own way through college, the dollars had to win. Slaps on the back and praise from the county team manager wouldn't put bread and jam on his plate in his cold and damp bedsit the following term. He failed to make the county fifteen so he was free to go.

The stress and tensions on the campus increased in the weeks leading up to the exams. This didn't bother Jack and his project team. They worked their smart plan and were confident that they would get their planned exam results. In Jack's mind, even though they hadn't put this label on it, they were successfully operating the input-to-output model. Their factual exam results – their output – had a direct relationship with the quality of their study approach – their input.

When the exams ended, Jack cleared out his bedsit and took his excess belongings home as he travelled to play what would be his last home club match for some months. His club mentors understood his financial imperative and, while they would have liked to have him for the summer games, they understood he had to go. They wished him well.

Jack flew to New York as planned. Paddy Joe met him off the flight in JFK airport. After a welcome drink, he took Jack back to their apartment where he became reacquainted with the lads. They wanted to hear all the latest gossip from Ireland and in particular who Jack thought would win the Sam Maguire Cup this year. Mick prepared the meal, and they sat around and had a few beers which lubricated their over-extended voice boxes.

Paddy Joe had arranged for Jack to get a start in a relatively new building site on 56th Street. Jobs on building sites were few then – without his football connections it wouldn't have been possible. He told Jack that the money was good and that the site generally closed at 3 p.m. This would allow lots of time to indulge in their main interest, which was to train and play football.

The job was scheduled to start on Monday morning. This allowed Jack a few days to get accustomed to the New York way of life again. On Sunday they all went to Gaelic Park and watched the matches, renewed acquaintances with old colleagues and drank beer. That evening they went to the Irish dance. They had fun. Jack was seen to be the new blood around, and many of the girls were keen to ply their attention on him. As a cool, laid-back character, he resisted the urge of his rising sap and instead played around without giving commitment to any girl.

Jack arose from bed early on Monday morning and made his way from the subway to the designated building site. He reported to Joey, his contact ganger. Joey was expecting Jack and, without many formalities, put him with the concreting crew. He was the only Irish man on this crew, which was made up of Africans, Italians and Portuguese. To Jack, they were a tough-looking bunch, but Jack had met worse in London. The site work was well under way with foundations and sub-floors of the apartment block already completed. They were working on the first floor on the day that Jack joined the gang. Over the coming weeks Jack got to understand the sequence of the job. They worked on a three-day cycle. The first day was to fix the steel, which was laid out according to the instructions on the architectural drawings and tied together by the steel fixers. Jack's crew had the task of drawing the steel from the storage area on a rotational basis to these fixers. The carpenters put up the timber shutterings.

During the second day, giant trucks poured the concrete. This concrete had to be poured as much as possible in the morning so that it could be spread, vibrated and screeded off before it went off due to the heat. In the summer heat of New York, the concrete tended to dry too quickly, which resulted in cracking and splitting. In order to slow down this quick drying-out process they added an acid to the mix. They then covered the completed floors with a gauze-like covering and kept watering the surface to prevent surface-moisture evaporation. The acid helped to slow the drying-out process.

Companies gave short shrift to complaints about health and safety – there was none. Jack and his colleagues had no protective clothing and they had no gloves. As they wiped the sweat from their brows, the acid from their hands mixed with the water of their sweat to create a corrosive mixture which scorched their skin. As a result, many concrete workers lost their hair and got ugly burn marks on their skin.

On the third day of the cycle, they stripped the shuttering and took it to the next steel deck, where the carpenters re-used it to erect the shuttering for the steel-fixers and thus started the next cycle. By sticking with this cycle, they completed pouring a new floor every three days.

Joey was never satisfied and ruled through fear. One of his tactics was to sack someone every Friday. This kept everyone in a state of stress. The work was tough and the conditions appalling. Nevertheless, the money was good.

Jack loved the money but found the working experience difficult. He got little sympathy from the lads in the apartment. Their view was that every job has a downside and that their own jobs were not much better, except that maybe they were more used to this level of hardship. For Jack, the combination of heavy work, high temperature and unrelenting humidity made his working life so difficult.

Every Friday morning, Fipi, the foreman, came onto the site to inspect the week's work. While he was demanding on the schedules, he nevertheless had a good way about him. He would walk about the site and speak on a personal level with the men. He had a good capacity for names, and although he was in charge of hundreds of staff, he got to know and remember Jack's name. On his Friday mornings rounds, when passing Jack he would say, 'How is it going, Jack?' before passing on.

Money was important to Jack, but the recognition of him as a person meant more to him than the money. This recognition by Fipi taught Jack an important lesson in his dealing with people. The cleaner of the lavatory is as important as the chairman of the board to the prosperity of the company.

Because of the good money earned, Jack didn't need a second job to supplement his income or to save for his college fees and keep. He could now concentrate on his football and have a more rounded social life.

Limerick had a better team this year and got to the final where they were beaten by a strong Donegal team. They considered their appearance in the final for the first time in the Limerick club's history to be a victory.

Jack had now solidified his centre-forward position and was well known for his James McCartan-like style of play. Although he hadn't played much hurling since he left school, he turned out for the Limerick hurlers on alternate Sundays. He played full forward and used both his head and finely tuned body to create havoc around the goalmouth. As Michael O'Hehir said, 'He raised dust in the square.'

Some of the lads in the apartment had issues about personal relationships with their girlfriends and partners, and problems at home in Ireland. Many of them were striving to save enough money so that they could get back to Ireland, buy some property and start their own businesses. For many it was an aspiration. For some it was reality.

Jack was seen to be educated and an outsider. Some confided in him – they wanted a trusted person to whom they could unburden their fears, who would understand their feelings and listen to their aspirations. As they spoke about their issues in this non-judgemental environment, they felt better and their own solutions crystallised for them. Jack and his friends developed a deep and genuine bond because of this trust.

When Jack walked in the door of the pub, it was buzzing with people talking and drinking. Many were people he had met on and off the pitch. The pub silenced suddenly and people paused. Mick was standing on a table beside the bar. He called for attention and began a speech. The speech was about Jack and how he had worked hard and played hard and how he was a member of the team and how all his friends appreciated him. Jack was stunned and delighted. The chairman of Limerick presented a cheque for $1,500 to Jack in recognition of his services to the team.

Contrary to the spirit of GAA amateur status, Jack was now a professional footballer. But neither he nor his Limerick colleagues cared. He was humbled by their gesture. In a way he felt sorry for them, because he was going back to Ireland to further his career, while many of them were stuck in a vicious cycle of good money versus hard work. They lacked management skills and forward planning, and they were stuck in a rut in a vicious cycle for life. They just dreamed of their objectives. Jack did not just dream of his objectives – he made smart objectives of his dreams.

At Dublin airport he went to the bank to lodge his dollars before taking the next train home. Mary Anne, Mick Denny Bill and those brothers and sisters still at home were delighted to see him. They understood that his studies and his work experiences were now the precursor to his life in the fast lane. He togged out with the local team at the weekend and came on as a sub late in the second half.

On October 1st he went back to Dublin and organised his registration and accommodation for his third year at university. Third year was considered to be the least academically stretching of the four years of the degree course. But Jack knew of the need to avoid being lured into a false sense of security.

Although formal lectures had started, the focus of students was elsewhere as they relived their life experiences of the summer-holiday period and recounted them to each other. The activities of these students over this particular time frame would be fertile ground for a socio-economic study. Some were conservative and returned to their parents' businesses. Some got safe jobs locally. Some, like Jack, went where the money was and did what it took to get it. Some used the opportunity to travel on adventure-type hikes and were indifferent to the money.

A sociologist might subdivide them into those who had their parents to back them, irrespective of their squandering of time, opportunity and money, and those who were selfish and self-gratifying and who borrowed and bummed money off fellow students, slept on their floors, and ate their food. This was the price they were prepared to pay in order to take adventures they couldn't afford.

This grouping could again be sub-divided into those who used this innate selfish streak to underpin their later successful commercial lives, and those who just acquired the 'bum' brand tag and later found the commercial doors shut in their faces.

Over time, Jack again pulled his academic project team together and set out their action plan with the methodology they were to adopt. Jack now saw that his formula had a value and presented his service to other select groups of students within the college. He set up a sort of franchise deal. The payment here was not money, but pints of Guinness in the students' bar – he used the barter system. This crystallised for Jack the concept of leverage, even though he didn't know that label at that time. He knew that the study formula they had fine-tuned doing their own academic projects could be reproduced elsewhere with equally good results.

Their Sigerson Cup team was strengthened by the addition of two new county players who had registered in the college that year. Jack was now the anchor centre-forward. They had a good run. However, they were unfortunate to lose by a point in the final to UCC. A last-minute controversial penalty was given against them, and the UCC star forward buried the ball in the back of the net to give them a one-point victory. But their disappointment was neutralised in the revelry afterwards. Jack now played regularly on the county football team. This was a great honour for his family and for his local football club. Action pictures and reports about his playing regularly appeared in the local newspapers and sometimes in the nationals.

When he allowed himself to reflect, Jack wondered what his career objectives following university should be. University or college life exists in an academic and social bubble and can be divorced from the realities of life where little external discipline is demanded or expected. Students tend to take on external causes and demonstrate on the streets because they are in a privileged position where time and atmosphere facilitate the generation of ideas and angles on causes. A mob element develops as vocal leaders suck impressionable students who are looking for excitement and attention into their cause. In some cases the students form extreme views or become polarised in their political views.

The troubles in Northern Ireland worsened. The events of Bloody Sunday incensed the student body, who were encouraged by vocal leaders and the media to come out in sympathy. After much debate and argument, it was decided that they should organise a march from the college to the

British Embassy. They would use the symbol of a coffin, which the students would carry on their shoulders and then burn it publicly in front of the British Embassy. Many students joined the march and were swept away in the wave of enthusiasm. This put fire in their bellies, but it also made them fragile enough to be manipulated by the leaders.

As the march made its way towards the British Embassy, some students saw the journalists, broadcasters, photographers and television cameras. Supposedly brave students took flight or covered their heads in case their parents would see them on the news or their photographs in next day's newspapers. They didn't want their mothers to see their hard-earned money being spent on activities other than study and furthering their academic qualifications.

This demonstration showed the ease of barking rather than fighting, being true to your mission and being prepared to pay the necessary price. The dynamics of the mob evolved much as predicted in the book *Animal Farm* by George Orwell. There were few leaders and many followers. The British Embassy was already on fire by the time this particular students' march arrived.

Now that Jack was a full squad member of the senior county football team, he felt obliged to give them priority over his commitments to the Limerick football team in New York. He trained hard. Meanwhile, his reputation increased. The team had a good run in the league, but their main focus was to win the provincial final for the first time in fifteen years. The intensity of this training commitment coincided time-wise with his preparation for his exams. This didn't worry Jack since he had his study-project team working the exam oracle for him. They won the first two championships games, which got them to the provincial final. In the meantime, Jack had remained in contact with the lads in New York and committed to fly out to New York as soon as his team ended their run in the championship in Ireland.

The flags and banners for the provincial final were everywhere. Younger people were on the streets wearing the county jersey with pride. The players tried with difficulty to insulate themselves from this euphoria and focus their thoughts and energy on winning the final. On paper they seemed to be as good, man for man, as the reigning champions. However, they lacked the team cohesion and experience needed to handle the tension on big days.

A hackney car collected Jack from his flat in Dublin on the Sunday morning of the game and drove to the hotel where the team was based. The team members had a light meal at 12 noon and a quick kick around in order to loosen up the muscles and their nerves. Their team coach gave them a pep talk in order to keep them focused on the task at hand. They went to their dressing room at 2.45 p.m. and were togged out and ready to go at 3.10 p.m. The team coach again called them to attention and re-emphasised their game-plan. Then the dressing room door opened. They were so pumped up that they burst through it and onto the pitch to be cheered on by the loud roar of their supporters.

The fife and drum band led the team around the pitch. Then they played the National Anthem. Jack's team was nervous and lashed into the task on hand. The reigning champions knew the score and absorbed their initial burst before starting to pick off their own scores effortlessly. By half-time, the reigning champions led by nine points to three points.

The coach had some very hard words to say to Jack and his teammates during the half-time break, but then used some reverse psychology on them. He told them that the game was now lost and that they, therefore, had nothing to lose. Based on this, they should go out there and play their natural game without fear or favour. They should show pride in their county jersey, their local clubs and their families. 'Let's go for it!' they shouted.

No longer under pressure of trying not to lose the game, Jack and his teammates went about restoring pride. They stuck into the reigning champions for twenty minutes of the second half and got within one point of them. The champions did not panic. They regrouped and picked off three unanswered points to close out the game. The dressing room was silent, and the supporters were too, but Jack and his teammates soon got over it. Players can get over these disappointments quicker than their supporters. Many supporters think that, just because they have paid their entrance fee at the gate, the players owe them victory.

Jack returned to New York the following week and helped Limerick to win their first championship. It was a massive occasion for the club and its loyal supporters. Jack again worked on the buildings, but this time on a different site. A number of Irish lads working in this building site made the work more tolerable than on the building site of the previous year. The money was good, but Jack had another view. He now saw this job as a means to an end and not an end in itself.

What Jack Learned from his Team Coach

- **People crave recognition.** There is no sound more golden than the sound of one's name said in praise on a stranger's lips. Jack's boss on the building site was never satisfied and ruled through fear never giving any recognition for a job well done. This was soul-destroying to Jack. One of the tactics of his boss was to sack someone every Friday. This kept everyone in a state of stress. Maslow's Hierarchy of Needs demonstrates the need for recognition at every level of development.

- **Nobody has a monopoly on good ideas.** Jack would understand the practical implication of this later in his career. Take the idea and redefine it in a way that's relevant to your situation. Then follow it up with appropriate action, measure your result and celebrate your victory.

- **We need to stretch ourselves to see the degrees of our potential.** Part of the value of university life is to stretch the boundaries, see what snaps, see what breaks and see what springs back to hit you.

- **Life is a bitch because we have to make choices.** Jack had to decide between dollars and the potential glory of winning the football championship.

- **It is easier to bark and be against everything, rather than to do the right thing.**

Chapter 19

A Day of Pride

Jack left New York and came home to Ireland to commence the fourth and final year of his engineering degree programme. He was now part of the furniture within the college campus and was appointed captain of the Sigerson Cup football team. He took on this responsibility very seriously. Over time he built a focused, cohesive team. They were tipped as favourites to win the cup this year. After a few disappointments on the road to the final, they won comfortably.

They carried Jack shoulder-high through the pitch. For the student interested in sport, this win was of biblical proportions.

The students pressured Jack to let his name go forward for presidency of the students' union. He was flattered to be identified and recognised, but he was more focused on helping himself than on expending his energies for the good of everyone else. He couldn't see himself getting too excited about parochial issues for minority groupings within the student population.

Many final year students focused more and more on their studies, attempting to enhance their final degree grades. These final grades were often used by potential employers, both in the public bodies and private sector, as their main criteria in their selection of graduates. Jack and his academic project team were confident that their methodology would get them their planned grades.

As this academic year progressed, more and more of Jack's colleagues were involved in getting their curriculum vitae together and making formal applications to a range of employers who tended to hire new graduates every year. The public service and the professional bodies were the usual hunting ground for these applicants. Jack decided that, based on his vision and practical life experiences, he would not apply. He also decided that he wouldn't do a Master's degree, as he felt that to do so would be to opt out from facing life's challenges now rather than in eighteen months hence. Because of his practical work experiences, he had an idea of what might work for him, but he kept it secret.

Jack did well, as expected, in the final exams. He decided that he would take some time out until after graduation in October in order to decide where he wanted to strategically reposition his career in the future. He decided to travel around Europe by train, by boat and by hitching. This was a fun tour, but he wanted to experience other cultures and seek other possible opportunities.

The university fixed graduations for October 10th, so he planned to come back to Dublin just in time for it. This was an important day for Jack as it marked the junction in the road from the trenches in London to his future professional career. It was a critical and exciting day for his parents, especially his mother. This day was the day Mary Anne had hoped and prayed for. It helped too to differentiate her in her local community. She was the mother of the first university graduate who had come from the parish and the local school. Jack was happy that he was able to facilitate the realisation of her dream. He felt that the trials and tribulations of her journey were worthwhile.

The day started with Jack meeting his parents off the train. His father was dressed in his Mass suit and his mother had bought a new costume for this wonderful and awesome occasion. She had her first new outfit in seven years. Jack had given her money to buy it when he returned from New York.

They took a taxi from the railway station to the college campus and arrived there well ahead of the designated time. Jack had pre-booked his conferring gown so he went off to collect it. When he came back, his mother wept with pride to see her own son dressed in his official graduation cloak. A photographer took mandatory photos. At 12 noon, the students assembled in the Great Hall for the ceremony.

Part of the hall was reserved for the students who were graduating and for the parents of those students. Supporters occupied the remainder of the hall. At the sound of the bell, the college president and his entourage appeared at the back door and made their way in military formation onto the stage at the front of the hall. The master of ceremonies profiled the stepped procedure for the ceremony. He then called on the president to come to the podium and deliver his address to the attendance.

The president spoke about the economy and the importance of education to facilitate the continued development of the graduates in the future. He spoke of the sacrifices the parents present had to make in order to get their children to this wonderful day. He congratulated the students for reaching this day and said they had overcome the many necessary roadblocks that were put in their way on their journey to this point. Now that the investment had been made by themselves, their parents and the State, they had an obligation to generate a return on it. He said they should do this through the quality and professionalism of their work in the future.

The attendance applauded. Mary Anne thought this was a powerful speech from such a learned man. She tried to internalise its implications for Jack.

Each graduate was called individually onto the stage to be presented with their parchments in scrolls and to have individual photographs taken. This formal part of the ceremony was conducted in Latin, which Mary Anne said added to the gravitas of the occasion.

The master of ceremonies announced that there was a special prize for the top graduate. The graduates looked around and nudged each other in their attempt to find out who was the winner. The master of ceremonies carefully opened the letter containing the name of the chosen recipient. Taking out the card and reading it, he announced that the chosen graduate was Jack. He said that he had been chosen because of his leadership, maturity and methodology for getting the job done. Jack climbed onto the stage for the second time to tumultuous applause in order to be presented with this coveted prize. He noted that the applause of some of his fellow graduates was muted – they were envious, and that was natural.

Mary Anne and Mick Denny Bill could not believe that their own son had been chosen for such a prestigious prize. They were overcome with pride. They were happy.

After the formal presentation, the president and his entourage marched out through the back door. The crowd mingled as the graduates and their families gathered together so that they could hug and congratulate each other.

Jack made his way to his parents and, over the tea and sandwiches supplied by the college, spoke with them and thanked them expressively and most sincerely for their support. He introduced them to his friends. Later he took them on a guided tour of the campus. They then went to a nearby hotel for a celebratory lunch. Mary Anne tried to absorb the enormity and significance of it all.

At 5.30 p.m., Jack called a taxi and took his parents back to the railway station to put them on the train home. He promised them he would be home soon. As the train moved away from the platform and they waved to Jack from their seats, it really struck him that he was now entering the next phase of his life. One door closes and another opens. Jack had arranged with the official photographer to post the graduation photographs home to his mother. When they arrived, she would have them framed and placed prominently on the dresser and the wall. This would ensure that everyone entering the kitchen would see them and be prompted to ask her about the events of the day and about Jack's professional career. She now lived her own unfulfilled life through glorying in Jack's life.

Jack got out of his formal gown and suit and into his casual clothes before meeting up with his fellow graduates for their last meeting together. The new graduates, now with their parchment scrolls safely stored away, spent the night telling stories about their undergraduate years. The issues and events they laughed at now were potentially the most serious and important at that time. They said that most of the things they worried about never happened. They said life would be so much simpler if they could have identified the minority of worries that become reality.

This was the first day of the next phase of Jack's life journey.

What Jack Learned from Great Achievement

- **In a team, the total can be greater than the sum of the individual parts.** While Jack was a good footballer, it was the cohesion and synergy strength within the team which facilitated them to win the Sigerson Cup which was of biblical proportions for their team. Teamwork squeezes more from us. This is the effect of synergy.

- **Competition is good for you.** Competition helps raise the sap in us, especially if we are competing against colleagues.

- **Milestone events influence our lives.** Jack's graduation was a milestone event. It marked the junction in the road from the trenches in London to his future professional career.

- **The emotional differences between the sexes make life interesting.** Billy Connolly said: 'Someone, somewhere, is playing a practical joke on us. Apparently, women need to feel loved to have sex. Men need to have sex to feel loved. How do we ever get started?'

- **Life is a series of doors opening and doors closing behind us.** Others can help you decide which door to walk through, but you must do the walking. Are you prepared to start taking more responsibility for your forward journey? The word responsibility can be broken up into ability to respond. You have the ability. Now go for it and be prepared to pay the price. You must make the investment before you can get the return.

- **Sometimes you have to create what you want to be part of.**

Chapter 20

Anything for a Job

Sitting alone in his Dublin city flat, Jack propped his degree parchment on the table as he ate breakfast and studied it and its important message with admiration. He, Jack Cronin, had a university degree in engineering. He reflected on the sacrifices and the influences that helped him achieve his goal.

Meanwhile back home, Jack's extra achievement of being declared the top graduate in the university gave Mary Anne and Mick Denny Bill bragging rights in the parish. Mary Anne said she had paid the price and now was her payback time. She fielded a range of questions from the neighbours. Some neighbours were genuine in their praise. Others, nice to her face, reacted with natural human jealousy. Mary Anne knew this. Some of the neighbours had dismissed her in her younger years. Now the books of begrudgery were balanced.

News of Jack's degree and news of his success was widespread. However, he now felt a certain anti-climax. He was surprised that potential employers weren't beating a path to his door and offering him jobs.

Jack's savings from his final year in college had dwindled to little. He thought about emigrating to New York or London again, but felt he had an obligation to try making a career for himself in Ireland. Before his conferring, he had put together his CV and sent it to targeted companies. However, no positive responses came. With his money disappearing, he was forced to generate an immediate income.

At a building site, he asked a foreman if there were any jobs available. The foreman told him that he had one job – the job of security man minding a building site on the north-side of the city. The foreman checked Jack's passport and student's card and told him to report for work that night.

As he sat in the builder's hut and patrolled the perimeters of the site, he had time to think. His mind wandered back to his building site days in Liverpool and London and to the navvies he worked with. He swore that he would not go back to digging trenches and pulling cables. As he reflected on where he was, and where he wanted to be, he started to plot his life's journey ahead of him.

As he reflected, he tried to visualise the journey and status of the successful people he had read about. He tried to build a picture of his own journey. He dreamt what it might be and where he might fit within it. As he built the visual pieces of this dream in his mind, he became more conscious of the gap between his present reality and the completion of his vision. He then gave notice to the foreman that he no longer wished to keep the job of security man.

Jack next applied for and succeeded in getting the job of night watchman for a large retail store in the centre of Dublin. He clocked in at 8 p.m., and his manager then locked him into the store opening next morning at 8 a.m. There was no induction training. He was merely told to walk around the store and ensure that there were no intruders. The company gave him no procedures to follow in the event of either a raid or a fire.

These security jobs gave him money, but he was frustrated and anxious to get onto the corporate ladder with a real job.

He had, earlier in the year, sent his CV to a recruitment agency. To his surprise, a letter arrived inviting him for interview. The Irish operation of a large multi-national technology company planned to set up a factory and a service base in Ireland. They wanted engineering graduates.

Jack's knowledge of the company was confined to what the agency had told him and what he was able to read in the college library. This was Jack's first formal interview. His previous jobs were arranged for him by his football colleagues or he just walked onto building sites and asked for a start.

He prepared as best he could by reading a number of books on etiquette and how to prepare for a job interview. He spoke with a few of his football team friends who had already been through this journey. A dark suit, a white shirt and a plain red or blue tie made up the formal and appropriate dress for business job interviews.

He arrived ten minutes before the appointed time. A member of the interview panel came to the door and called him in. He followed the etiquette as written in the book, which instructed him to shake hands with each of the three interviewers and then stand beside his chair until he was invited to sit down. The chairman of the interview panel took him through the details of his CV and said he was happy with his answers.

Jack explained his methodology for gaining good marks in his final exam and described how he had formed and managed his study project team based on his observations on the building sites in London. This stirred interest amongst the other interviewers who quizzed him on how he came up with the idea of gaining the most from the least input and how he had managed the dynamic of the team so that the planned end results were achieved. This was a critical issue for the interviewers. Jack was smart enough to tell them how he integrated his football management skills into this academic model. He gave them the message that he was not just another raw engineering graduate.

In addition to his basic academic qualifications, he showed signs of leadership and smartness in his approach. To Jack, this was natural and nothing to boast about. To the interviewers, this was the differentiating factor that set him apart from the other applicants. While he had no electronic engineering skills, they knew he had the capacity to absorb the functional training for the job and that he was streetwise enough to eventually work away from strict supervision. Jack hadn't prepared for the final question from the interview panel.

'If I was talking in the hotel tonight with people who knew you and asked them what sort of a fellow is Jack, what would they say to me?'

Jack was stuck. He knew he had built brownie points and didn't want to blow them away with a wrong answer. He thought for a few seconds and answered, 'It depends on who they are and their relationship with me.'

He didn't develop his answer any further. He left the interview feeling that he had performed well. He was pleased about the prospect that he would be offered his first real job by this company.

He continued his cash-generating job as a watchman as he waited for a response. As the days rolled into weeks, he oscillated from degrees of optimism to the depths of despair as he was concerned that this was the only job in town for him.

He collected the formal looking letter when he returned to his flat. As he looked at the envelope, he trembled. It reminded him of incidents during his school years, opening letters containing his school results or the first letter he got from his mother after he made contact with her from London. All kinds of thoughts and emotions went through him. The longer he delayed opening the letter, the more stressed he became.

The most stressful times in our lives are those before we make major decisions. Once we make the decision, for better or worse, our stress levels evaporate. Ninety per cent of things that we worry about never happen. We tend to beat ourselves up by procrastination.

Jack went through this pain process as he looked at the envelope and kept delaying its opening. He brought himself to a point in the kitchen where he took the envelope and opened it. As he opened the formal looking letter his first thoughts were that it was short. This was, he predicted, an indicator of 'thank you, but no thank you'. However, the letter called him for a medical examination and said that, provided he passed the examination and that his references checked out, the company would offer him the position of trainee engineer. He was to report for work on January 2nd.

Jack couldn't believe it. He read and re-read the offer letter. He now believed that the road towards his vision was now opening up. He arranged to go for his medical exam. When the results said he was fit and healthy, the company sent an offer letter which gave him the details of his contract. It advised him to sign one copy and hold the other for his own records. As he heard his reply letter falling into the post-box as it slipped from his fingers, he knew for certain that the security business was history – electronic engineering was his new route.

Now that he had completed the formalities, he wrote a letter to his mother with this great news. As he wrote the letter, he found that it was easier to express in writing rather than in conversation his genuinely felt appreciation of her vision and the sacrifices she had made to get him to what she had called a 'collar-and-tie job with a pension'. He carefully placed it in an envelope and posted it. He then went to the office of the security company and gave them notice that he would finish the job as watchman on the Thursday night before Christmas. He arranged to collect his P45 and back-pay on that day.

The postman told Mary Anne that he had a letter from Jack. He recognised the handwriting, he told her. He enquired how Jack was doing. Mary Anne, not knowing about the exciting news contained in the letter, played the game. She spoke in vague but glorifying terms of how Jack was gaining valuable experience and was doing well. When the postman finished his tea and left, Mary Anne opened the letter and digested its contents. Her heart jumped with joy. She got more excited than she ever thought she could. She danced around the kitchen and knelt by the statue of the Blessed Virgin and thanked God for making her vision become a reality.

Jack's father and the workmen coming in for dinner sensed a change, an air of excitement, even though Mary Anne tried to play it cool. She told Mick Denny Bill that Jack had been offered the engineering job with a new technology company and that he would be starting on January 2nd. They sat around the table and wondered what he would be working on and then worried if he would be able to understand it. She told them that his starting salary was £2,000 per annum, plus benefits. To them, this seemed like a great fortune. They rationalised that it was just the start of an executive journey. Mary Anne now had a further feather in her cap to crow about to the neighbours.

Jack worked out his notice without incident. During his quieter moments he visualised what his new world would be like and where it might lead him. He was both excited and frightened by it. He discussed it at length with some of his ex-college friends. They offered exciting angles such as the opportunity to gain valuable skills and experience, and the opportunity to travel, not as an immigrant but as a company professional.

At the end of his last working day, Jack went to the office and collected his papers and outstanding pay. He had the same feelings that he experienced on his last night in secondary school when he organised a bonfire to burn his books and class notes.

He then went into town and bought Christmas gifts for his mother, father and rest of the family. He went to the friary and got a Mass said for his Aunt Sheila, who was now expected to die.

He took the train home and hitched a lift from the train station. Mary Anne gave him a welcoming hug. The family was euphoric. They questioned him about the new job and when he would be getting a promotion.

Jack and his mother visited Aunt Sheila in the local general hospital. The nurse told them she was dying. Jack and his mother took turns in conjunction with some neighbours to sit with her. She was unconscious. The medical people told them that, even in their unconscious state, patients still know who is present; this helps them move from this world into the next in peace. Aunt Sheila took a turn for the worse at midnight. The nurse tended to her and told Mary Anne that she was ready to go. The hospital chaplain came by and prayed over her, providing a sense of security to all present.

In moments like this, a deep-rooted religious belief of the hereafter supports both the dying and their family and friends through the unknown. Aunt Sheila was pronounced dead at 12.30 a.m. Mary Anne gave out the prayers and sat beside her for a long silent farewell.

Mary Anne, Jack and the neighbours went to the hospital reception area, got a cup of tea and went through the funeral arrangements and high points of Aunt Sheila's life. Aunt Sheila's husband was in a county nursing home. He suffered from Alzheimer's Disease so he was unaware of his wife's death. Mary Anne was, thus, the chief lady mourner. She depended on Jack for support.

Jack contacted the parish priest, the undertakers and the grave diggers next morning. He drafted the death notice. Mary Anne and the neighbours then discussed it in detail before they released it to the undertaker who would arrange to publish in the newspaper. Who should be named as relatives was a sensitive issue. Joe McCarthy, who was a first cousin of Aunt Sheila's husband, seemed to have visited her more often in the last few years. When he wasn't at the morgue that night, they agreed to notify him. Would this cousin inherit the farm, or was Jack still in the running? Such issues weren't spoken about but were in everyone's minds. Emotions of jealousy and greed were evident from their body language.

Aunt Sheila was laid out in the cold and dull hospital morgue. A 5 p.m., the neighbours and friends started to drift in to pay their last respects. Joe McCarthy and his wife, Sheelagh, were now present and, along with Mary Anne, assumed the role of chief mourners. Most of the people sympathised with Mary Anne as they didn't know Joe. The crowd was so great that it crushed and pushed as they filed in and out through the single door of the morgue.

The neighbours had hushed discussions about the life of Aunt Sheila, how she had married into the farm and had to deal with such hardships and how she devoted her life to minding her husband. One said he was a spoiled only child who had more streaks of grandeur than streaks of work on his back. Joan, a neighbour, gave out the Rosary and all its trimmings at 6.45 p.m. The Rosary captured the focus of the people within the morgue. Those outside the door mumbled the Rosary and meanwhile chatted away about the common enemy, the weather, a non-intrusive subject. In reality, the weather had a major impact on the local economy. It determined the quality of the hay and the dryness of the turf, which were central commodities in their local lives. Talk about the weather provided a context for the talk about the life of Aunt Sheila.

Tim, the undertaker, moved in and quietly cleared the morgue of the people so that the chief mourners could have their final moments with Aunt Sheila. Mary Anne, Joe and their immediate families circled the coffin to say their last farewells. Tim closed the coffin and brought it on a trolley to the door of the hearse. The funeral moved towards the church. En-route to the church it stopped for a minute's silence at the gate of her farm. Father Ryan met the funeral at the church doors and said prayers. The coffin bearing the remains of Aunt Sheila was placed in front of the main altar. After the final prayers, Father Ryan left. When a short silence in the church elapsed, Julie, an old neighbour, went to the front seat to sympathise with the chief mourners. The crowd followed her like sheep.

Jack and some of the neighbours went to the local pub where the life of Aunt Sheila was a talking point among the many other issues of a world where people died, lived and moved on. They eventually made their way home and prepared for the funeral the following day, which was Christmas Eve.

Three priests concelebrated the Mass, showing the extent of Aunt Sheila's influence and popularity in the parish. The crowds scattered after her burial. Some cousins went to Mary Anne's house for tea where the men were given large bottles of porter and the women small glasses of sweet port.

Joe McCarthy told Mary Anne he would call some day for a chat. This raised her concern as she wondered what he knew about the will. As the days went by, Mary Anne wondered, but she didn't take part in any of the conversations about Aunt Sheila's affairs. She had overheard comments at the wake about the likely inheritor, but pretended not to hear. Jack himself had both physically and mentally moved on; to him Aunt Sheila's will didn't matter.

When Jack got home from the funeral he saw that all the fuss was about getting ready for Christmas. Jack placed Christmas presents in the corner of his loft room and, in the quiet of the night, reminisced about all the times he had spent on Aunt Sheila's farm, the freedom he had there and how this had acted as a counter against the harsh school regime, giving him a more balanced view of life. This experience and philosophy had helped with his progress through the building sites, college life and the real life experiences he was exposed to on his journey to this day.

Jack was now about to turn off the roundabout of this life's road to his first professional job starting on January 2nd. Irrespective of Aunt Sheila's death, he was going to enjoy this last Christmas. He understood that his college life and now this professional job would naturally isolate him more from his local friends, so he was determined to give it one last lash with them over the next week.

He joined the throngs of people at Midnight Mass on Christmas Eve where the singing and music in the church set a scene of wonderment and awe. The church was fuller than normal, an indicator that the emigrants were home for Christmas. The returned emigrants were easy to pick out. Most had brighter clothes and jewellery and some had gold teeth fillings instead of white enamel. Neighbours and emigrants shook hands and trailed into the night wishing each other a 'Happy Christmas'.

Back home, Jack took out the Christmas presents and distributed them. His father opened a bottle of Irish whiskey. 'Happy Christmas' they wished each other and prayed for the repose of the soul of Aunt Sheila.

Christmas Day was a day off for the men while the women took command of the cooking. Mary Anne had the Christmas dinner ready at 2 p.m. and announced to all to sit down. She sectioned the goose and distributed the vegetables and gravy. Mick Denny Bill did nothing. To this day, Jack associates Christmas with the smell of that Christmas dinner.

The conversation around the table roamed around diverse issues including football, politics, what would happen to Aunt Sheila's farm and Jack's new job. Jack's new job was virgin territory for a family from a rural parish with no knowledge or experience of corporate life. Their imaginations ran wild. Some of the angles were so wide of the reality mark that they were hilarious. Jack explained the job as best he could. He took out a pocket diary and showed them that, since he was going to be so busy with various tasks, he needed a planner. This fascinated those who lived mundane lives with each day having a sameness about it, dictated only by the light on the sky and the weather, with no need for a planner.

After dinner, they fell asleep in their chairs, allowing Mary Anne's scrumptious fare to be digested. The neighbours stayed away from each other on Christmas day. That was custom. It was supposed to be a family day. For those whose families were not getting on, it was a difficult time.

Young lads didn't observe the non-rambling culture. Jack went to Johnny's house to meet up with some of the local lads. They had a few bottles of porter and a sing song. A few of the lads went off with the local girls for a shift. Many shifts were encounters of convenience to beat the boredom of the day rather than a search for love or the satisfaction of driving hormones. These were more likely to happen on St Stephen's night when the pick was bigger and the sap higher.

Jack glided home, went to bed and slept off the physical effects of the overeating, the porter and the periodic, intermittent sadness of Aunt Sheila's death, remembering his time on the farm and how she encouraged him and defended him in times of crisis. He slept late next morning, and when he arose, Mary Anne was pitching together a cocktail of leftovers from Christmas Day in order to prevent any waste and to make up a dinner. She supplemented cold meats with freshly boiled potatoes and re-heated gravy. The Christmas pudding was more delicious on St Stephen's day than on the previous day.

The big issue for the young was to be ready for the big dance that night, to organise outfits and transport to the venue. The young women spent most of the day getting themselves spruced up to snare the young men of their dreams that night.

Recovered from his exertions for St Stephen's night, Jack relaxed for the rest of the week. He reflected on his new journey. He was both excited and fearful about it. He wondered what he would be doing, how he would settle in, and who would show him the ropes. He spent this final night twisting and turning as his mind raced with all sorts of scenarios. He observed the time on his bedside clock on the hour, every hour.

He celebrated the midnight ringing in of the New Year and the follow-on celebrations.

What Jack Learned from Drifting

- **Securing a new job is an act of selling.** Most candidates will be suitably qualified and able to do the job, but it takes a relevant spark to distinguish you from the crowd. What is your relevant spark?

- **Others will live off both your glory and your misery.** Can you identify instances in your life where this happened? In Jack's case, his mother lived off his growing reputation. This was her payback for her critical input to his earlier life. She had earned her bragging rights.

- **There is always a smarter way of achieving your objectives.** Jack used his project team to smoothen their exam preparations in the smartest way possible. Are you a disciple of the sweat approach or the smart approach?

- **The most stressful times in our lives are those before we make major decisions.** Once we make the decision, for better or worse, our stress levels evaporate. Ninety per cent of things that we worry about never happen. We tend to beat ourselves up by procrastinating.

- **Experience is not only a factor of time; it is the factor of the breadth of experience within the given time.**

- **The cost clock keeps ticking.** One of the certainties in life is that whether you are earning money or not, it costs you a certain amount to live.

- **Drifting in a vacuum is more stressful than trying to meet pressing deadlines.**

Chapter 21

A New Career

Mary Anne shook Holy Water on Jack, and as she wished him all the best for his exciting professional career, he put his bag on his shoulder and took the train to Dublin.

Next morning he got up at 6.30 a.m. and boiled a kettle of water so that he could shave and have a cup of tea. He had brought back some butter, milk and soda bread from home. His anxiety translated as he nipped himself with the razor and bled. The traditional cure for bleeding was to lick a piece of paper and place it over the wound. When it dried, he removed it and cleaned away the excess blood to leave it hopefully traceless in time for work. He ate his brown bread and got ready. This was his first time to put on a crisp new shirt and tie to go to work. It was another first, another milestone in his life.

On notification of his new job before Christmas, he had done a dry run of the bus journey from his flat to the company's office. Armed with this knowledge, he knew he should leave the flat at 7.10 a.m. to catch the bus and reach the office at 7.55 a.m. for an 8 a.m. start.

He was determined that he would not be late on his first morning. You get only one chance to make a first impression. He got the bus as planned, paid the conductor and sat on his seat observing all the people in transit at this hour. Most had sour expressions on their faces as they made their way after the festive season back to their cubicles and another year of mundane activity in the rat race.

Jack arrived into reception excited but tense about this next stage of his life's journey. He was early for his appointment with Tom, his new line manager. He waited around and observed his soon-to-be colleagues coming in and signing the register. When Tom arrived, he welcomed Jack and spoke with him during a short meeting. He gave him some idea about the business. There was no formal induction at that time. Tom told Jack to move around the various departments and, because he was a new pair of eyes, to observe what was going on. They would meet later to go through work issues. Jack was perplexed by the loose and open-ended instructions for starting. He had been used to direct instructions in rough language on the building sites.

He drifted uncomfortably through the huge offices. He rambled like a rudderless ship through the building. He felt useless. He didn't know whether to introduce himself to his future colleagues or keep out of their way. A senior lady with glasses on the base of her nose, asked him in which area he worked and what he was supposed to do. He gave a general non-committal answer and moved on. He endured this unanchored and uncertain existence for the first week. Tom, his boss, had gone to another office at the other side of the city and hadn't catered for Jack before he left.

Jack longed for someone to bark an instruction at him or pile undone, hard work on him. But no one did.

Employees make up their mind about their employer within the first few hours of employment. They then spend the next forty years proving or disproving whether or not this initial judgement was correct. If Jack had had an alternative that week, he would have quit his job in the first few days. He would have been gone before Tom returned.

On the Friday of that first week, Jack drifted into another department. Suddenly he recognised Dave O'Connor working on a bench repairing some electronic apparatus. Dave was two years ahead of Jack in university and had played corner back on the Sigerson Cup team in his last year. When Dave spotted Jack, he called him over. They chatted at length about their college days and nights. He gave Jack a rundown on the culture and style of work in the company. He told Jack that there was an open-style management and that the graduates tended to sit together and work hard and play even harder. He introduced him to the other employees. Suddenly

Jack's cloud of depression evaporated. He saw why he had been excited about the job. Dave invited him to join him and colleagues for pints in the local pub after work.

Dave introduced him to more colleagues. Jack got over his awkwardness as the lubricating affect of the alcohol loosened his tongue. A girl who was part of this social group walked over to him. Excited by her approach to him, he shifted her. After the shift, he walked to his flat in Ranelagh.

Jack arose early on the following Monday morning, showered and just had time to have breakfast before going to work. He expected to meet Tom, his new line manager, this morning to get some direction about his job. They met at 8.15 a.m. Tom enquired how he had settled in and questioned Jack on his initial impression. Jack was afraid to tell Tom that he felt useless and unneeded for most of the week and was very anxious to get some tangible job to do and a space to work in. Tom was observing him and, in a way, was playing with him to test his limits.

Tom drew out an organisational chart and then revealed a more detailed chart of a major project. He explained the core of the project and that Jack would become a member of his project team. He told him not to worry about the technical details as he would be fully briefed by the technical engineers. He gave Jack some technical manuals and asked John to act as Jack's mentor. He said that this was to both induct and indoctrinate Jack into the business. Now that he had a designated space and the outline of a tangible task ahead of him, Jack allowed himself to relax and began to read his way into the job.

Over time he got to know the agreed methodologies, who was who and what the critical deadlines were. He found out that his line manager, Tom, was highly regarded within the business and was ear-marked for promotion in the company.

One of the girls in the canteen asked Jack how he managed to get on Tom's team. It was the 'A' team she said. In Jack's case it just happened, but over time he came to understand its importance.

Jack settled in and learned the skills of the business. His tactics for passing his exams were important here. When he hit an information deficit, he understood that it was best to go and find out from someone who knew and had been down that road before, rather than slavishly sweating it out by himself. This tactic got him down the project road faster than going solo. Tom and his colleagues noticed these tactics. They were looking for potential capacity and future stars rather than today's absolute knowledge and skills' base.

Jack found out that the electronics business is a fast-growing sector where the solutions of today will be redundant tomorrow as a better solution is developed by some cutting-edge project team. Groups such as his created solutions for tomorrow's issues, not today's issues. The lifecycle of end-products was getting shorter and shorter. Hence, operating smarter and building capacity for change, rather than building absolute degrees of knowledge and skill for today, was critical.

Within his project group there seemed to be the full range of diverse skills and personalities. The core left-brained engineers were complemented with right-brained visual engineers, and the guys in between seemed to have a balance of both left and right. Within the team there was a balance, even though many of the individuals were biased either left or right. Over time, Jack saw that he could empathise with both. This indicated to Tom that he was more balanced. A profiling of Jack's personality in a test conducted later by the company confirmed this.

Another observation made by Jack was that his project team had one left-handed person. Jack didn't then know the significance of this person. As Jack got his feet under the table, he got more excited about the prospect and sometimes reflected on the attractiveness of the current opportunity versus the brain-dead job he had had on the building sites. Reflecting on this gap encouraged him to take this opportunity within the lifetime of the opportunity.

Jack didn't yet have enough experience to understand the manoeuvres and politics which go on in the business environment. He was aware of national and local politicians and some of the things they did to survive and become Ministers. They were masters of guile. However, he had no idea that corporate internal politics can be more deceitful and treacherous as people trample on the bodies of their colleagues in their mad rush for recognition and the vertical movement of their careers.

A member of the project team focused on Jack's link in the chain and observed the practical angles he brought to the issues. At the next project review by Tom and the senior management, this member made a professional presentation on an angle that Jack had produced as a solution to a project problem. He presented this as if it was his own invention and left out reference or credit for Jack in his presentation. Jack's own ideas were subtly stolen from him. This was a first lesson for Jack on the politics of survival in the corporate jungle. He learned that the tactics of licking up to critical bosses, kicking the lads below and stealing their concepts were commonplace.

Management talk about groupthink and that the project team was bigger than any individual was wonderful, in theory. In practice, at least 20 per cent of the team gave this lip service and, in their cunning and ruthless way, pursued their individual agenda to get noticed by upper management. As Jack learned, some senior managers were also adept at the sucking up and kicking down tactic. The only difference was that they operated at a higher level.

Jack was no fool. He was streetwise from the breadth of experiences that he had gained from the building sites. This now innate capacity would be good in his professional career and business journey. He knew from his football days that the game wasn't won until the final whistle was blown. Flashy corner forwards put on a show at the beginning of the game, only to be followed up by a slower and smarter corner back who, over the course of the game, sucked the blood out of them; eventually the flash corner forward had to be substituted. The corporate game is no different. Corporate life is a full-length game; it's not just a flashy exhibition for the first quarter.

The project they were working on was to develop next generation technology that would be cutting-edge, intuitive, user-friendly and could be brought to the market in an eighteen-month time frame. The reporting lines between Tom as project manager and Jack's line manager became blurred as the project grew and many mini project teams were created for the various links of the total-value chain they were developing. The blurring of roles led to all sorts of manoeuvrings for personal positioning within the team. The result was that those at the lower steps of the food-chain were used in subtle, and not so subtle, ways.

Since Jack was still on this lower rung, many tried to manipulate him. They didn't realise that Jack was not just another raw, wet-behind-the-ears engineering graduate. He was a survivor, and he drew on his breadth of survival instincts to manage this manipulation. He continued to be co-operative but also strove to make meaning of his small contributions. Holding onto that vision allowed him the time to reflect. He gradually gained respect beyond his limited short amount of experience.

As the main project team fragmented, more and more bosses emerged. Jack was uneasy because of this confusion and lack of clarity. He was gaining no forward motion. The clock concentrated the minds of those responsible for delivery of the project within the original eighteen-month time limit. As timelines tightened, panic developed, and Tom became more and more involved in the project. He banged heads and pulled all the diverse groups together in order to get the whole team working for delivery on the due date.

This focus on delivery by timelines eliminated much of the pessimism within the team members as they focused on a common cause. Idleness and too much time allow people to focus on personal agendas and waste valuable resources and energy.

A stretched team will always outperform a limp team whose capacity is dissipated in different directions of self-satisfaction. No longer counting weeks, Tom was now counting the time deadline down by hours. The team burned midnight oil, ignoring the hours set in their employment contracts, working till dawn if necessary. They may or may not get time off later. Tom kept driving the project, based on achieving planned outputs by specific timelines. He didn't accept excuses. He said, 'You are responsible for your link of the chain and nothing else is on the agenda.' He measured tangible outputs, not promises, and ensured that he brought the project home on time and within budget.

This reminded Jack of the thinking he used as team captain when his team won games that on paper they seemed not to deserve. It's all about who, in sporting parlance, has the silverware at the end of the day. The silverware here was the tangible delivery of the project within the time frame. From this final peak performance, the team members were exhausted, but they were proud and relieved. They released their pent-up emotion at a night out, organised by the company for them. As the alcohol loosened tongues, they voiced many previously unspoken angles on the issues. This allowed Jack the opportunity to observe who was who and who was jockeying for position and glory.

One swallow never made a summer. The harsh reality of corporate life soon hit Jack in the face, as he was immediately challenged by Tom to drive a new project. The previous project was now history, and the gloating about this past achievement had to stop. This culture was in stark contrast to Jack's experience on the football pitches and the building sites where the current victory was reflected upon long after its delivery.

Jack was still green but was more streetwise than other raw graduates. He strove to succeed by consistently delivering measurable outputs as per the agreed parameters. This facilitated him to get noticed, which is necessary for vertical career movement.

Having acquired a name for delivery, Jack found himself being pulled in many directions, which tended to dilute his effectiveness. In the matrix structure which existed, successful managers achieved their own delivery agenda based on their ability to grab and exploit necessary resources.

As the months rolled into years, Jack matured and began to perform well in both his personal life and career. This refocusing from just having a job to establishing a career was natural, but partly surprising to him.

Jack fell in love with Áine from the first time he saw her in the office. Her blue eyes, with her hair groomed to hang over her left eye, defrosted any reluctance that Jack had previously perfected to defend himself from other girls who became too serious too early for him. Prior to this, Jack wanted the advantages of a relationship without the accompanying obligations.

Their relationship deepened. Jack and Áine understood that they were developing something special, something unique, a *je ne sais quoi* that meant they would be together for life. This balancing of career and relationship in Jack's life made him more rounded in his behaviour and more understanding in his mind-set.

To underpin their growing relationship, Jack knew that he needed to build a parallel suitable career. He realised that, as the quality of his current input to the work projects grew, it led him to better-than-average outputs. His enhanced outputs got him the attention of senior management. In corporate land, attention from management is critical. In a changing workplace there are always opportunities and threats which management are often stretched in their desire to tackle. If you are noticed for the right reason, you may match your perceived talents with passing opportunity.

The board of management of the company asked Jack's boss, Tom, to examine the best options for the development of a new tangent technology which had emerged from the Research and Development department. The R&D department estimated the probabilities of the success or failure of the proposed product. In testing solutions, combinations of variables can throw up an unexpected angle which may represent another opportunity. This tangent technology discovery was such a potential opportunity. It might become commercial or it might fail.

Firstly, Tom was faced with a task of recommending to the board if this opportunity was worth scaling up. Secondly, he was faced with deciding whether it should be developed in-house or outsourced.

Tom was streetwise and had the breadth of practical experience to sniff out possibilities. He analysed it, listened to his intuition and decided that it had commercial possibilities. He knew it couldn't be developed in-house because it was a tangent project, which wouldn't sit pretty within the culture and preconceived ideas of the corporate world. He knew that its development was risky and that it would need space and oxygen which would only be possible when managed independently of the corporation.

He developed a business plan for this project which scoped out areas including the resources, structure, and space it would need for it to live long enough in order to become successful. Within the structure section, he recommended that a new and separate company be set up away from the corporate company so that it could focus exclusively on the further development of this product and its commercialisation. This new company would have a separate board of directors, who, in turn, would appoint a chief executive officer who would build its business model. It would also have its own budget and be responsible for the planned commercialisation of the product or service.

Tom had difficulty in convincing the board to cut this project loose from other projects being developed – this was a new strategic option. Like all change there was outright resistance from some directors and bullish support from others. The debate went on for weeks until the managing director called for a final decision to either support it or kill it. When faced with this contrasting choice, the sceptics gave it their passive support but told Tom it was on his head. This allowed them the comfort that, in the event of its failure, they could blame him and say 'I told you so'.

Some people manoeuvre themselves into positions where they can slither away and avoid the point of winning or losing. This results in stress and indecision. They are usually purposeless and fruitless. They find it difficult to answer the question, 'What do you stand for?' Their personal survival is their only objective. They would be shocked and paralysed if faced with making a major decision.

The board signed off on Tom's proposition. He then set in motion his implementation plan. He rented an old warehouse which offered office space. He drew up Articles of Association and a Memorandum of Association. He registered the new business with the Companies Registration Office as required by law.

The human aspects of the business caused him anxiety. The first of these human dimensions was the formation of the board of directors. The signed-off deal stipulated the number of members of the board who were to be drawn from the corporation and the number who were to be outsiders. This process was a new experience for Tom, but being streetwise, he anticipated that landmines would be planted for him and that he would have to bypass them or defuse them. He eventually got decisions about the board structure.

At their first board meeting, the directors appointed Seamus to be board chairman and confirmed Tom as CEO. The chairman organised with the corporate head office that he could be seconded for a period of two years. Tom took on the role while still retaining ultimate responsibility for the outputs of his old department.

He took on the task of putting together the physical set up of the new facilities and the installation of necessary equipment and telecommunications. Next, he pulled together the initial team and agreed a road map with them. Because of his networking capability, he was able to negotiate the release of some people from various departments of Ramu Plc. He supplemented them by recruiting externally. He seconded Jack to the team. He continued to work from his current office within the corporate head office.

Over time Tom built an enthusiastic team, which was drawn more by the initial burst of energy rather than by brain power. The roadmap was still vague, and this lack of clarity percolated down to the individual activities so that, over time, the team members felt frustrated. They felt they were driving in a fog. This, in turn, appeared as a foggy performance to the board. While the board had a long-term vision about the project, they were unclear about the stepped journey that had to be managed from starting point to end game.

Tom was the positive driver of the car in the metaphorical motor rally. He struggled to clarify the roadmap ahead both for himself and his team. This made it impossible for him to give clear instructions. Each piece of clarity is equivalent to one wheel of the car getting traction. Each lack of clarity is equivalent to the other wheel of the car merely spinning, with one wheel spinning and the other gaining traction. The car merely goes around in circles rather than forward.

Because of the initial euphoria about this project, the board members were unconcerned. They believed that it would quickly get over its teething problems and gain traction to move it toward the dream end-point.

The business digested huge resources as Tom tried to tackle the vagueness of the issues with more resources.

As the months drifted into a year and the year drifted into two years, Tom and the board grated on each other. They strove to get hold of the issues and develop an agreed roadmap for the business going forward. This required a lot of soul searching, resulting in many arguments and blaming of each other. It was a necessary process to facilitate the venting of feelings and the clarification of issues.

At the end of this stormy process, they agreed on a basic roadmap. Tom would return exclusively to his day job back at Ramu Plc and a new, uncontaminated general manager would be appointed to drive the business. They agreed that the new jockey should be drawn from the existing team. They scoped out the job and advertised it internally. Tom indicated to Jack that he should apply for it as it represented a real opportunity for him to advance his career.

Lessons that Jack Learned from his Boss

- **Ride on the tail of a vertically moving manager to get ahead in corporate life.** Successful managers have a vision of where they are going and they cause it to happen by pulling together appropriate project teams and resources to make it happen. Jack was good enough to optimise the opportunity of getting onto Tom's A team.

- **We tend to get blinded by our surroundings.** Tom told Jack to move around the various departments and, because he was a new pair of eyes, to observe what was going on. What is the message here for you?

- **Uncertainty can be very uncomfortable.** Jack drifted uncomfortably through the huge offices. He rambled like a rudderless ship through the building. He felt useless. He didn't know whether to introduce himself to his future colleagues or keep out of their way. How good are you at inducting new recruits into your organisation? The sooner they are up and running, the sooner you will start to get a return on your investment in them.

- **You get only one chance to make a first impression.** Employees make up their mind about their employer within the first few hours of employment. They then spend the next forty years proving or disproving whether or not this initial judgement was correct. If Jack had had an alternative job to go to that first week, he would have gone.

- **Corporate politics is often more intense than national politics.**
Corporate internal politics can be more deceitful and treacherous
as people trample on the bodies of their colleagues in their mad
rush for recognition and the vertical movement of their careers.
Success has many sponsors, but failures have none.

- **You need to be street-wise to succeed in business.** Having
formal qualifications represents only the starting point. You must
know how to play the game and win. Experience is not necessarily
a factor of time; rather it is the factor of the breadth of experience
gained within the given time frame.

- **Keep stretching.** A stretched team will always outperform a limp
team whose capacity is dissipated in different directions of self-
satisfaction.

Chapter 22

The New Boss

When the job advertisement appeared, Jack read it and reflected on it carefully. He tried to understand how the gaps in his own profile could be bridged to fill the requirements sought in the job advertisement. He considered too the potential impact of the job on his growing love of Áine. They spoke about the impact of this advertised job and whether it would be an enabler or a hindrance to the continuing development of their relationship.

Being young and with little to lose, they agreed that Jack should give it a go. If he was lucky enough to get the job, they could then decide to either accept or refuse it. Jack put his CV together as best he could so that he could hit as many of the key hot buttons as he could. Áine read it. She was surprised at the extent of Jack's work skills and experiences. From her perspective, it clarified what she knew. 'My Jack is a treasure. He is special to me. Together we can face the world and conquer it. Ní neart go cur le chéile.'

Jack submitted his application and waited for a response. During this time frame, rumours circulated through the company about who had applied and who was going to get the job. Jack's name was not mentioned.

In a letter to Jack, the company told him that he should present himself for interview for the position on the following Thursday at 3 p.m. He and Áine were initially excited about the prospect, but on reflection they were frightened as well. Áine told him to understand the importance of the difficult road he had travelled to this point and how he could draw from this breadth of practical experiences to make this new business work. Between them they sussed out that the logic of company's decision to invite him for interview was Jack's innate potential and his willingness to take on new stretching experiences.

They read books on how to prepare for interviews and role-played the interview process several times, with Áine in the role of chairman of the interview board. This was a team effort and gave them the opportunity to jointly develop their relationship at a different level. Even if he didn't get the job, they were already winners in their own minds. They were now a performing unit.

Áine had Jack's suit and shirt ready for Thursday. She took time off work to dress him and provide support and encouragement in his moment of need. He had similar butterfly feelings in his stomach to those he experienced before important football matches.

Jack arrived ten minutes before time for his interview. He noticed one of his colleagues coming out of the interview room; he was one of the people rumoured as likely to get the job. Instead of being frightened, Jack now felt challenged to go for it. His football experience came into play. He remembered the football philosophy of his team coach: 'The bigger the star, the harder you can make them fall by applying appropriate tactics on the day.'

The interview panel comprised three company people – one of whom was Tom. In the first part of the interview they reviewed points from Jack's application form and CV.

Interviews are just another form of buying and selling. The company has an opportunity to buy the best candidate for their pre-defined task, while the candidate has an opportunity to sell his or her relevant skills and experiences. The final decision is based on the judgement call of the interview panel. This often turns on what might appear to be a small issue. While it might be small, it can nevertheless be the critical one.

Jack and Áine had earlier in their preparation tried to guess and tease out what the critical issue might be. Through trial and error they worked out that it was the answer to one question: 'Why should we appoint you in preference to other applicants who have more capacity than you?'

This was a sticky issue for Jack during preparation, but they rationalised it out. Jack waited for this crunch question to come in some format. He wasn't disappointed. Tom asked it in an innovative way. He painted a practical scenario about the critical points facing the business and then asked Jack how he could successfully address these issues in spite of the fact that he didn't seem to have as much experience as some of the other applicants. Jack reflected on and dissected the question so that he could draw on the rational thinking he and Áine had gone through. His resulting answer was different from what they expected, which in an interview scenario is always good.

Jack showed maturity in his answer. First he tackled the issue of experience and told the interview panel that experience wasn't a function based on the number of years. What was important was the breadth of the experience. He explained that one could be several years in the same job, but have only the equivalent of one year's experience. This is because one should have conquered that job within this period whereas spending more time at it was the equivalent of going around in circles. He referred to his own breadth of experiences and how these survival traits would be critical to succeed in this job.

He could see from their body language that the interview panel had not expected this answer. He said that his management response to the scenario painted by Tom could at best be a general response and that he would need to be in the job to fully understand the angles of the real issues. Then, he could formulate more precise strategies and tactics and cause them to be successfully implemented. He then went silent in order to let the impact of his answer sink in.

The interview panel members looked at each other and brought the interview to a close quickly. They told Jack that he would be informed of the outcome within one week. Jack got up, shook hands with each member of the panel and walked out of the interview room with, as he saw, his reputation enhanced. Like winning a football trophy, you have to be prepared for whatever tactics the opposition throws at you on the day. Thanks to Áine, he was prepared for the encounter.

Áine and Jack celebrated the end of this step of his journey. They felt closer together as a result of their joint effort to get to this level of performance. Like all proactive people, they were prepared to stretch themselves, perform at the optimum and accept the results, no matter what. If they achieved the planned result, they would celebrate more. If they didn't achieve their planned result, then they would learn from the experience, dust themselves down and move onto the next opportunity, but from a stronger base.

On Friday, Tom called Jack and told him he was the chosen one. Jack had yearned for this offer, but now that he had it, he was frightened and unconsciously allowed negative thoughts to control his mind and sap his enthusiasm. He had thoughts about the critical issues facing this business, how he would deal with identified problem team members and how he would manage the board and his team.

Although the negative issues swam around in Jack's head, he felt more comfortable by the hour.

For Jack, Áine's reaction and advice was his critical intervention during his moments of doubt about this new opportunity. By asking him questions and actively listening to his responses, she facilitated him to verbalise his thoughts and give them air. He could now see that his initial negativity and fears were groundless. However, he still hadn't reconciled the price to be paid for repositioning himself from his current comfort zone versus taking the supposed opportunity being offered to him.

Áine's methodology was good in that her interventions challenged him rather than directed him. She understood that this strategic decision had to eventually come from Jack after he weighed up the pros and cons and understood the price that he had to pay for either accepting or rejecting this presented opportunity. There is also a price to be paid for deciding not to change. The price Jack had to pay was the opportunity cost of not being able to experience the rewards from this opportunity.

Jack asked for a meeting with Tom and the board in order to clarify the relevant issues. As the meeting time approached, Jack increasingly lost the positive debate in his mind. As he walked over the door saddle on the way into the meeting room, he decided that the job wasn't for him. He had not prepared for this circumstance. He got into discussion about the business issues with Tom and the board and felt a certain degree of excitement and challenge as they focussed on a mutual development of the vision for the business. As the thinking process continued, Jack couldn't find either the nerve or the opportunity to inform them of his snap decision. They assumed that he was already in the position, and their thinking was now focussed on how best to agree the business vision and development of the model to make it a reality.

The chairman stood up, shook Jack's hand and welcomed him on board. Now there was no going back. He was snookered by default or by design. Like all capable people, he now snapped into the mode of 'let's get on with it and do what I have to do'. At that moment his mind was firmly on driving and looking through the windscreen rather than through the rear-view mirror. He left that room feeling elated.

In Jack's case, the impetus for change came from the challenging excitement of the new opportunity. This now became stronger than the hold or hankering of the old role. He quickly agreed his departure terms from his current job and set about implementing his new role in a professional manner. As he departed, leaving old colleagues, he was mindful of his mother's advice: 'Be careful about standing on people's toes on the way up, because you may need their support on the way down.' This basically sound advice was nevertheless negative or limiting in that it was anticipated that one would have to eventually retrace the trodden road. Her complementary follow-on advice was better: 'Don't burn your bridges behind you.'

Unlike other countries, Ireland is a small place with its network of networks, which have the capacity to either enhance or ensnare you over time. In his own way, Jack played by this principle and managed his exit very professionally, leaving the door open for future contacts and, perhaps, business opportunities. As he cleared his workspace he was driven by mixed emotions. Nevertheless, the new challenge and its opportunities now won all the debates in his head.

Áine said that the messages and wishes of good luck to Jack from his old colleagues at his going-away party hosted by the company were genuine. He read somewhere that women are more intuitive about feelings than men, and that men tend towards being more one-dimensional. Men, therefore, miss many nuances and also critical enabling angles. Jack was smart enough to know his male shortcomings. Áine's opinion on the sincerity of his colleagues boosted his confidence for the new challenge.

Jack decided that it was best not to take too much time out between the departure from his old job and his entry to the new opportunity. He finished on Friday and started on the following Monday. He was restless for the weekend, driven by excitement and anxiety about the mammoth task ahead of him.

Everything in life is relative. This was just another logical step and, in relative terms, was no greater than his decision to step onto the cattle boat at the North Wall and sail into the unknown. He now realised the lesson from this experience. He had survived, and he had later used this baseline to successfully kick-start the first phase his professional career. Now was his opportunity to stretch himself, and kick-start the next phase.

He twisted and turned all night, got up early, showered and shaved. After a quick, stand-up breakfast, he made his way to his new office. He allowed himself plenty of buffer time. He wasn't yet sure of traffic. He arrived near the new office an hour earlier than the start time of 8 a.m. He pulled his car into a side street and parked. If he arrived too early, he might inadvertently give unintentional signals and mixed messages of arrogance and power to his new colleagues and staff.

As he waited, his mind raced and his heart pumped. He remembered the advice from his one-time football coach, Dick, about the tactics to adopt when faced with a football opponent who had a fearsome reputation. Size him up first, rather than striking first and then having to live with the consequences. Jack would first size up the situation in this business; only then would he allow himself to act. He would do this by adopting the tactic of listening, observing, asking questions and verifying, and empathising (LOQVE) so that he could build a profile in his own head about the dynamics that existed. He would then decide his action plan.

At 7.55 a.m., he started his car and quietly eased it out of the side road and into the nearby company car park. There were function-specific car spaces, one of which was for the managing director. The space was vacant. He had to make a snap decision whether to park there or park in the general parking area. His snap decision was to park in the general car parking area. This decision was driven by his uncertainty about his positional power and the possibility that Tom would arrive and expect the space to be there.

He straightened his jacket and walked into reception. He introduced himself. Paula, the receptionist, welcomed him to the organisation and advised him that Sheila was now his PA; she would come and meet him presently. As he stood there, he witnessed the early morning movement of people into the building, who, he observed, were ignoring his presence and getting on with their routine. He knew he wasn't invisible to them. He knew that when they got to their work stations the main topic of their conversation would be him. Tit bits of information about him personally, his style and hot points would be shared and added to. He felt, for the first time, the experience of the fish in the fishbowl – watched by all with most things private on public view.

Sheila arrived smiling, shook hands with Jack and welcomed him to the job. Sheila was blonde, perfectly formed and seemed to be in command of herself. She was the film-star image of personal assistants to corporate executives. She saw her job as the shadow and support to the managing director. Jack reminded himself that he was now the managing director. She said she would attend to his administration and secretarial needs. She told him that Tom was on his way, and they would have a meeting. She took him to his office, which was guarded by her own office. She gave him a rundown on the communication equipment on his new desk. The black button on his phone was the most important – that buzzed Sheila.

Tom arrived into Jack's new office. Sheila took their orders for tea and coffee and left. They discussed the weather, sports, politics and the economy, the precursor to business communication. Tom said he would be going back to corporate headquarters to focus on his core project. He advised Jack to read his way into his new role and to look around. He advised him that his fresh pair of eyes and ears would spot angles on issues that those longer on the team, including himself, would have been blind to.

Tom then walked Jack through the offices, introduced him to his immediate management team and then brought him to the factory floor where he introduced him to key players throughout the plant. This was an artificial, but necessary, process. It gave Jack the opportunity to meet those he would be depending on to help him take the business in the strategic direction he would shortly decide on. It also marked the hand-over from the outgoing managing director to the new.

By lunchtime Tom was gone. Jack now had both the responsibility and the authority to make this business work. First impressions are important. He declined Sheila's offer to go to the canteen and fetch his lunch as she had always done for Tom. Instead, breaking tradition, he queued like the rest of the staff and went to the nearest available table, asking those already present for permission to join them. He introduced himself as Jack. He listened and addressed them as each, in turn, shook his hand and welcomed him to the business. He then teased out which department each worked in and their individual roles there. This gave him an initial, bottom-up impression of the place. The conversations drifted to issues other than work. Sport was a common theme, a universal currency and medium through which Jack could communicate with most of the staff.

Jack knew from his practical experience gained in the building sites that he was being observed by everyone. Because he was now the managing director, he was conscious that he needed to gain their genuine respect rather than their artificial friendship. This would be his management style going forward. As a novice in the new role he was conscious of his incompetence for the job today, but was also aware of his capacity to become consciously competent and eventually, like Tom, to become unconsciously-competent. He knew that when the unconsciously-competent phase arrived, it would be time for him to move to a new challenge and again go through the process of equipping himself to move from his new conscious-incompetence level through the stages to become unconsciously competent in the next new role. The cycle would repeat.

After lunch, Jack returned to his office and fielded calls from friends who wished him all the best in his new role. He flicked through the critical files Tom had handed over to him. Sheila gave him copies of the management accounts. He sat down with Mick, the financial controller, for a quick overview of the financial model and how work was progressing against budgets.

By 5 p.m., Jack knew that his first day as managing director – Day 1 as he marked in his diary – was a success. Now with his feet under the desk, he had a better feel for the strategic positioning of the business and the various enabler and check points that would take the business forward.

He would park in the designated car space next morning, sending out the signal that he was now in charge and that this business would never be the same again.

He met up with Áine, and they went out to their local pub for a celebratory meal. Áine was good for him. She didn't crowd him, but generally debriefed him about the various events of the day and how she felt about these. This cleansing of his mind gradually relaxed him. They grew more comfortable with each other's company and closeness.

Jack and Áine were now less defensive and more open with each other – and they were very much in love. They thought that their relationship was special. They believed this, and then this belief became true for them. They were on a mutual journey together and had a common mission.

Together they knew that their love, mutual respect and support for each other would, in turn, equip Jack to have renewed confidence to build the company one step at a time.

Jack arose an hour later next morning and, being more relaxed and confident, parked his car in the designated car space for the managing director just before the scheduled time for the start of the work day. He planned to now define the size of the elephant and decide what bites he would digest or reject.

Jack had trained in management techniques. He knew that the skill of good managers is to perform these techniques under the stress of the real commercial world. None of us knows our real capacity until we are faced with a new challenge beyond our comfort zone and must decide how to react to it. The issues or events we face in life are important, but more important is how we react to them.

Jack spoke to his management team and staff, not because he had to say something but because he had something to say. Say not always what you know, but always know what you say. His initial tactic was the LOQVE technique –listen, observe, question, verify and empathise.

The first few days were a honeymoon period, where there was a lot of 'sucking and seeing' both by Jack and his staff. There is a survival instinct in all of us. Irrespective of the circumstances, we can adjust after the initial shock to our survival mode.

What Jack Learned about Power-Play

- **We are less successful because we are encouraged to conform.** To be more successful, you must be unsatisfied without being dissatisfied. You are unique. You can decide what you want to become. People with a purpose can break the pack. Differentiate yourself from the crowd.

- **We are all travelling the journey of life with no idea about the length of that journey.** If you want to do something that you are passionate about, then go and start doing it. Encouraged by Áine, Jack decided to face this career opportunity and was prepared to pay the price.

- **You can react differently.** Instead of being frightened, Jack felt challenged to go for it. His football experience came into play. He remembered the football philosophy of his team coach: 'The bigger the star, the harder you can make them fall by applying appropriate tactics on the day.'

- **Don't undermine your case.** Interviewees often make the mistake of diluting their main point by offering too many follow-ons and alternatives. Jack was aware of this. He underpinned his case with his best evidence – just one point at a time.

- **Elation is the natural feeling you experience when you replace the stress of indecision with definitive decision.**

- **People may doubt what you say, but they will always believe what you do.**

Chapter 23

Conflict and Change

The appointment of the new managing director sent waves throughout the organisation. The employees stood back, observed and interpreted the signals coming from their new boss. They tried to identify his hot and cold buttons. When they received blurred signals, they pushed their luck and waited for reaction. When there was no reaction to their first press of the buttons, they pushed them again until they got a reaction. This reaction then represented the outer limits of the area in which they started to build their new comfort zone.

Jack had practical experience of this while working and surviving on the building sites. He and the other navvies had to quickly learn the style of their ganger. Based on this interpretation, they then adjusted their behaviour.

Jack knew he would be tried out on a range of situations so that the staff could 'mark their own cards'. He counter-played their tactics by keeping his head down, listening, observing and resisting the lure of the bait laid out for him.

As he read his way into the job, he walked around the various sections of the plant. He stopped spontaneously at stations and spoke with the operators there. This appeared to be casual, but Jack used the management tactic of asking specific questions such as 'What are you doing here?' His walk-around tactic gave him a feel for the range of activities happening on the ground and who was doing what. This would later be invaluable as he became more dependent on the system output and his information conduit in managing the business.

Tom had already established a system of management meetings, and Jack decided that he would first follow this system and observe what happened at them to see if they were productive. His first finding was that there were many meetings about meetings, producing little output. The length of the meetings was not to be determined by the relative seriousness of the issues, but rather by the availability of time. The more time that was available, the longer the meetings went on.

At the end of his first month, Jack had to attend his first board meeting. This was a new experience for him – he was apprehensive about it. He had received copies of the previous minutes of the board meetings from Tom, but they were inadequate for his need to visualise the real state of the business. Being his first meeting, he assumed he would be allowed to feel his way through this foreign territory.

This first meeting was very structured. Following the initial review and sign off of the minutes and matters arising, the chairman quietly addressed the items on the agenda he had drawn up in the weeks beforehand and then quickly got to any other business on the agenda. The directors had their eyes down and gave no response. Before he closed the meeting, he turned to Jack and asked him to report on his initial observations of the business.

Jack hadn't expected this direct challenge and hadn't been prepared. Drawing on his practical experiences of survival on the football field and the building sites, his instinct told him not to dig holes for himself. He remembered the advice of his football coach, Dick: 'Don't go in for the full frontal tackle and get mortally wounded. Instead, go into the tackle sideways and live to fight another battle.' He gave a few general observations and said that it was still too early for him to make definitive observations about the critical issues and to formulate the necessary follow-on action plans.

The honeymoon period quickly passed, and the harsh reality of commercial life started to kick in. Jack was unable to keep kicking to touch and had to become confident about his decisions as they arose. He learned on the football pitch that you must win the first real tackle with your opponent. This would then set down a marker for the remainder of the game. Being streetwise, he understood that there was no advantage in going to battle with the workers' union. He had to attack their main player as he had done in the All-Ireland final all those years ago. This then would put down a marker and would send out a strong message to the rest that, contrary to initial perceptions, Jack was a strong managing director.

When Jack first applied for this job, Ted was already the internal pretender to the throne. Ted had the technical qualifications and experience, but he lacked the strategic perspective – even though he didn't know that himself. He was very disappointed about his failure to get the job. He feigned support for Jack in his presence but criticised Jack when he was out of sight. Jack himself would probably have done the same if their roles had been reversed. He sensed that Ted was sniping at him, so he waited to take his opportunity to define Ted's boundaries.

He was guided by the principle that the opportunity of a lifetime must be taken during the lifetime of the opportunity. Ted's project team had worked for the last eighteen months on the Connacht Solution. They tried to develop a cutting-edge solution which could, in turn, be incorporated into the core company product. From his analysis, Jack understood that they were struggling to meet their targets and had wasted much of their budget on tangent activities. They had missed their output timelines on three occasions, and therefore the opportunity for this planned solution was passing by.

When Ted came with a proposal to Jack for both extra time and budget in order to bring the project in, Jack told him he would reflect on it and make a definitive recommendation to the board at their next meeting. He was upfront with Ted; he pointed out to him how badly the project was managed and how it had probably missed its strategic importance in the family of solutions currently being developed. This straight talking from Jack shook Ted as it was his first time to be challenged with reality in his patch.

Ted had the ability to deliver the project, but he got diverted in his self-fulfilment journey towards the role of managing director. His competition with Jack now had the elements of trench warfare. Jack held his factual ground, and Ted looked for an opening to win the battle. Jack wanted to win this battle, so that he could use it to then win the war.

Having done his analysis on the strategic positioning of the business, Jack decided to terminate this project. Instead of patching the leaking bucket, he needed to dump the bucket. He prepared his case to underpin his recommendation to the board and advised his chairman what he proposed to do. He also proposed that Ted should be invited into part of the board meeting in order to put his side of the argument. The chairman reluctantly agreed, and Jack informed Ted so that he couldn't later use the excuse that he was ambushed. Various rumours went back and forth throughout the company about this warfare. They were fuelled by Ted, who now played the dirty game of whispering into the ears of various people about how he and his team were wronged and how Jack used this opportunity to shaft him.

As Jack became more aware of the background game, he was more determined to challenge Ted and the board, if necessary, to justify their continued support for the project.

To his face, Ted was all smiles to Jack. But he wasn't fooling Jack. This evolving scenario was being observed and commented on from all angles within the company. It reminded Jack of the dynamic with his school team in the hours before they played the All-Ireland. Rumours flew around about the opponent's key players. These rumours weren't based on fact, but they still became reality for the team. Jack longed for the whistle to be blown and the game to start.

On the night before the board meeting, Jack and Áine role-played the scenario. This pre-playing of the case helped to sharpen Jack's angles as he built his case to justify his recommendation to pull this project. He was now able to bring a dispassionate, intuitive discussion about it to the meeting.

The project issue was the last item on the agenda and, because he anticipated intense discussion around it, the chairman transacted the business of the meeting with precision and decisiveness. Drawing attention to Jack's proposal on the agenda, the chairman informed the meeting that he had invited Ted to join this section of the meeting to give him the opportunity to hear Jack's proposal and to then put forward his counter argument. The board would then excuse both executives and consider the pros and cons of the case in private, where they would make an informed decision.

When Ted joined the meeting, the chairman asked Jack to formally make his proposal and present his supporting case. Jack presented a factual case, with figures and projections based on the available data, and in conclusion proposed that the board should terminate the project.

Ted was seething. This was the first frontal challenge he had experienced in a long time. His judgement and management performance were now being questioned, and this was very uncomfortable for him. He made his pitch profiling the steps of the project to date. He glided over the missed milestones and tried to paint a picture about its future.

The more he tried to build his case, the hazier Ted became in his presentation. He tried to defend the indefensible. Instead of using the ladder to get out of the hole, he dug a deeper hole. When both sides had made their case, the chairman asked Jack and Ted to leave the meeting so that they could discuss the options in private.

When Jack and Ted re-entered the meeting, the chairman informed them that the board had decided to freeze the decision until the next meeting and that it depended on finalising the corporate strategic business plan and clarification of Ted's project. Jack had already signalled that Ted's project wasn't sitting well within the corporate strategic plan. This angle gave some of the doubters on the board the escape hatch they needed to delay the definitive decision.

Over the next month, Jack drove the finalisation of the strategic plan onward and got buy-in from the stakeholders. This strategic plan defined the vision for the business going forward. He got agreement on the vision statement, mission statement and corporate objectives. He now had clarity about the strategic position of the business within the targeted, but evolving, external trading environment. Having achieved that, he drew up an action plan detailing how the business was to reposition itself and gain competitive advantage in this redirection.

When completed, Jack presented this strategic plan to a special board meeting. He was smart enough to involve them in the process, so that now they were signing off what they had already agreed to. After a lengthy debate, one director proposed the plan and another seconded it. There being no counter proposal, the chairman and Jack signed the plan, making it legally their collective decision. This plan was the equivalent of their new road-map. It showed where the business was, where it was to be driven and how it had to get there.

Now that this strategic plan was signed off, it was an easy decision for the board to back Jack's proposal about Ted's project. It was now obvious that his project had to be killed so that the drain on company resources of time, labour and finance could be stopped.

Ted was very upset. He felt that he had been screwed by Jack, who, he believed, had hidden behind the veneer of the new strategic plan. Jack had often seen emotional outbursts on the football pitch, in the dressing rooms and on the building sites. These emotional outbursts eventually end. Ted had won some earlier battles, but he had lost the war. He was now a yesterday's man as far as the business was concerned. Over the next few months he withdrew more and more from the business. The corporate company gave him a supposed trophy task back at the headquarters office.

This victory demonstrated Jack's resilience, his clarity and his capability to make things happen.

Managing directors occupy very transparent positions. They are in a fishbowl where their every action, reaction and non-action is observed and interpreted. They are always giving out signals.

Jack signalled strongly that he knew where he was going and that he was capable of getting the various stakeholders to support him in his quest to allocate limited resources towards high-performing stars and away from dogs that have an insatiable hunger for consuming scarce resources. These signals set the tone and determined the culture of the business. The evolving culture combined clarity of purpose and optimisation of resources so that the agreed objectives of the business would be met on time and within budget.

Those who bought into this enhanced pattern of productivity thrived; those who resisted it gradually weakened or left the company. Jack now led the business according to its mission statement and action plan towards its goals and ultimate objectives.

The winners and losers percolate through the layers of the organisation. Jack was now seen as a winner with the status of a god whose decisions were less likely to be questioned.

Jack and Áine continued to grow in their relationship. In the early days, Áine challenged Jack and supported him as he prepared for the initial interview. She supported him through his leading-in period and then later during his big battle with Ted.

During this period they got engaged and then married. Now they were the proud parents of beautiful baby, Maura. This experience helped Jack to become more rounded making him more mature and responsible. In this exciting period of their personal lives they learned to live, love and support each other. Áine had run her professional career right up to the birth of Maura. They decided that Áine would take a leave of absence so that she could devote quality time to the baby and reduce the pressure on Jack to perform both at work and at home. Their social life now centred on the baby and home.

Because of his job commitments, Jack had to frequently travel to other countries. He was also responsible for entertaining business guests when they visited Ireland. On the surface this seemed attractive, but it was more of a chore than a pleasure. Sometimes Áine's mother was babysitter for Maura so that Áine could join Jack at business and social events.

One decision they made was that they would take a holiday, no matter what happened. It allowed them to enjoy the income that Jack now earned. Baby Maura further solidified their union, and as a threesome they were a mighty force.

On return from their recent holiday, Áine found she was pregnant again. After the initial shock and denial and who was to blame, they realised how lucky they were. They conditioned themselves in anticipation of the baby's arrival. The arrival of the new baby kicked them out of their group-think comfort zone and opened up new and exciting possibilities for them.

Jack was guided by both the strategic direction and pace as documented in the company's corporate strategic plan. This involved the building up of a stable of complementary projects, whose outputs were to be used as inputs to the major projects being worked back at corporate headquarters. Jack's company was basically a strategic supplier of critical solutions to the corporate projects.

Because of the demands of the corporate board of management, Jack had to manage his business unit both efficiently and effectively. The effectiveness part was to ensure that they resourced the right projects. The efficiency part was to ensure that they were efficient at completing the projects, so that their unit costs were kept competitive as input costs. This process involved a lot of pre-planning and the gathering of necessary resources for competing projects within the corporate portfolio. The process taught Jack about corporate politics. He was aware of national politics and how politicians jostled for position. He now realised that if you weren't successful at playing the corporate politics' game, your future would be jeopardised. Knowing the theory and successfully putting it into practice were two different things.

By nature, Jack was highly principled and had simple tastes, but he either liked or disliked people. Because of his personality profile, he had to discipline himself to play the political game until such a time that it became a habit and he was unconsciously competent at it. But it wasn't his natural style, and he tended to slip his guard on the odd occasion, particularly when people rubbed him up the wrong way.

About this time there was a change of chairman of the board, because the original chairperson had been promoted to a senior position back at corporate headquarters. At first, Jack got on well with John Joe, the new chairman, but over time they started to irritate each other. John Joe's personality profile was similar to Jack's – people of similar personality types tend to compete with each other.

John Joe had his own vision about his role. He had read the book about the job of chairman. Over time he tried to manoeuvre himself from the position of non-executive chairman to that of executive chairman. This caused problems for Jack, as John Joe tried to get increasingly involved in Jack's patch. The person who has too much time to kill can be dangerous. While they had an externally good relationship, Jack became more and more frustrated with John Joe's interference. Jack assumed that he did it deliberately to undermine him.

The world economy went through a tough period and put pressure on the financial performance of the company. In turn, this had a ripple effect on Jack's area where more stringent demands for reduced unit costs came from corporate level, and high-profit expectations came from his own board. Jack was under pressure to square this circle. John Joe's interference was sabotaging his attempts. Jack could manage the dynamics of the market, but John Joe's irritating interference and undermining of his position frustrated him.

Jack kept much of his frustration from Áine since she had her hands and head full with the babies. He knew that if he told her the full story, she would have told him to tell John Joe that he was leaving. Jack didn't want this outcome. He decided that he wasn't going to give in and let John Joe have the satisfaction. It became a war of attrition. Jack knew that his decision wasn't rational. Nevertheless, his strong stubborn streak dictated that he risked the opportunity of going forward by resisting John Joe's interferences. It became like a cancer within him, continuing to eat his self-worth and satisfaction.

How it was working around in John Joe's head, Jack had no idea and could care less. On the surface everything appeared professional – but under the surface, the swan paddled like hell but made little progress.

During this difficult commercial period, Jack had a number of disasters and successes. The successes out-balanced the disasters. Jack was still winning but by only a short head. As the projects progressed, the financial opportunities started to grow, and Jack's business was fit and lean enough to grab opportunities and move forward again with success.

During the bad times, Jack decided that, as the ship's captain, he wasn't going to abandon the leaking vessel. Now that their ship was mended and back sailing the waters of opportunity and tranquillity, he was determined to manage the business professionally. He felt also his responsibility to the various stakeholders. Jack could now refocus on himself and start to dream of his own personal mission statement. Now that he had survived, won the different battles and had his ship sailing in calmer seas, he felt better; the negative influences and interferences from John Joe became less relevant.

In a restructuring of the corporation, the board put John Joe into semi-retirement where he could graze in pastures away from Jack's business. The rising economic tide and the departure of John Joe put Jack into a very good place in his own mind and allowed him to establish a new comfort zone. His former boss, Tom, was appointed his new chairperson.

Jack, Áine and their two children went abroad for a sun holiday. As he relaxed on the beach, he let his mind wander. He realised that, although now in a very comfortable place, he was too young and ambitious to stay in his present job and spin on the spot for the remainder of his working life. He and Áine had many discussions about issues of security of employment and income, the cost of the children and their education. These issues presented logical excuses for them to do nothing but spin faster on the spot. The more they teased the issues and scenarios and opportunities out in the relaxed atmosphere of the holiday, the more they realised that their reasons for not changing were just convenient excuses.

Jack had successfully guided the ship through the troubled commercial waters. The business was focused and professional in its delivery of planned projects, and now operated as a productive strategic partner to the parent company. There was genuine mutual interdependence between them. Jack was mindful of the strategic repositioning of Ramu Plc and how his own company had made its contribution to that manoeuvre.

Jack's work conditions were good, so the impetus for change from his comfort zone would have to come from the positive side. At Jack's current level there was no possibility for share options in Ramu Plc.

The new opportunity would have to be so attractive that the impetus could beat the resistance. As Áine and Jack prophesied and discussed the future, they realised that they would never create real wealth for themselves while working for someone else.

Jack's Lessons from Adversity and Experience

- **Change is always difficult.** For change to happen, there has to be enough impetus to kick you out of your comfort zone. From the negative side, this impetus may come when your boss sacks you or the firm goes into receivership. From the positive side, it may come when an opportunity is so attractive that you kick negativity out of the way and have a go. Jack raised himself to the change possibilities.

- **Winning requires a particular type profile.** The strategic manoeuvring conducted by Jack demonstrated his resilience, his clarity and his capability to make things happen.

- **Managing directors occupy very transparent positions.** They are in a fishbowl where their every action, reaction and non-action is observed and interpreted. They are always giving out signals. Jack signalled strongly that he knew where he was going and that he was capable of getting there. His practical experience gained while working and surviving on the building sites stood to him.

- **If you want to succeed in business, you must be prepared for the landmines which will be laid out for you.** Ted was obviously disappointed that Jack got the job ahead of him. He feigned support for Jack in his presence but criticised Jack when he was out of sight.

- **Facts stand up to scrutiny.** Those who perceive the facts are not to their advantage tend to waffle. At the board meeting, Ted was waffling. He was trying to camouflage the facts.

- **Those caught with their trousers down quickly look for who and what to blame for their predicament.** Failing managers flail out at all those around them.

- **Your business objective should be to optimise your wealth, as you see it.** Unless you get part of the action, it is nearly impossible to create wealth for yourself while working for someone else.

Chapter 24

Towards a Higher Goal

Jack managed and drove the business based on the principle that business success is measured by tangible results. His star was rising, not only with his board and peers, but also with the senior management of the parent company. Board members approached him many times to consider letting his name go forward for senior management jobs within the company. Because he was happy with his own vision of his future with Áine and the children, he decided against these management jobs. He was, nevertheless, mentally uncomfortable with his level of comfort within his own ship, which now glided on calm, still water with the wind at its back. He was no longer stretched or tested. He could now manage the business with his eyes closed. He knew he needed to do something; his difficulty was in answering the question: 'Do what?'

This need to change challenged him to look at other opportunities outside of the parent company. There were options, but none jumped out at him. He considered the option of advanced management studies.

This further formal education for someone who found secondary school traumatic and boring was a surprise to his aging mother, who had a narrow definition of education. He decided to study for an MBA, otherwise known as a Masters in Business Administration. He decided to pursue his studies on a part-time basis. This would allow him to continue his job and keep cash flowing to support his ever increasingly expensive family. The board agreed to pay his course fees provided he agreed to stay with the business for a minimum of two years following completion of the course. Because of the expense of the fees, Jack was happy to accept their sponsorship.

This new challenge was both exciting and frightening for him. He knew he wasn't a natural academic, but he wanted to know what the academics knew about business. He was smart at getting to his agreed output, as demonstrated by how he project-managed his way at undergraduate level. Because of his preconceived view about his own scholarly endeavours, he approached the first module with fear, stress and trepidation. He assumed that the other participants would be high-achieving academics, with more brain power and experience than he had. He assumed he would struggle. Nevertheless, he now had no option but to go ahead as he had declared his plan to the board of directors. If he failed, his credibility and reputation might be damaged. He felt that, regardless of success or failure, he would gain from the process.

He attended the first module at the MBA college. There were twenty-five participants drawn from a range of business types, professions and public services. He later discovered that the group had been carefully chosen by the college so that there was a good balance between private and public experience and so that no one was in direct commercial competition with anyone else within the group. This was a critical point for the group dynamic because if competitors were present, they would feel uncomfortable about disclosing their procedures, strengths and weaknesses, and this would create a negative atmosphere within the group. The facilitators from the college asked the participants to agree to have a code of ethics which stated that what was said and explored within the room, stayed in the room.

By the end of the first few modules and the interaction during the coffee breaks, it gradually dawned on Jack that the supposed high flyers were no better or no worse than he. Various challenges to them peeled back their veneer of academic achievement. The programme provided knowledge, but its true value was to challenge the participants to think differently about themselves and their role within their respective businesses.

The lecturers encouraged the individuals within the group to challenge everything and assured them that there are always faster, cheaper, more effective and more efficient ways of doing things. While this better way was not always apparent, the knowledge that there were other options challenged Jack and his college friends to search for them.

As the programme continued, it demanded more of Jack's time. He had to juggle his time between the three busy variables in his life – his family, his job and his study. Having to work out a priority schedule for this was a good learning experience for him. He realised that everything has a price, and he had to decide either consciously or subconsciously whether he was prepared to pay the price. Áine and his children were paying some of the price. Jack's time at the programme of study was eating into their family time. He and Áine had discussed this beforehand, and it was only with her support that he decided to do it. In other words, he had got planning permission from home to do this.

Now that he was in, he was in to win. Áine knew that and was prepared to back him. Synergy within a team is vital for achievement. Where there is synergy, 1+1 is never equal to 2, it is always 3+.

They worked out a rota so that Jack could have quality time with the children, even if it was restricted in terms of quantity. He committed himself to study from 6 a.m. to 8 a.m. before going to work. At the weekend, he did blocks of early study and was then available for quality time with the children for the rest of the day.

Jack found the range of experiences within the group stimulating and satisfying. The code of ethics within the group provided a safe environment where everyone had the opportunity to be uninhibited and was free to express themselves.

The safe environment was so refreshing to Jack that he decided it was an opportunity for exploration. He constantly expressed ideas about possible opportunities and gauged the reaction of the group. This was a form of focus group, drawn from a particular stratum of society. He was aware that this group might not be representative of his target market for any new business proposition he had in mind. Nevertheless, Jack continued to use this once-in-a-lifetime opportunity to test his ideas. The more he opened up and challenged the group members, the more respect he gained from them and the better the feedback he got. This was the Law of Attraction working at its best.

There are few leaders and many followers. Jack became accepted within the group as being reliable and trustworthy. They reasoned that he had many experiences which gave him street wisdom that the well-heeled members of the group didn't have.

His progress towards natural leadership of the group was gradual. It reminded him of the football teams and the building site gangs where the flash guys always felt that they had to say something while those who understood the local dynamics spoke only when they had something to say. In the football teams, you would never win a match with a team of fifteen flashy corner forwards who darted all over the place. You would have the work horses of corner backs, the steadying influence of the middle player and the creative playing of the centre-forward. These would make space for the flashy guys to take their scores. The balance within the team made the team.

Jack became the reference point for the group when they sought sound advice. This was a two-way street. As time went on, the Law of Attraction worked better. The more challenges Jack threw at the team, the more angles they came back with. It's difficult for a group of twenty-five to be fully integrated. Over time, while everyone is still part of the total, there is a natural osmosis towards the birth of subgroups.

A natural subgroup of five people evolved. No one planned it. The five members of this subgroup worked well together. Jack tended to project manage this group, using it to deliver the necessary programme projects in a smarter way, just as he had done during his undergraduate days in university. As the members of this group worked and ate together, they challenged each other to develop a vision for themselves for the future. They issued a challenge to themselves of: 'Do you want to do more of the same or do you want something else in the future? If it is something else, then what is that to be?'

By opening up this challenge and letting it ferment in their mind, they challenged their subconscious minds to search their subconscious database for options. Martin Luther King, Jr., famously said, 'I have a dream.' Jack and his subgroup members asked: 'What dream do you have?'

The safe confines of the academic environment allowed them to be liberal with their lateral thinking and allowed their minds to work outside the box. They knew that their dream would have to be converted into a goal. In addition, measurement parameters including timelines would have to be applied to the goal – a dream without a deadline is still just a dream.

As the two-year time frame for the course programme progressed, Jack and his colleagues settled into a rough pattern that allowed them to become institutionalised in this unreal and safe bubble. The group members became mutually interdependent. But for the necessity to return to the commercial reality of their day jobs, they could have easily drifted permanently into this new comfort zone.

As part of their programme outputs, each participant had to write a thesis on a single topic: 'How are you going to manage change in your business going forward?' They had to use their own businesses as the model.

This challenged Jack to look anew at his business unit and analyse where it could be strategically reprioritised within the strategic journey set for the corporate company. During this reflective analysis he thought also about his personal mission. As a fulfilling condition for the company's sponsorship of MBA programme, he had agreed to stay for a minimum of two years beyond the programme. This put time limits on his agreed personal journey.

He decided also that it would take enormous time and energy to do his MBA thesis alone. Instead, he decided that it would be smarter to empower those above him and those below him within his business unit in the company by involving them in his thesis. He would use it to tease out the strategic options for his business unit. He would use the external excuse of the thesis as the catalyst to get his necessary agenda considered.

Back at the office, he conducted a number of brain-storming exercises with the various staff members in company groupings in order to empower them and encourage them to come up with their own view of the strategic position of this business unit. Their ideas ranged from more of the same to wild and wonderful. Within these ideas lay possibly good answers. The value added from the process was that it challenged Jack and his board to think strategically and closely question what the best corporate structure and credible mission for the business unit might be.

During some think-tank discussions by Jack and his subgroup from the MBA programme, it emerged that, if they wanted to be commercially successful, they would have to have part of the action. They suggested that if they were to pay the price for initiating change in their business lines, they had to work a formula where they had part of the reward built in. This principle was embedded in Jack's mind as he facilitated the investigative, strategic thinking process within and without his business unit. One of his unpublished issues was: 'How can I manoeuvre myself to get a part of this action, and if I can't, when should I leave to set myself up so that I may gain from another opportunity?'

As the programme progressed and his mini thesis was teased out, Jack planned for life after completion of the MBA programme. He and Áine thought out the implications for them and how they would readjust to Jack's re-entry into their lives on a planned and more regular basis. The future was as yet unknown, and they were fearful and excited as they tried to put the pieces of the jigsaw together to complete their vision picture.

As Jack's mini-group worked together, they became mutually interdependent. They explored the options of pooling their resources and doing something together beyond their MBA commitments. They generated many wild business ideas, but no one was prepared, at that stage, to develop one of these ideas. On reflection, the reason was not that the ideas were wild or for the birds, but that the opportunity cost was too high for them as individuals at that stage. They all thought that the idea of a joint project was good, provided someone else within the group took responsibility for it.

Innovation tends to come not from comfortable situations, but from uncomfortable situations. The members of this mini-group were well-off in a relative sense. They were satisfied with more of the same.

There is a deep chasm between the idea and commercial success – it is known as the Valley of Death. The drive and passion to fuel this journey through the Valley of Death to the new vision has to come from an uncomfortable base. This discomfort can arise because your present situation is extremely uncomfortable. Or it can arise because the identified opportunity is so attractive. To realise the new vision, you need positive energy to pull yourself out of your current comfort zone and push yourself through the pain barrier.

The board of management agreed to sign off on the agreed strategic plan for the business; Jack left the structure section of the plan vague enough to allow him options in the future. He allowed doors through which he might escape to spring his real agenda when the time and opportunity would be right for him and not the board.

Some MBA participants showed withdrawal symptoms as the finish date approached. The reason for this is that people always settle for what they already have if they don't have the wish to chase a greater cause.

There were students who complained about incidental issues and lecturers. In one sense, their participation on the MBA programme was bad for them – the experience had awakened in them the reality of their pre-programme positions and a felt need to change. They had failed to successfully make the transition and create the new legacy for themselves.

Once you have looked out through the door of your patch and seen greater options, even though they may have large price-tags on them, you will never be the same again. Politicians and government run the same risk with their constituents. If they raise their constituents' expectations beyond their capacity to deliver, they create more problems than they can solve.

For those within the group who had more clarity about their future, this regeneration of possibilities was healthy. Jack was one of these. He worked out that more of the same was not the option for him in the future. While he hadn't worked out in detail how the future would eventually happen, he had planned a route towards his defined goal. This goal was to build wealth for himself, not for its own sake but as an enabler for a greater, more principled vision.

Jack edited his final thesis, and he and his mini-group members went to the programme's office to submit it before the stated deadline. It was a great feeling to have this tangible project completed. Now they were released from the burden of preparation and could start their individually-planned implementation plans.

The MBA course participants, their partners and the academic staff attended a celebration dinner that marked the end of the programme. This was an important milestone for Jack and Áine in their joint journey. Áine was very excited about it, as she really looked forward to meeting some of the other participants and their partners. Like many of these occasions, there was a combination of celebrations for successfully arriving at this point and for recognising that the group and their good experiences were at an end.

Some of the events of the previous two years were relived in the formal speeches. The recall of particular crises tended to get the most hilarious responses. They appeared to be real crises at the time – in hindsight they were trivial.

The celebrations came to a natural end. Jack and Áine eventually retired. This was the first night away from the children for some time; they were determined to exploit the uninterrupted opportunity. The earth moved for them and reconnected them with their genuine love, pride and respect for each other. This healthy base was critical for them to kick off the next stage of their life's journey.

Jack returned to work on Monday feeling as though he was walking on water. He found it difficult to understand that the rest of his work team hadn't the same exhilaration and buzz as he had. In reality he forgot that, while he was away in a safe academic environment, the team members were still producing the outputs of their planned projects. Within a day or so, he was mentally back at base, but now with a different perspective. He focussed on how to use his camouflaged escape doors to his advantage and, ultimately, to the advantage of the greater stakeholders. Though he didn't presently know how, Jack was confident that, armed with his new knowledge, he was going to achieve his objectives by adapting the appropriate tactics on the day.

The college looked well on this special day of the graduation, with the trees of October shedding their leaves. There was calmness around the college grounds. Jack and Áine and the children arrived early so that they could soak up the once-in-a-lifetime atmosphere and allow the children to know what Dad had spent his time doing – perhaps sow a benchmark seed in their little heads. We are all the products of our genetic make-up and the environment through which we come. Áine or Jack could do nothing about their own respective genetic pools, but they had the opportunity to create a supportive and challenging environment for their children and themselves. This was an ideal opportunity on this journey.

After lunch, Jack and his colleagues went to the changing room to don their graduation gowns. They then marched out to the hallway and posed for mandatory university photographs as well as family photographs to formally record this great event. At 3 p.m., an usher rang a bell and called the group to attention to line up so that they could enter the conferring hall in a military formation. Another usher showed their supporters, including Áine and the children, to already designated seats. When all were seated, another bell signalled the arrival of the dean, professors and ordinary lecturers in their gowns, who all marched to the stage. The dean addressed the group. He said they were a privileged group, but those privileges carry responsibilities and that, as potential future captains of industry, they must deliver to their potential.

The president of the college presented a parchment scroll to Jack as Áine and their children watched excitedly and proudly. They were even more proud, when towards the end of the ceremony, the master of ceremonies called out Jack's name and asked him to come to the stage to receive a special recognition award; Jack was chosen as the outstanding student based on a number of criteria, other than just his academic achievements. Jack felt elated that he had merited this special award. His fellow students had opened a betting school about who would be chosen but felt that the weighting given to pure academic achievements might have tilted the scale away from Jack. He was now being specifically honoured.

He thought how proud his mother would have been if she had been healthy enough to attend. Her vision and mission for Jack had not only been achieved, but it had been surpassed. He thought, as tears came to his eyes, that she wouldn't have dared to think that big, but, by God, she would have been so proud. He thought how she would have used his achievement in her interaction with her local community and within her wider family. She sowed the seed and cultivated its germination. Jack eventually tended to the resultant plant which flowered and grew fruit – he was now starting to pick some of this fruit.

The output of the MBA programme, as far as Jack was concerned, was not the theory he had been exposed to, but rather the change in his way of thinking. He now looked at various issues and incidents from different perspectives and through powerful filters and analysers. This process, in turn, guided his decision and follow-on actions. His team observed subtle and tangible changes. They seemed to be incremental changes, but they went as if directed. The accumulation and the manipulation impact of these little incremental changes caused a strategic repositioning of the business unit within the corporation.

Jack now operated more as a manager and less as an operator. He was causing things to happen and put appropriate measurement systems in place to ground and solidify these changes.

The strategic linkages into the corporate value chain were good, but the culture and the evolving management style had changed uncomfortably. The only reason that business continued between both was that Jack's unit continued to deliver critical solutions for them.

When you allow an alternative agenda to brood in your subconscious and conscious brain, it gradually makes the present situation less and less attractive. During the two-year time frame following his MBA, Jack's main focus was on alternative strategic options for himself. He was content to just keep his business unit going in that period.

He considered strategic options based on crazy outside-the-box thinking. He gave each of these crazy ideas due investigation. He used the safety of his mini-group from the MBA programme to think aloud and get their feedback. Over time he built his options. He broke the options into three broad categories:

Continue as is;
Leave and start a similar type business; and
Leverage current business away from Ramu Plc.

On further reflection, he decided to eliminate Option 1. His mind had been opened up to bigger things and there was no going back to his former comfort zone.

Option 2 was a live option, even though he hadn't yet worked out the how bit of it.

He understood the business niche and was comfortable that he could identify any emerging problem for which his new business could develop an appropriate solution. He fleshed out the details of funding, structure and market. He knew that, over time, he could put together a successful business model to make it happen.

Option 3 emerged from their brainstorming within the mini-group. Sometimes opportunities can be so obvious that we can't see them. We have to give ourselves space in order to see the picture that is already before us. The group teased this option out and rocket-tested it in many different ways. During this process, Option 3 survived its research, financial, market, operational and legal tests, and it looked viable enough to be developed to become a thriving business entity.

What Jack Learned about Making Things Happen

- **Nature is governed by a series of natural laws.** One of these is known as the Law of Attraction. If you clarify what you want with focus and passion you will attract to you the enablers to make it happen.

- **Managing a business is a pragmatic process.** Jack managed and drove the business based on the principle that business success is measured by tangible results.

- **Most of the things we get so stressed about never happen as we perceive them.** When you are going through a crisis, stand back and visualise the occasion when you and others will recall this instance and laugh about it. Will it matter five years from now? This will give you a more realistic view on life and its happenings.

- **In business there are few opportunities to be your true self.** There are always games and corporate politics going on in business and in the workforce. People look over their shoulders to avoid the brain/ideas thief, or they take the opportunity to do the same themselves. Jack found the 'safe' environment available within the MBA group to be refreshing, as it provided him with the opportunity to try out some of his ideas. The safe confines of the academic environment allowed students to be liberal with their lateral thinking and allowed their minds to work outside the box.

- **Pettiness prevails in the absence of a great dream.** Innovation tends to come not from comfortable situations, but from uncomfortable situations crystallised by the greater vision.

Chapter 25

The Munster Project

Jack survived the football fields and the building sites in the UK and New York with success. He was streetwise from this experience. He instinctively understood the tactics and the dynamics of negotiation. His participation in the MBA programme gave him the theory behind the concepts which he already knew worked in practice. He now knew that the theory worked in practice.

He believed that the strategic options available to him were:

Option 1 – Continue as is;

Option 2 – Leave his current job with Ramu Plc and start his own business; or

Option 3 – Acquire or purchase the current business trading as Ramu Developments.

Based on these options, he understood that he needed to continue to work Option 2 and Option 3 together. He reflected on these options and analysed them at length. He put them in priority order. He put Option 3 as his preferred first option. He put Option 2 as his second option.

While he was investigating the options and trying to formulate an action plan, he was approached by a headhunting agency and asked to consider changing employers. They offered him an attractive MD job with another company.

He participated in the recruitment process merely to gain experience and to see what was out there. He eventually decided that his own planned mission was more attractive to him. It was, nevertheless, interesting to get a valuation of his worth by the market. This, in turn, helped him in formulating his exit strategy from the present business. Jack met with a number of venture capitalists and tested their criteria for supporting one option over another. In addition, he looked at Business Expansion Schemes (BES). He met also with fund managers who were looking for investment opportunities for their high net worth clients.

Armed with this knowledge, Jack and his advisors got together to write a Business Plan to reflect his vision. As they brainstormed the options, their hazy picture of a real business opportunity gradually became more focussed. This was still a preliminary understanding of the likely opportunity. But at least it was positive and encouraging.

Parallel with investigating this start-from-scratch option, Jack still had his day job which was managing his business unit. He researched how he might be able to open some of the camouflaged escape doors that he had built into the already agreed strategic plan. While his relationship with Tom, his chairman, was good, he became more intolerant of the increasingly frequent interventions being made by some of the other directors of the board.

At this time, senior management back at head office were putting together a strategic plan for the Ramu Corporation.

Their purpose was to align it with anticipated emerging international trends in computer technology. This challenged them to decide how best to restructure their business model so as to reflect this strategic repositioning.

Jack thought to himself that if he had his way, he would, in one fell swoop, strip Ramu of this Ramu Development tangent business, do a management buy-out and retain Ramu Plc as his main customer.

He saw the possibility of separate ownership with a continuing trading strategic partnership. It was still too early for Jack to reveal his plan. The time delay allowed him to get his thoughts together and plan as best he could without breaking any confidentiality or doing anything wrong. He adopted the concept known as zero-based planning, whereby he started with a blank sheet of paper and doodled out possible scenarios to see how he could put together a buy-out team and get funding. He would need a clear mind about the possibilities and would need to be ready to take the opportunity if and when it would arise.

Jack adopted the tactic of laying small, but awkward, landmines during his business interactions with the senior executives who were formulating the strategic plan for Ramu Plc.

He wanted to influence their thinking about the difficulties of having the Ramu Developments type of business sitting within the corporate culture. The interaction of the culture of Ramu Developments versus the culture of Ramu Plc was a potential flashpoint. Ramu Developments needed a different culture based on short, intense project delivery followed by slack periods.

As the investigation process continued, Jack became more convinced that the emerging Ramu Plc corporate strategy would recommend that problem tangent related businesses should be sold off and that a tight supply agreement could be negotiated with the new owners as part of the exit model. If his judgement was correct, Jack knew he needed to be ready.

Jack put this option on the table in front of his A-team. They listened to his plan, tore it asunder and then put it back together again, but in a different way. They agreed that Jack would speak on a confidential basis with his two most trusted work colleagues and gauge if they were interested in joining a management buy-out team if the opportunity arose.

As Jack picked his way sensitively through the negotiations, he was surprised to find out that they too had discussed the possibilities and had decided to approach Jack to see if he was interested in leading a buy-out. They agreed in principle that they were on board if the opportunity arose. Jack arranged that the two would meet up with his advisors. Depending on the reactions, he would invite them to join his potential management buy-out MBO team. They met several times, and the contrasting styles and skills of the two lads helped to round off some of the edges of the MBO team.

Success often boils down to timing and inches. This was a delicate time, and Jack was highly sensitive to the importance of timing and whom to speak with. His streetwise skills came into play. He knew he needed to make a proposal to Ramu Plc before its final corporate strategic plan was signed off.

He led the preparation of the proposal to its final format and then waited for his time to pounce. This was a stressful time for Jack. He knew that, once he had made the proposal, he would have to stand down from his role as managing director. If they rejected his proposal, he would have to leave the company. The process was high risk, but that's business.

When he judged that the time was right, he spoke first to Tom on a confidential basis and explained what he was proposing and that his proposition made sense within the context of the emerging corporate strategy. He explained to Tom that Ramu Developments would still be available as a strategic partner to Ramu Plc and would accept contractual responsibility for the output of the range of products required by Ramu Plc. This would relieve Ramu Plc from having to manage Ramu Developments.

After some reflection, Tom said it was a good idea and that it should be attractive to the main board. Furthermore, Tom gave Jack guidance on how, when and to whom he should make his proposition.

Fight not because you hate what is in front of you, but because of your love for what is behind you.

Áine kept talking with Jack about his plans and kept challenging him to look at various angles. They both agreed that from the time he declared his hand, he would be walking down a road which may not take them to their preferred destination. Having 'planning permission' from home for high-risk journeys is critical. Áine and Jack were at one in their understanding of the pros and cons of his proposed plan. They were confident that if this proposal didn't work out, other opportunities would come along. They were also confident that they would have sufficient resources to keep them going from the time of termination of his job to winning a new job or setting up a new business.

Their children were getting bigger, and they had the general children's issues which ranged from real joy at their little achievements to disappointment when they kicked the traces. It was all part of the building of the tight, loving family unit, the base from which Jack could go forward with confidence.

When Tom gave Jack the nod, Jack asked the CEO of Ramu Plc for permission to make a presentation to him and his board. In order to get a hearing, Jack had to indicate to the CEO the broad outline of his proposal.

Jack was happy with the response and, after some coming and going, the CEO fixed a date for the board meeting and the window of opportunity for Jack's presentation. For transparency purposes, Jack took leave of absence from his job as managing director, using the time to prepare for his presentation. In preparing his presentation, he stepped into the shoes of the corporate board members and anticipated what their needs would be and what their walk-away point might be.

He decided that the hot points for the corporate board would be:

- How his proposition would fit within the context of their emerging strategic plan;
- Security of supply of contracted services and products;
- Capacity of the management buy-out team to make it happen and to grow at the pace required by Ramu Plc;
- Detailed plans on how the transition would take place; and
- Valuations.

Jack addressed the corporate board members on each issue individually and in enough detail to show that he and his team had the capacity and credibility to make the proposal work and to grow the business at the required pace. At the end of his presentation, Jack fielded questions from the board members. He diverted technical questions to the appropriately qualified members of his buy-out team.

The CEO thanked them for their initiative and agreed that they would respond in principle as soon as their own corporate strategy document was signed off. He told Jack that he was to continue on leave of absence in the interim.

Jack's judgement call was that they would get a positive response, so he decided with his MBO team to continue their preparation on the basis that the deal was going to happen.

Jack spoke with various venture capitalists (VC) and, over his period of absence, he and his A-Team finalised their business plan. They included in this plan the purchase of the shares from Ramu Plc at a yet-to-be agreed price and over a yet-to-be agreed time period. This indicated that they would take over the business as a going-concern. Thus they would take all the assets and liabilities. Included in this package would be the staff that would automatically transfer across to their new employer and who would carry with them all their contractual rights.

Ramu's CEO contacted Jack three weeks later and told him that the board was agreeable in principle to the proposal. He said that he was appointing an implementation team and asked Jack to do the same. These two teams could work out the details, and both he and Jack could make policy decisions about any issues the team members were unable to sort out. They both signed a confidentiality agreement. It was now full-steam ahead.

Jack and his MBO team acted as support to their negotiating team. Everything went smoothly for a time, but as always, the devil is in the detail. On a number of occasions during the process it looked as if the courtship period would not result in a marriage or that the marriage would not be consummated. On and on went the two teams in debate and disagreement over small issues. There seemed to be no end in sight. The CEO and Jack spoke and agreed that they needed to put a time deadline on the process with which Jack agreed.

In the meantime, Jack and his MBO Team worked with their designated venture capitalist company to finalise their package, subject to the final details being signed off and the deal completed. They agreed the equity percentage split and the exit methodology for the venture capitalist company within a targeted five-year time frame. The negotiating teams crystallised the deal and listed the outstanding issues which had to be agreed at a higher level.

The CEO and Jack agreed to meet with both sets of advisors to deal with the outstanding issues. As in any negotiation, most advantage is either won or lost in the last 20 percent of the negotiating time frame. Jack and his team had agreed their walk-away point and had also advanced their alternative point in case the deal fell through at this last hurdle.

This last stage of the negotiation was tough, but professional. Jack and his team negotiated from a point of mental strength. This allowed them to squeeze some vital final points from the deal.

They eventually finalised the deal. But it was subject to the CEO getting final clearance from his Ramu Plc board member. This board meeting took place on the following Friday. On the following Monday, Jack received a letter from the lawyers for Ramu Plc, officially notifying him of the timeline for the completion of the deal and change of ownership.

Over the previous weekend, they had worked on the preparation of three draft statements for delivery to the stock markets and the financial press. One statement anticipated failure. One anticipated deadlock and one anticipated success.

The negotiation process had escaped the attention of the press over the last few months of negotiation. Now that it was a *fait accompli*, they could issue their press release announcing agreement and success.

Before the news broke in the press, Jack re-entered Ramu Developments, now in two roles – one as managing director of the new business, and one in his new role as part owner of the business. He called a full meeting of the staff and announced the deal. He reassured them that it would have no immediate impact on their jobs or conditions of employment. He indicated in broad terms some of the strategic options being examined by the new owners. So it was back to work for the team, and Jack had to now regroup and refocus since he was not just an employee any more.

The deeds of his assets were now stored in the lending bank vaults. Jack's new board consisted of his MBO Team plus a representative from the venture capitalist company. They had a big opportunity ahead of them. Jack was in a hurry to drive on the business and take all opportunities. Jack was now driving the business with strength and with speed. His management style was to have current projects running efficiently. He spent up to 80 percent of his time focusing on the possible strategic positioning options for the business. He set up an advisory strategic group, drawn from the general Information Communications Technology (ICT) area and others. The mission of his team was to develop a strategy which would drive the business to identify and conquer a niche space within which it could develop an innovative solution. This solution had to have an international application and be attractive to those who controlled the critical distribution channels to the targeted markets.

The team adopted a step-by-step process in which step one was to agree the broad mission, and step two was to find support pillars for this mission. They brainstormed and reflected on a number of possible opportunities within their defined strategic space. Having reflected on these opportunities, they continually eliminated the less viable ones until they had reduced the list to two options. They again reflected on those. Jack decided that both options needed to be worked to the next step of their possible life cycle. At that stage they would be better informed about which option to go with.

He set up two project teams whose term of reference was to complete the initial feasibility study in order to find commercial possibilities. Jack put strict deadlines on this first step. Both project teams scoped out their respective projects and set about identifying market niche possibilities and the profiles of these niches.

Based on defining this potential, they tried to investigate how they could develop an innovative solution which would give the business the opportunity to work out its competitive advantage. Each project manager reported to Jack at 10 a.m. every Monday morning and in more detail at 10 a.m. on the first Monday of each month. Running parallel with this initiative, Jack kept driving the core Ramu Developments business. This business was the cash-cow which helped to finance the R&D budget allocated towards the development of new products.

Within this time frame, the project to which they gave the code name Munster, to identify it and to meanwhile protect it, began to look exciting. It was focused on the mobile telephone market and had identified a possible issue which seemed to be sexy. This involved technology for conversion of voice recognition into text. This was to make texting more user friendly.

Jack and his team tested the potential of the product from a technology perspective, a market perspective, a financing perspective and a return-on-investment perspective. They concluded from their research that this was a new star product which must be nurtured. They decided to concentrate their resources on this project.

Jack was influenced in following this strategy by some of his building site experiences where he observed the waste arising when crews were changed from one job to another without any measurement of the consequences. This poor resource management generally led to panic towards the end of the job.

Jack strengthened the Project A team and also added his financial controller as an ex officio member of the team. Jack himself adopted the strategic role and kept the project team focused towards the defined end product. He and his business development manager decided that they needed to build tentacles out into the global market. They used every opportunity to network with their future possible strategic partners for the products currently being developed by their project team. They were also conscious of the need to avoid wasting resources on developing a solution for a non-existent problem or need.

Jack himself wore out shoe leather in their target market to get a good feel for the reaction of the market to their developing product. He could see where the new product might be more precisely positioned so that the early adopters would commit and later influence others towards their products.

He understood that this is a fast-moving market and that the identified opportunity must be optimised during the shortening time of the opportunity.

Jack attended relevant conferences and cold-called relevant people to inform them that their business existed. He kept gathering as much relevant, up-to-date information as he could about market trends, economic trends, demographics, fads and fashions so that he could feed this critical information to his development team and guide them in their development.

Jack had a clear exit strategy from the business in his head. This involved building as much potential value into the business as soon as possible, in a niche which was critical for targeted big operations. If he and his team could develop their solution uniquely and relevant enough, Jack was sure that he could raise enough buyer interest out there in the market to sell the business. His preference was for a trade sale, but he needed to keep an initial public offering option (IPO) alive as an alternative negotiation option.

As part of their agreed strategy, Jack and his team had set a business objective to have 50 percent of their revenue coming from clients other

than Ramu Plc over a five-year period. This would be achieved not by con-
tracting the Ramu Plc business, but by initiating new business with targeted clients. They agreed that 15 percent of the venture capital money
they got would be allocated to establishing a new R&D department to
develop prototypes of new products. These products would then be scaled
up to test their technical and commercial viability. As this process developed, more and more of the budget would be spent towards the development of a stable of new stars.

The business developed as budgeted in the first year, which helped to
give it credibility from all the important success criteria measurements.
During the second year, the business hit a wall when it was decided that
their potential star product based on Bluetooth technology wasn't going
anywhere and had to be scrapped. This was a severe decision for Ramu
Developments but it had to be done. They secured some extra funding
through borrowing and focused on a joint venture with a major player.

A major global player code name (Rathme) contracted Jack's team to
develop and provide critical software to facilitate them to develop their new
sexy product which had to reach the market to optimise the Christmas
trade. Jack had negotiated the contract in such a way that they were able to
hold onto the intellectual property (IP) for their part of the work. When
the end product hit the market, it had phenomenal commercial success.
This provided tax-efficient royalty income to the business and thus became
the next cash cow that banked the development of other interesting products.

Meanwhile, their core traditional business with Ramu continued to
grow in the absolute sense, even though it was continuing to drop as a percentage of Jack's total business. This was because of its development of
other new businesses. By the third year, it had dropped to 25 percent of
their total business.

Entrepreneurs operate mostly through the right brain and work the big
picture; they then get left-brained people to do the detail.

Jack had a clear vision for the commercial journey ahead for the
business. This vision was expressed in the mission statement that they had
written for the business:

Our Mission Statement
To build a serious business in its chosen, tightly-defined niche through a combination of in-house development and precisely related acquisitions so that the total is greater than the sum of its individual parts.

To energise this vision, Jack needed to drive in-house product development and acquire underperforming businesses which had the potential to give his business bridgeheads into suitable emerging markets. To fuel this, he raised capital through a series of borrowing and another 10 percent equity sale to venture capitalist investors. He was the one with the big picture. He was acquiring the relevant pieces of the jigsaw so that all the pieces would together create his agreed picture. The more clarity Jack gained, the more the pieces of the jigsaw became available and fell into place.

This was a challenging but exciting time for Jack. He sometimes had to stop and pinch himself in order to refocus on where he and the business was and, even more importantly, where they were headed. As he travelled this journey, Jack quickly recognised those around him who had the capacity and the confidence to travel it with him. On all challenging journeys, there are winners and losers. There is no hiding place for less-than-excellent performance.

What Jack Learned about Negotiation

- **Be unsatisfied without being dissatisfied.** Jack was driven by the vision to take ownership and thus have the real opportunity to create wealth for himself. This made his current situation appear unsatisfactory from this perspective. From this he got the energy to have a go.

- **Set your ideas high enough to inspire you and low enough to encourage you.**

- **We become prisoners of our current situation.** Jack adopted the concept known as zero-based planning, whereby he started with a blank sheet of paper and doodled out possible scenarios to see how he could put together a buy-out team and get funding for his proposition.

- **A smart way to get decisions made in your favour is to influence the circumstances before the decision is made.** Jack adopted the tactic of laying small, but awkward, landmines during his business interactions with the executives who were trying to rebuild the new corporate business model. He wanted to influence their thinking about the difficulties of having his type of business sitting within the corporate culture. Often you get only one shot at some opportunities.

- **Success often boils down to timing and inches.**

- **Love is a more resilient motivator than fear.** Fear tends to pass.

Chapter 26

A Family Decision

Áine fought a war of words with Jack. She was paying the price for Jack's business success through the strain on their personal relationship.

Eventually she had bought into Jack's vision. She was then prepared to pay the current price so that she could reclaim Jack after his exit from the rat race. Her friend, Margaret, told her that all improvements, whether in personal or business life, costs now to gain benefit later.

Áine was now prepared to make the necessary investment. She tried to act as both parents to their children so that they could, as a family unit, enjoy the return on Jack's investment later.

Her friend, Margaret, told her over a cup of coffee that there is a relationship between money and happiness. You may have little wealth, but if you have friends and freedom, you won't be unhappy for long. Wealth is not necessary for happiness – the possession of riches does not resolve the agitation of your soul. To avoid acquiring what you do not need, or rejecting what you cannot afford, you must challenge yourself at the impulse moment and rationally decide if you really need 'this'.

Top members of Jack's team had to face the challenge of managing this paradox, and paying the price. Some decided that the price was too high to pay for the possible future return. They dropped out. This was the right decision for them.

In commercial life it's sometimes better to walk away rather than become a dead hero while playing to someone else's definition of success.

As Jack's commercial journey became more demanding, Áine became more assertive and started to manage him. Other than Jack's mother, she knew him better than anyone else. We are all actors on the stage of life, and the more out of character our exposed active role becomes, the more stressful the journey for us becomes. Áine knew that Jack was a country boy at heart who liked his football and a few pints with the lads. She knew that his core value in all its manifestations was honesty. He used say to her, 'If you don't stand for something, you will fall for anything.'

Of necessity, he needed to play other games in his current commercial journey, but within the bosom of the family, Áine readjusted him to his honest roots. This internal strength and support allowed him to act successfully on the public stage and then recharge himself within the safety of his family. A true friend is someone with whom you may be comfortable enough to think aloud and get honest challenges and responses.

Jack was privileged to have his genuine home sounding board to help anchor his external manoeuvrings in business.

Margaret explained to Áine that life is a series of s-curve cycles. The natural shape of the s-curve cycle is that you falter at first, then grow and, if left to your own devices without support, you will falter again. The plants in the field go through life cycle stages, starting with germination where the seeds die in order to put out roots so that they can absorb the necessary food nutrients to support their future growth. Then shoots appear and, through the process of photosynthesis, provide the food and energy for the plants to grow and produce flowers, which the bees pollinate. Seeds are produced, and the cycle is ready to start again as the change in seasons kick starts the new cycle.

Áine was aware of the s-shaped journey and was determined that her creative and timely interventions would ensure that her personal relationship with Jack wouldn't naturally follow this s-shape. She understood that their relationship needed to be reinvented at many critical inflection points on this natural s-curve cycle. She understood that life wasn't just one curve, but a series of mini s-curves. Each succeeding curve had to be generated while the previous one was still in a healthy ascending direction, rather than trying to rescue the relationship as the previous curve was going downward.

In order to keep the series of s-curves of life flowing, Áine and Jack challenged themselves to reflect on what was most important in their lives. They discussed their problems, reflected on them and decided that the ultimate achievement for them, both as individuals and as a unit, was peace of mind. In order to achieve peace of mind, they had to manage the variables which played into that highest goal.

The tactic they used was to stop in order to reflect, always assuming that they had lost what was most important or dear to them. They tried to think and visualise how they would then feel and react. They knew that the reality is that it's too late to decide this after the event.

Áine understood the importance of initiating the series of curves on time. She understood that she had been married a number of times, but always to Jack. Jack now understood that he too needed to remarry Áine, This involved creating a new curve while the flame was still burning. He now understood that it wasn't just good enough to remain faithful – he needed to positively contribute as well. The genuine, home-appreciated, mutual support of his personal self allowed Jack to more confidently play his commercial self on the public stage.

What Jack Reflected on about Life

- **Wealth is not necessary for happiness.** You may have little wealth, but if you have friends and freedom, you won't be unhappy for long. The possession of riches does not resolve the agitation of your soul. To avoid acquiring what you do not need, or rejecting what you cannot afford, you must challenge yourself at the impulse moment and rationally decide if you really need 'this'.

  What is success for you?

  What is your life's cause?

  What is it that gives meaning to life for you?

- **Can you be your personal self and your commercial self at the same time?** How can you manage this paradox? Eventually Jack and Áine worked it out in a way that was good for them.

- **Don't confuse emotion and passion.** It is easy to become passionate about managing the issues around your meaning. Jack was clear about his vision and meaning in life.

- **A true friend is someone with whom you may be comfortable enough to think aloud and get honest challenges and responses.** Jack was privileged to have Áine as his genuine home sounding board to help anchor his external manoeuvrings in business.

- **As we travel life's journey, we go through a series of cycles.** This challenges us to remodel our approach. We all need to remarry several times but to the same partner.

- **How would you feel if the person nearest and dearest to you was gone?** It's too late when it happens to be lamenting about what you would do if you had a second chance. You currently have that second chance. Go and grab it.

- **What footprint do you want to leave behind?**

Chapter 27

A Better Deal

Jack, now with renewed home-based strength, drove his business model on at full-speed. Part of his strategy was to build capacity into the business away from the attention of the media or potential competitors. He followed this tactic for the following two years. Jack and his team built a robust business model, specialising in a family of related products which had the potential to penetrate the value chains of a number of the big boys who controlled the final delivery to the market.

He reached a development point where he felt that it was time to market his products aggressively. He and his team could then measure the reactions of their target market and potential competitors. In order to do this, they secretly formulated a publicity and promotional campaign that would inform their target market of their existence and their plans for the future.

Their big plan was to attract one of the big players to buy them out. They decided to adopt a negotiating tactic known as the reluctant bride tactic. When the excitement is at its most intense, the reluctant bride holds back in order to raise the sap in her potential husband. In negotiating, you create excitement and desire, then pull back and force your prospect to come and get you. Play hard to get, treat them mean and keep them keen.

In order to achieve attention, interest and desire that would lead to action, they created a media campaign. For this media campaign, they decided on a rough budget. They then allocated half of the budget to an advertising agency to advertise on selected media channels in a sharp, burst campaign over three weeks. For the second half of the budget, they engaged a public relations company in an attempt to convey their messages to target audiences through journalists and broadcasters on radio, television, newspapers and magazines.

Their campaign quickly created recognition of the business and an excitement around it. Telephone calls came from well-known investors, fund managers and IT companies. Some were predators eager to make a killing on a quick sale. Some were on a fishing expedition and eager to find out the market value so that they could put a value on their own business. Just as the Pareto rule proves, 20 percent of the respondents were genuine and had the potential to do the deal.

As the excitement and the positive press coverage took effect, Jack had calls from genuinely interested suitors looking for permission to come and sit with him in order to talk about the possibilities of a deal. The more he played the reluctant bride tactic, the more the sap rose in some suitors. Jack's shadow-boxing helped to screen out the tyre kickers and wasters.

Jack screened the list of suitors to those with potential. Jack was the majority shareholder in the business, and he had to keep the other shareholders in his business informed enough to keep them supportive. They were betting on Jack to be professional enough to do the best deal possible for himself and consequently, for them.

Eventually, two serious suitors, both potential strategic partners, emerged from the process. Both pitched for an exclusive option to get into formal negotiations. Jack reflected on their potential and the synergy possibilities arising from the acquisition of Ramu Developments. He decided to sign an exclusive option to negotiate with the Mewx Corporation. Jack was upfront with the other suitor. He informed their team that he would enter into negotiation with them if his first option failed to deliver an acceptable deal. He put a definite time frame on the process and charged them €3 million for the initial exclusive negotiation option to concentrate the minds of all involved.

He and his team were mulling over the progress of their negotiations when his personal assistant came more briskly than usual into the office. Seriousness, concern and stress were written on her face. She whispered the news in Jack's ear that there was bad news from home. She told him that a message had come from his sister on the phone that his mother, Mary Anne, had passed away suddenly an hour ago. Jack was overcome with grief. He broke down and sobbed his heart out, witnessed by his unknowing business colleagues.

His best friend, his guiding light through the progress of his career and his life to this point, had died. He quietly reflected on her life, on her commitment and her support against all the odds through school, college and his graduation, and on her determination to get him to achieve his goals and her own goals. He was proud that she was so proud of him. He immediately informed the team; they, in turn, informed his colleagues and the negotiators from the other side of the sad death of the most important person in his life.

He left the office to meet with Áine and the children so that they could travel home. Jack's father Mick Denny Bill had already passed away a year ago at eighty-nine years of age. Jack and his siblings agreed to give Mary Anne a send off that she would be pleased with. Business leaders, politicians, priests, community leaders, old friends from the community and from his football and college days thronged the church and the graveyard to pay their last respects as Mary Anne was laid to rest with Mick Denny Bill. As he wiped away the tears and took the many handshakes, Jack reflected on his parents' lives and the sacrifices they had made in order to give him and his siblings stretching opportunities.

Three days at home and then, as Mary Anne would have advised, it was time to get back quickly to work. He bade farewell to his brothers and sisters and as Mary Anne would have advised, sped back to his office and his purpose. Now he felt, for the first time in his life, that he was without his reference point, without the person he most wanted to impress. But he carried her philosophies in his soul.

Jack got back to his office and he and his team resumed the negotiations with the Mewx Corporation. His team and their lawyers agreed on a confidentiality agreement and options' contract. They signed off the contracts and paid for them. Mewx sent in their mergers and acquisition team to start their due diligence process. They had to work under cover as much as possible so that rumours wouldn't slip out to the Press and the market. This was difficult. They adopted the tactic of spreading a number of false rumours and laying banana skins so as to confuse nosy people and trip up those seeking the real story. They completed the critical work off-site at a secret location, which helped to preserve confidentiality.

As is normal in these situations, the due diligence analysis by Mewx threw up various questions regarding possible liabilities the business may be exposed to in the future. Jack and his team were able to kill off these questions with informed answers on the spot.

As the option time deadline approached, the shape of a possible deal emerged. Jack and his fellow shareholders took over from their negotiation team and entered into a focused negotiation process with their corresponding opposite team. Jack had on-the-ground, practical negotiating skills. Because this was a massive potential deal, he was intelligent enough to understand that he needed specialist professional help here.

Bill, a specialist with a lifetime experience of many mergers and acquisitions, coached Jack's team on the art of negotiation. They first agreed that the deal should be a win-win deal as otherwise it would not work for either side over the long term. Bill next told them to 'never assume you know what the other side's real agenda is'. He then laid out the negotiating steps for Jack and his negotiation team:

- Assess your own bargaining power and that of the other side. Tease out the relative strengths and weaknesses of both sides;
- Identify matters of principle which you are not prepared to negotiate away, irrespective of the consequences;
- Clarify your preferred end game; and
- Flesh out a possible implementation plan.

Bill then coached them on the stepped phases that negotiations tend to travel. These generic phases are in their numbered steps:

Step 1 – Exploration phase;
Step 2 – Movement phase; and
Step 3 – Agreement phase.

Having a better understanding of the dynamics that tend to play during each of these steps, Jack and his team role-played the possible tactics they would utilise during each of the phases. Bill showed them how to use the various tactics. These included the use of bluff, threats, manipulation and promises.

Bill told them that, as they used a combination of these tactics, they had to be very mindful of argument dilution. This involves giving too many reasons to support your proposition. This, in turn, gives the other side too much ammunition. If they are effective negotiators they will then focus in on your weakest supporting argument and rubbish it. By implication, they are then undermining your total proposition.

Bill continued to coach Jack's team as the process stepped along at snail's pace. He established the following negotiation principles for them:

- Know what you are negotiating about;
- List the issues you perceive the other side will have difficulty with;
- Define their ideal end point;
- Decide beforehand what your best alternative to a negotiated agreement is;
- Decide your walk-away point;
- Use silence to your advantage;
- Decide which tactics to use during various scenarios; and
- Decide what role each team member is to play – Jack would play the role of the good cop, since the negotiating team was playing the bad-cop role.

Bill coached them on how to manage the time frame to their advantage. He told them that most of the advantage tends to be gained in the last 20 percent of the time. 'The party most urgent has the weakest hand,' he said. They now understood that it is easier to resist at the beginning than at the end. Therefore, they needed to play their negotiation according to these guidelines.

The overriding negotiation tactic Jack used was that of the reluctant bride. Now impregnated with some of the above useful negotiation tactics, especially the use of silence, his team decided that they were going to listen to the offer from the other side and refuse it upfront. They would then utilise their enhanced negotiating capability to gain an upper hand as the negotiation progressed. They would use a series of appropriate tactics of bluffs, threats and promises as they tried to manipulate the other side to get nearer to their bargaining zone. They anticipated that, in the meantime, the other side would use their own tactics in order to gain some competitive advantage. In reality, this process is a game – one has to do what one has to do in order to gain advantage.

Because Jack's business was relatively new and very much at the development stage, its balance sheet didn't reflect its true value. The net asset on its balance sheet was €4.5 million. Their important bargaining chip was its potential to enhance the value chain of its acquirer. The intellectual property (IP) it already had built and which it was working on growing further, plus its tentacles in the market, represented its true value. When the direct negotiating teams sorted out their identified issues, the stage was set for both sides to get in there and complete the deal. Jack and his team had already agreed that their preferred deal was €70 million, which was based on a multiple of sixteen, and their walk-away point was €40 million.

Armed with these agreed parameters, they grew psychologically stronger because no matter how the process went, they had already agreed the outward parameters of the deal. They were now prepared to live with the net results of this negotiation process.

After more shadow-boxing, the other side put their initial and, as they said, final offer of €30 million on the table. Jack and his team had already agreed they would reject the first offer in any event. When they received a refusal of their offer, Mewx Corporation's team asked Jack's team for their proposal. Again Jack's team had agreed that they would not name their price until Mewx had made an offer higher than their predetermined walk away price of €40 million. Jack's team invited Mewx to make a realistic offer, as it would otherwise be best to call a halt to negotiations at this point. After some consideration, Mewx put a second offer of €45 million on the table, but with a number of stipulations about its structure. Jack and his team asked for time to consider their offer. They agreed to respond to Mewx on the following day by 9 a.m.

Now that the offer was beyond their walk-away point, Jack agreed that they would respond positively and that they would be prepared to enter into active negotiations. The critical issues to be negotiated were:

- The actual price and the formula to be used for the earned-out bonuses and their accompanying time lines;
- The tied-in contract for Jack and his management team; and
- The proportion of the agreed price, which was to be paid by cash and by shares in Mewx.

At the 9 a.m. meeting, Jack and his team put their preferred price of €70 million on the table. They invited the other team to enter into meaningful negotiation so that the now defined gap between both offers could be bridged. In order to concentrate their minds, both sides agreed that the process would finish one way or the other by 3 p.m. on the following Friday.

The negotiation process hit high and low points during the week. Jack and his team understood that a certain amount of posturing was required and that the real gains and losses were likely to happen in the final twenty-four hours. They therefore played to their game-plan.

They teased out each parameter of the deal. They had previously agreed that nothing would be agreed until everything was agreed. By lunch time on Friday, much of the common ground about the details had been finalised. The big question about final valuation and its payment structure was still the elephant in the room. They finally agreed that Jack and his counterpart from Mewx, George, would lock themselves in a room without advisors and either do the deal or kill it off.

The chemistry between them was positive. Jack took a blank sheet of paper and drew a line across the sheet one third of the way down. Then he divided this bottom two thirds of the sheet in half. At the top he recorded where the common ground was and what was agreed by both teams. On the left section he documented the Mewx offer and on the right side he documented his team's offer. This clearly demonstrated the gap they had to bridge in this final effort at negotiation. They agreed that they would stop playing games and see if a successful business formula could be agreed upon.

Bit by bit they reduced the negotiations to one sheet of paper which contained the emerging agreed formula. They finished with one definitive sheet on which was detailed the agreed valuation and its structure. They both signed and dated this as a Heads of Agreement.

This Heads of Agreement would later be converted by the lawyers into a legally binding document with all the various issues tied down under law. Jack had to sign certain warranties indemnifying Mewx against certain issues which couldn't be killed off 100 percent at that point and which had some very small possibility of becoming issues over the next two years. This is normal in such deals. The bones of the agreement included the following:

- A final valuation of €58 million was agreed. This was structured as follows:
- €20 million cash up front plus €20 million of shares in Mewx at that day's valuation according to the stock exchange;
- The remaining €18 million to be based on an earned-out fee formula over the next two years, 50 percent of it to be paid at the end of year one and the remainder at the end of year two. This total of €18 million was contingent on agreed performance indicators being achieved or part thereof;
- Jack's team was to be tied in contractually for three years and Jack himself for two years; and
- Jack to become a director of the main Mewx board.

As with all such deals, the devil is in the detail. Once the Heads of Agreement was signed off, it was up to the legal, financial and regulatory people to sort out and agree the fine points of the agreement.

Running parallel with his process, they agreed a joint PR campaign with their public relations consultants. They prepared a carefully-worded press release for announcement to the Press and the market so that the relevant stakeholders could be informed at the appropriate time and to influence positive commentary from the analysts and the stock market to boost their share value.

When the deal was finally washed out, Jack's stakeholders initially finished up with cash and stock in Mewx worth €40 million. By staying on and driving the business to meet its agreed stretching targets, Jack and his stakeholders were playing for this €18 million. There were three variables:

- That the business could deliver the agreed targets;
- That the Mewx stock valuation would at least hold its base price as of the date of the signing of the deal; and
- That Jack could operate within the confines of the inevitable corporate constraints from Mewx.

The market reaction was generally positive to the deal. All kinds of valuations were touted around the city about Jack's pay-off. Jack was determined that he would be professional enough to energise his side of the bargain and keep his core team focused. The other stakeholders had varying degrees of excitement or disappointment about the deal.

Jack learned a critical lesson from this process. This lesson was: Everyone is selfish at the end for their own agenda – they ask, 'What's in it for me?'

The honeymoon period was pleasant. Jack drove the business onward adhering to the agreed business development map. Jack flew to New York to his first board meeting of Mewx. After a ritual of welcome, it was down to commercial business. The meeting was very structured with the focus on measured outputs against budgets. Jack soon realised that this was a very different corporate structure from anything he had previously experienced. It was also a different culture. No prisoners would be taken here.

Now that he had the name of having wealth from his public windfall, Jack was targeted by people from many walks of life and business, ranging from charities' organisers to financial advisers, who offered all sorts of attractive deals to manage and spend his wealth for him.

Jack now had a huge amount of money, but he instinctively knew that there was no such a thing as a free lunch. He had come up the hard way. He had been smart at the way he had strategically manoeuvred the buy-out and got the business into a model type that was attractive to outsiders. He was now playing for the final stake of his earned deal. From his football days Jack understood that the match was won over the sixty minutes and not merely by the first flashy score. Because of this, he ignored all the flashy advice and invested his money in a good yielding, but mundane, bond for a year.

Over time, Jack found that he was really being isolated as more and more of the communication between his team members took place directly with their counterparts back at corporate headquarters in New York. This worried him because he felt that, while he had the responsibility, his authority to deliver was being ambushed and taken away from him. Some of the executives back at Mewx headquarters looked for all types of reports and in very subtle ways began to integrate this business within their culture and procedures' map. As the slack on this rope was being pulled in, individual team members felt the strain. In all change situations, there is a natural initial reaction to resist these changes.

Jack found himself getting very defensive at the corporate board meetings and even now his own in-house management meeting back in Dublin became more and more uncomfortable.

Áine and Jack spoke about this change and its effects. They debated whether it was the factual interference of the corporation or whether it was because Jack now had options and didn't have to listen to rubbish. They concluded that it was probably a bit of both.

At the end of the first year, the business had performed up to 90 percent of its projected agreed targets. Jack's earned-out deal was calculated on the percentage of this projected agreed output. After some difficulty from the resistant financial controller of Mewx, Jack collected his 90 percent of his year-one earned-out deal. Having collected this money, a total of €5.4 million, Jack decided he didn't have a future in this corporate structure. He planned that he would withdraw from the business as much as possible and would take his chances with the last of the earned-out money at the end of the second year.

Once he made this private decision, he was happier in himself. He understood that the corporate strategy by Mewx executives was to make it so uncomfortable for him that he would leave before the end of year two and they wouldn't have to pay his last payment.

The Mewx stock he had acquired as part of the original deal was doing well on the stock exchange, and he was now free to trade them after having held them for the first year. He phoned his stockbroker and sold them, making a capital gain of €5 million after paying his capital gains tax. He had now got his reward, even if he hadn't got the last payment of the earned-out deal.

Jack found that his fellow directors were isolating him more and more at corporate board meetings. At a board meeting during year two, the CEO accused Jack of poor judgement calls and said that his professional input was suspect. Jack rose to this challenge and used this trigger to tell the CEO to stuff his job and directorships and go fuck himself, and he walked out. He remembered his football mentor's advice: 'Speak when you are angry, and you will make the best speech you will ever regret.'

The CEO took Jack at his word and put in place the legal procedures to normalise his departure from the board and the business. On the following Monday morning, the operations vice president, Joe, formally informed Jack that he was now taking charge and that all the legal papers for his departure were being prepared for final signing.

Jack was shocked that the Americans were so blunt, brutal and clinical. He wanted change, but not in this heartless manner.

Jack now closed this chapter of his life's journey. He could now focus on his next step. He sent an internal letter to all his staff informing them that he was leaving and introduced Joe as their new boss, wishing them the best for the future. He physically and psychologically left the business immediately, conscious that he caused the earned-out deal to be broken, which cost him in the region of €4 to €5 million in earned-out payments.

He told the news to Áine over lunch. They decided that they would immediately take a family holiday and be out of the country early the following morning. Jack would not be around when the media got a hold of the press release announcing his departure. The media and the market would try to put all sorts of spins on it as they tried to make a story about tragedy when, in fact, Jack was as happy as could be.

Lessons that Jack Learned about Achieving Better Outcomes

- **Expectations are the foundation stones of motivation.** Jack entered the negotiation process with high expectations, based on the fact that they had value to bring to the Mewx Corporation table. You have to win the debate in your own head first before you can win it out there in the market.

- **Every proposition has a value.** The absolute figure depends on the intersection of the supply and demand curves.

- **Most of the advantage in negotiation tends to be gained in the last 20 percent of the time.** The party with the most urgent need has the weakest hand. It is easier to resist at the beginning than at the end. Jack understood this and played to this dynamic.

- **Everyone is selfish at the end for their own agenda.** The question they keep asking is: 'What's in it for me?'

- **Be considered in your responses when emotional.** Speak out when you are angry and you will make the best speech you will later regret.

Chapter 28

Jack's Legacy

Jack, Áine and their children left Dublin airport early next morning for their quickly-arranged sun holiday. This was their first real, long family holiday where they didn't have to worry about the price of it. They now had more money than they ever imagined.

Their real mission for this holiday was to regenerate their love for each other. They could now allow themselves space, relaxation and time to court again. This was their opportunity to remarry again – to each other. They needed to prepare for this next s-curve event, and this courtship period was going to be important.

Jack needed to rearrange himself and satisfy his desire to become a meaningful, participating father rather than just a provider. He looked forward to this opportunity and this time to reflect on this current juncture of their life cycle. It would let enough space and time pass so that the next phase could infiltrate their minds easily and allow their complementary lacks to synchronise.

It took them a few days to wind down. Now relaxed, Jack spoke with Áine about the details of the last few years and how he had felt through the various phases. Áine facilitated him with a safe, loving environment in which he could debrief himself and try to close the door on that stage of his life's journey. In reality, he had achieved the tangible results he had planned. He was now looking for the intangible output he could extract from his great breadth of experiences so that he would be better equipped for the next step of life's journey.

The harvest-time came earlier for Jack and Áine than for most people. They were going to enjoy its space and possibilities as they followed their own agenda rather than someone else's agenda.

Jack was anxious to facilitate Áine to express her own ideas, feelings and the vision she had for herself as an individual and the family as a unit going forward. In this two-way probing and active listening process, they were able to rekindle the fires of their original relationship and become excited in each other's company again.

Money cannot buy this special gift. Nevertheless, money allowed them to have space to stop and reflect, rather than continue to struggle under the unrelenting pressure and stress to pay their bills. Everything in life is relative. To them, they now had a large amount of money. They were multi-millionaires. To others in the world, it was merely petty cash. In reality it was large enough to be meaningful, but small enough for them to keep their heads.

The holidays drifted into weeks, and the weeks drifted into months. Jack and Áine returned to Ireland so that their children could get back in time to go to school in September. By the time they got home, the news of Jack's departure from his previous business was history and only rose occasionally when journalists were trying to fill space. Jack and Áine tried to return to a routine for the sake of the children. The tangible difference for the children was that Daddy was around for breakfast and took them to school in the mornings.

Jack leased space in a serviced office block and got into the routine of going to the office after dropping the children off to school. This allowed him time to reflect on his interests and read books that he wanted to read. It also gave him time to have lunch and cups of coffee with contacts from the banking and industry world. Jack was a chaser and doer by nature, and in this reflective period, he felt purposeless and impatient. He had time, capital and capability, but he wanted to put his great capacity to work.

Jack constantly looked around for excuses to travel. He and Áine travelled to all sorts of business-related events such as trade shows and business seminars. They generally built in a few days' holidays around these events. A business-training organisation identified him and asked him to become a public speaker to present his own business life in the form of a case history to students. Their idea was that, by profiling the stepped journey he took and the context of his various decisions, he would give others a road map for their own future strategic journeys.

This floating around was interesting, but Jack wanted to get his teeth into something more tangible. Having reviewed his options, he decided that it was too early for him to start another large business.

He allocated €100,000 to a trading account and became a day trader. He geared up electronically with the equity and commodity markets so that he could automatically take market positions and bet on the market going in particular directions. It was an interactive trading activity, and there was real money involved. This helped to raise his sap and give him a real interest without having to answer to anyone. As a day trader he closed off all positions at the end of his trading session, and he had either instant satisfaction or dismay as his net balance from his day's trading was either positive or negative.

Between his public-speaking engagements, his day trading activity, his active management of his wealth portfolio and his focus on family commitments, Jack had readjusted to his new comfort zone.

Áine went back to college to do an advanced course on psychology. Jack supported her timetable through his shuttling of the children from one venue to another. This precious time together in the car helped Jack to focus on the children's agenda and satisfy their craving to be recognised and heard. Into this schedule, he integrated frequent weekend retreats for the family to their new holiday home in the Canary Islands. They became efficient travellers by taking the minimum of hand luggage, since they held clothes in a wardrobe in their new holiday home. They also brought their timing in and out of airports to a fine art.

Jack still had a need to utilise his vast talent for the good of others. The view of his late mother Mary Anne was that you always get back a multiplier of what you give. This payback comes in many manifestations, and when it comes, it is very satisfying, she had told him. Jack kept reading the life stories of others who had travelled this road before him. He was trying to crystallise his vision to create his future mission. Only then would he be in a position to make definitive decisions about the optimisation of his talent and his capital for the good of others. He would get a unique return on his investment.

In his office, he surrounded himself with the portraits and books of people he admired. He often sat there in his office and looked into the eyes of these people asking aloud the question: 'So what would you do if you were in my position?'

He would then stop, reflect and try to think what answer the real person behind these portraits would give. He was trying to answer the questions:

- Who should he be targeting?
- What should he be doing for them?
- How should he go about it?

Áine encouraged him to go back to college and do an advanced programme on personal development. His first reaction was to do a PhD on some aspect of business. On reflection, he quickly understood that he was not an academic but that he was a doer. He signed up instead for a short intensive course in the graduate college titled 'Who Are You?' He found this refreshing and challenging. He was now able to enjoy the full experience, since he was neither driven by exam nor certification requirements. He was there because he wanted to be there. He thus absorbed the bits that were relevant and interesting to him.

As the programme progressed, he got to know the other participants, two of whom sought his help. Gradually, he found that he had informally become their mentor. He found this rewarding in that he had the opportunity to tease out their visions and planned journeys and advise them on how best they might achieve their objectives.

Patrick impressed him. He seemed to have clarity about the journey ahead of him but didn't have the necessary resources to begin this journey. Jack could see himself in Patrick and got excited about the possibility of kick-starting him on his defined journey. Jack challenged him to draw up the stepped roadway he needed to travel to his defined destination. In addition to challenging him, Jack gave him some angles about the strategic positioning and the necessary structures he needed to build.

Jack encouraged Patrick to get his business certified for the Business Expansion Scheme so that potential investors, including Jack himself, could invest in the business in a tax-efficient way. In addition to this BES funding, Jack decided that he would take a 40 per cent equity stake for an investment of €50,000. He also agreed that he would become a non-executive chairman. Jack was excited about this new venture.

Jack's strategy was to identify and back good jockeys in particular horse races. Patrick's race was a new and potentially satisfying race. Jack knew that a number of talented people could energise their vision as they explored the business opportunities in the evolving trading environment. Jack wanted to play his part by leverage.

As the project with Patrick progressed, Jack was re-energised. His intervention package would be useful to others starting out on business roads that were similar to the business road he had successfully travelled. Jack realised that issues create a burning desire until such time as they cease to be issues.

Money was an issue for Jack throughout his youth. His late mother, Mary Anne, was his first financial controller. Her money-management techniques influenced him through his navvy days in London and Liverpool when he kept his hard-earned money in his socks, through his college days and the earlier part of his married life. Now money was no longer a burning issue for him. He now had far more money than he or his mother Mary Anne or his wife Áine could ever have dreamed of.

Wealth is relative. There is a big difference between a wealth level reached from above and a wealth level reached from below. The road from €15 million to €1 million is not as pleasant as the road from €0 to €1 million.

With this immediate burning issue out of the cycle, other issues came to the fore. One of these was: how could he, Jack, use his intervention package to facilitate others to achieve their goals and, in turn, allow Jack to successfully reach his higher goal?

Jack's new commercial goal was to optimise his own wealth by helping other budding entrepreneurs to reach their goals. In addition to this commercial goal, Jack was conscious of his own core values and the importance of bringing a workable balance into his family unit.

In Jack's case, stretching points and defining moments on this journey were his home upbringing, his time on Aunt Sheila's farm, his football and school experiences, his relationships with girlfriends, the building sites he worked on, college life, corporate life, married life and the negotiation of his departure from his last business.

As he won and lost on this interesting journey, he subconsciously learned the rules of the game as he saw it. These unwritten rules then became the benchmark against which he subconsciously or intuitively made or avoided decisions along the way. In Jack's case, values such as genuineness, honesty, love for his dearest, value of his work, understanding his roots, intolerance for shapers and passion for success made him what he was.

We are drawn to expensive things because they seem to provide plausible solutions to needs we do not understand. They are presented to us through advertising that mimics in a material way what we need at a psychological level. Be confident enough to make decisions that are right for you.

Jack now had the opportunity to start afresh, and he was determined to align this next phase of his life to be in harmony with his core values.

In hindsight, his life's experiences to date were merely the price he had to pay for this opportunity to align his goals with his values. It was a means to an end, not an end in itself. As we saw earlier, you have to make the investment before you can collect the rewards or returns. Stress is caused when your goals, as you see them in your mind, are out of alignment with your values.

Jack advised Patrick to grow his business to a commercial point first, and then he would have more opportunity to align his internal personal goals with his business objectives. He told him that this growth had a cost. He asked Patrick if he was prepared to pay the price.

As Jack went through his life's journey, a number of people and events influenced him and challenged him to ask, 'Why not?'

We all reach watershed points which influence our decisions about which road to travel from these points. These decisions have a direct impact on who we are today. Influencers of our decisions can be grouped into home, school, sport, Church, media, what gets punished and what gets rewarded and so on. All are influencers of our basic values, so that our resultant actions conform to predetermined acceptable standards. The tactic of guilt and reward has been successfully used by influencers to shape us into who we are today.

- What is past is history, and we can't change that. We can change the issues and events out ahead of us.
- Look at your own core values. Who and what are your influencers? Make a decision to align your goals more precisely with your core values. This will make your life worth living again and give you a sense of achievement, excitement and fulfilment.

In a mind-storm meeting with himself, Jack said:

'I have been commercially successful networking with the supposed right people; yet why is my life so unfulfilled?'

Jack now had the opportunity to stop and consciously admit that he had been commercially successful but that he was personally unfulfilled.

Do you have to wait for the big event so as to kick-start this realignment of your goals with your values?

In Jack's case it was a positive event. Others haven't been so lucky. Often in these cases the big event tends to be a disaster of some sort which is the catalyst for their questioning and looking for answers.

Jack was, at one time, a cog in someone else's wheel. Now his mission was to facilitate others to build on their personal and commercial dimensions and achieve their mission. He wanted to become a small but critical cog driving their larger wheel.

If you do work that stretches your latent talent and raises your passion while doing something worthwhile, then you are making a valuable statement to yourself and others who might use you as a role model. This is the ultimate definition of success.

Build-in a series of little victories for yourself so that you gain genuine confidence to get to know your worth. You need to know this before you can influence others.

Participation in the self-development programme challenged Jack to reflect on his genuine worth. Only now had he the space to utilise it for the good of others and achieve his own objectives in the process.

People seem to follow 'How To' advice, rather than 'What' advice. Many agencies advise people on how to achieve their objectives rather than guiding them about choosing their objectives wisely. If your objectives are wrong for you, knowing how best to achieve them is pointless. Unless your objectives are truly yours and right for your situation, you won't have the patience, determination or energy on a consistent basis to reach them.

They are not right for you when you keep forgetting them, or changing them, or going after them with the attitude that they are a chore you must tackle. If this is reflective of your situation, you will never have the necessary passion to make them happen.

Profit comes not from the end job itself, but from the idea behind it. Become the ideas generator and let others sweat at its delivery.

Jack, as the ideas' generator, was now advancing in the direction of his dream. He was doing so in an energising, planned way. As he coached Patrick, Jack advised him to set smart business objectives and understand the critical role his proposed product would play in the value chains of his targeted customers.

Jack had the luxury of being able to align his own objectives to his own personal priorities. Patrick had to earn the right to reach that same luxury. Jack could see the path Patrick needed to successfully travel in order to reach it. Jack felt he had to challenge and also support Patrick to work out in his own head if he was prepared to pay the necessary price.

You can't claim the treasure if you are not willing to dig for it. Make sure you are digging for it in the right spot.

The price often consists of having to work through objectives which are more commercially aligned than personally aligned at that point of the journey.

Jack delayed the alignment of commercial objectives with his personal-private objectives until he reached a notional prize point. In reality, you may not live long enough to reach that point. So start your own realignment today and have your own debates about the price you are prepared to pay in order to achieve each of your individual objectives. Ask, 'What do you want to do sometime? What do you really want to do with the rest of your life?'

If you want it badly enough, then you have the time. It just needs to become priority for you.

Living your life without a clear personal vision is like driving a car in a fog. You do not know where you are going. As you know, if you drive a car at night in a fog you may go over a cliff. With a clear personal vision, you can drive the car of life fearlessly in clear daylight.

Jack was now driving in daylight and felt a renewed level of energy and excitement. This energy came from the clarity of his vision about where he was, and more importantly, where he was going. He was determined to wear away rather than allow himself to rust away. This clarity made him realise that only mediocre people are always at their best.

If you want lasting success, create a life that matters to you, and you will find that it's difficult to retire from the obsession.

Success is about energising your plan in order to achieve your objectives. Happiness is wanting what you have. There is no point in waiting around for what you have to do – just go and do it. There is no point in saving up pleasure until you are old – do it now.

Do what you love, and your thoughts and actions will be naturally focused on those issues which have real meaning for you. If you don't love what you are doing, you will eventually lose out to someone who does. Love is a more resilient motivator than fear. Fear tends to pass.

Some have work and wealth, but they have no time to enjoy it. 'I will do so and so when I retire,' they say, but they may not live that long. Others have all the time, but no work or money. Their attitude is to get the most income for their least input.

In Jack's case, he had taken the benefits of his efforts in money form. Now he wanted to take it in a different currency – one that was synchronised with his inner worth.

Jack's mission now is to utilise his own resources so that those he chooses to facilitate can energise their own mission and work towards a life where their objectives are aligned as soon as possible with their inner self.

Jack's methodology was to challenge them to have a clearer vision of their chosen journey and then to provide them with the necessary support so that they might build their own capacity.

In mentoring his chosen budding entrepreneurs, Jack expected to identify one star jockey who would be capable of bringing his horse over the winning line. He worked on his belief that commercial success comes from a clear vision driven by an appropriate strategy, supported by necessary capital and other resources. Jack was capable of making all these critical parameters available for the right jockey.

He did it and relived his life's journey through his chosen entrepreneurs. Real generosity is doing something for someone who will never find out. In Jack's case, the immediate significant ones knew, but not the wider public.

Before his death, Jack reflected on the footprint he had made on Earth. In order to be an inspiration and role model for others, he ordered that his representatives put on his headstone the inscription:

'Jack made a difference to _____.'

What Jack Learned about Making a Difference

- **Give and you shall receive.** Jack's mother's view was that you always get back a multiplier of what you give. She had told him this payback comes in many manifestations, and when it comes, it is very satisfying.

- **Fathers have more than a one-dimensional responsibility.** Jack needed to rearrange himself and satisfy his desire to become a meaningful, participating father rather than just a provider.

- **No one has a monopoly on good ideas.** Jack surrounded himself with the portraits and books of people he admired. He often sat there in his office and looked into the eyes of these people asking aloud the question: 'So what would you do if you were in my position?' He would then stop, reflect and try to think what answer the real person behind these portraits would give.

- **Wealth is relative.** There is a big difference between a wealth level reached from above and a wealth level reached from below. The road from €15 million to €1 million is not as pleasant as the road from €0 to €1 million.

- **Success means living your life in synch with your basic beliefs.** In Jack's case, values such as genuine honesty, love for his dearest, value of his work, understanding his roots, intolerance for shapers and passion for success made him what he was. What are your basic beliefs?

- A typically empty cry is: 'I have been commercially successful, networking with the supposed right people; yet why is my life so unfulfilled?'

- **What is your solution to solve your wants?** We are drawn to expensive things because they seem to provide plausible solutions to needs we do not understand. What is your answer?

- **Influencers of our decisions can be grouped into categories.** They include our home, school, sport, Church, media, what gets punished and what gets rewarded and so on. The tactic of guilt and reward has been successfully used by influencers to shape us into conformity.

- **The ultimate definition of success might be: If you do work that stretches your latent talent and raises your passion while doing something worthwhile, then you are making a valuable statement to yourself and others who might use you as a role model.**

Life Lessons from Jack

- **Commercial and material success without meaning tends to result in dissatisfaction in the longer term.** Having paid the price by focusing on achieving material success, many are unhappy and unfulfilled with the resultant output. They are cheated by the absence of knowing what really matters to them in life. Many people achieve outward success, but are at war with themselves internally. They realise in hindsight that the price has been too high. It is never too late to become that which you really want to be, but it is difficult to regroup off your current base which you strived so hard to get to.

- **Start by being honest with yourself and by being yourself.** Live the values of the type of person you want to be and you will become that person.

- **Never worry about where you have come from.** That can't be changed. But you can change the direction you are going in.

- **Genuine honesty, love for his dearest, value of his work, understanding his roots, intolerance for shapers and passion for success were the values that made Jack a success.**

- **She must have something he lacks, he something she wants.** Every lack loves another's lack. Lust dies, Love lasts. Jack and Áine were in love many times over.

- **With age, maturity and the means comes the harvest-time of your life when you can be more considerate and blissfully irresponsible.** Jack saw this as an opportunity to give back something to society.

- **Your values make you what you are.** They are the subconscious rules which you learn by trial and error throughout your life. You weren't born with them genetically; you acquire them as you stretch yourself on life's journey.

- **Be true to yourself.** Stop living a lie. Start to live the values of the type of person you want to be and you will become that person. Act the part and then become the part. Be yourself, but do it well.

- **People grow not by what is given to them, but by what is expected of them.**

- **If you can synchronise your objectives with your core values, you will have the wind to your back as you travel life's journey.** Peace and fulfilment comes from living in harmony with what matters most to you.

  Who has been the most influential in shaping you to date?
  Who or what is really important to you?

- **Don't wait until there is a corpse in front of you to say sorry for some outstanding misunderstanding or to say 'I really love and appreciate you'.**

- **Your life is limited, so don't waste it living someone else's dream.**
  Whose dream are you living?
  Is this right?
  What is your future action plan?

You must be the change you wish to see in the world.
– Mahatma Gandhi

A Challenge for You

The captain of a sailboat in a storm is unable to direct the wind. However, he can adjust the sails even if the wind is blowing against him. When the wind blows in a different direction, he can set the sails at different angles and move through the storm to calmer waters.

Life is similar. You can adjust your planned journey to synchronise it with your values. If your values are out of synch or out of harmony with your plans, you will have increased stress. The day-to-day lives of thousands of people are in disharmony with their values. They are living a lie. They are not true to themselves. Are you?

Synchronise your plan of action with your values.

If you want lasting success or happiness, whatever you perceive success or happiness to be, create a life of meaning or purpose that matters to you.

The purpose of life is to live a life of purpose.

Rather than try to manage the many variables over which you have no control, manage the few variables that are immediately around you and over which you have control.

Practical education cannot change your genetic map. However, it can make it easier for you to get the most from it.

Now, define success for yourself. What do you want from life?

What are the rules that guide your life?

If you want a better life, bring it into harmony with your value system.

Be true to yourself. Stop living a lie. Start to live the values of the type of person you want to be. You will become that person. Act the part. Become the part. Trust yourself to make it happen. It does not matter what happens to you. What matters is how you respond.

Do you want to make it happen?

Intention without action is still only intention. A dream without a deadline is still only a dream. Set a deadline.

Do you want to try?

It's up to you.

Jack

This Jack, joke, poor potsherd, patch, matchwood, immortal diamond,
Is immortal diamond.

– Gerard Manley Hopkins (1844–89)

This ordinary Jack, in 'Nature's Bonfire (That Nature is a Heraclitean Fire and of the Comfort of the Resurrection)' by Gerard Manley Hopkins, was a joke, a piece of broken pottery, a mere patch on some trousers, a piece of matchwood – but in the eye of God the potter, he was an immortal diamond of inestimable value.

You too, dear reader, are an immortal diamond of inestimable value.

You are the limiting factor

Unlocking your True Business Potential

Blaise Brosnan

You are the limiting factor

Unlocking your True
Business Potential

You are the limiting factor in your personal life, your career and in your business. That is good. Why? Because the variable you have most control over is yourself. The person who has enough insight to admit his/her limitation is the person who comes nearest to perfection.

This book focuses on facilitating and challenging you to achieve your optimum potential. By reading and reflecting on the concepts contained here, you can immediately begin to build your own capacity. With this enhanced capacity your personal life, your career and your business will improve, ensuring that you optimize your wealth.

'Managing your career has always been important but I believe it is even more essential in today's very uncertain world. Blaise Brosnan's You are the Limiting Factor gives very practical advice in helping you develop your career by both challenging and guiding you on your career path. This book could help you reach your optimum potential in business.'

– Philip Lynch, CEO, One Fifty One plc

'This is one of the most practical books on business skills that you are likely to come across- buy it, more importantly use it.'

– Dr Sean Mythen, CEO, Wexford County Enterprise Board

'All good managers must maximize their own output, while ensuring that those around them are contributing to their maximum potential. This book is a must read if you are to achieve its goal.'

– Denis Brosnan, former Group CEO, Kerry Group

ISBN: 978-1-906926-00-7
Available from: Management Resource Institute (MRI), Hospital Road, Wexford, Ireland
Tel: 00353 (0) 53 914 7774 | E: info@mriwex.ie | W: www.mriwex.ie

About the Author

Blaise Brosnan is an independent management consultant, trainer and businessman. He possesses a unique blend of practical senior management experience gained over twenty-one years in his role as chief executive of a number of large businesses. His successful completion of a portfolio of assignments in Ireland, the US and in Russia has gained him further national and international experience.

Born into a small rural retail business in Killarney, County Kerry, in Ireland, he has gained hands-on experience of dealing with customers and with the other variables of business from a very young age. From there he worked in a range of summer jobs in the UK and the US to earn his college fees.

His first management opportunity arose at the age of twenty-four, when he was appointed chief executive officer of a dynamic multi-purpose business. There, he quickly learned to initially survive and then succeed in business and, as he learned by 'doing', his experience and success often arose through the school of hard knocks. Blaise subsequently underpinned this practical business experience by successfully completing his post-graduate studies at Trinity College, Dublin.

Eighteen years ago, he established his own management consultancy/business training enterprise known as the Management Resource Institute, Wexford. As senior strategy specialist within the Management Resource Institute, he facilitates business owners and their teams to stand back from the 'fuss' of their day-to-day activities and focus on how best to drive their businesses forward. This he achieves through a combination of direct consulting and focused training.

More than 2,000 owner/managers have successfully participated in his Owner Management Development Programme (OMDP).

He is also founder director of International Dispute Resolution (Ireland) Ltd, which specialises in providing disputants with alternatives to the normal litigation routes in solving their commercial disputes.

He is former regional chairman of the Irish Management Institute, founder of IDW, founder member of Enniscorthy Rotary Club and board member of the world-famous Wexford Festival Opera.

In 2009, he published his first book, titled *You are the limiting factor – unlocking your true business potential,* which received national acclaim.

Profound Quotations

cogito ergo sum • I think, therefore I am

facta non verba • deeds not words

natura abhorret vacuum • nature abhors a vacuum

necessitas non habet legem • necessity has no law